Funeral Rituals and Christian Witness
in East Asian Contexts

Edited by Gregory and Amy Whitsett

Global Mission Series Editors:
Rick McEdward, Homer Trecartin and Kleyton Feitosa

Editors:
Gregory Whitsett and Amy Whitsett

Assistant Editor:
MaryAnn Conrad

Cover Design:
Adriana Suzuki, Suzuki Agency

Interior Text Design:
Amy Whitsett and Adriana Suzuki

Cover Images from:
Gimi Totori/ gaobon372023/ pngforest/ tohamina/ mahmoodakhtarsms/ pnglava/ Premium Access via Freepik, and imtmphoto Premium Access via Gettyimages

Produced by the Center for Adventist-Buddhist Relations (CABR) of the Global Mission Centers.

© 2015, 2024 by the General Conference Corporation® of Seventh-day Adventists.

Printed in the United States of America. All rights reserved. Second edition, 2024.

ISBN: 978-1-943507-46-7 (pbk)
ISBN: 978-1-943507-47-4 (ebook)

https://cabr.globalmissioncenters.org/contact

CEV: Bible quotations marked CEV are taken from the Contemporary English Version®. Copyright © 1995 American Bible Society. All rights reserved.

ESV: Unless otherwise noted, Scripture quotations are from the ESV® Bible (The Holy Bible, English Standard Version®), copyright © 2001 by Crossway, a publishing ministry of Good News Publishers. Used by permission. All rights reserved.

HCSB: Scripture quotations marked HCSB are taken from the Holman Christian Standard Bible®, Copyright © 1999, 2000, 2002, 2003 by Holman Bible Publishers. All rights reserved.

KJV: Scripture quotations marked KJV are from The Authorized (King James) Version. Rights in the Authorized Version in the United Kingdom are vested in the Crown. Reproduced by permission of the Crown's patentee, Cambridge University Press.

NIV: Bible quotations marked NIV are taken from the Holy Bible, New International Version®, NIV®. Copyright © 1973, 1978, 1984, 2011 by Biblica, Inc. ® Used by permission of Zondervan. All rights reserved worldwide. www.zondervan.com The "NIV" and "New International Version" are trademarks registered in the United States Patent and Trademark Office by Biblica, Inc.™

NKJV: Bible quotations marked NKJV are taken from the New King James Version®. Copyright © 1982 by Thomas Nelson. Used by permission. All rights reserved.

Table of Contents

Section III: Reflections from Former CEAR Directors

Appendix

Foreword

As Seventh–day Adventists, the biblical teaching of death is one of the core doctrines of the church. The state of man in death touches on the theme of the great controversy, the character of God, creation, and the definition of the soul. Over the past few decades the biblical doctrine of the state of the dead, as taught by Seventh–day Adventists, has gained traction in some evangelical communities, becoming a more accepted view in some seminaries. Even though new light on the subject of death is being brought forth in the western world, there still remains a significant gap in how to convey this biblical truth in mission settings.

In 2014, under the direction of Gregory Whitsett, the Mission Issues Leadership Conference was held in Bangkok, Thailand. This conference offered an opportunity for practitioners and academics to wrestle together on how to present, teach, and contextualize issues related to death. In the Asian context this issue represents the most important of all mission issues, death rituals make up the core of all structures in both culture and religion. Ancestor worship is a common challenge for new members, trying to balance honor the culture demands without worshipping a dead loved one.

The book you hold in your hand represents a valuable collection of mission insights presented at the conference. This volume could not be considered exhaustive or conclusive, but represents honest attempts to understand how to present this vital subject in the Asian context. As you read, pray for the guidance of the Holy Spirit, that Seventh–day Adventists may better share the hope we have, in preparation for the fast approaching day when Jesus will come again and raise those who have died in the Lord to live eternally with Him.

The Center for East Asian Religions is one of six Global Mission Centers that are sponsored by the General Conference as a part of the Office of Adventist Mission. Each of the Global Mission Centers bears a special concern for a particular religious or cultural group.

God is the great lover of mankind, and it is because of His great love and the immense sacrifice of Christ on our behalf, that the General Conference seeks to empower all Seventh–day Adventists to share that love with the world around us, a world that is made up of infinite variety. As Seventh–day Adventists we bear a special responsibility to share Christ with the world. The role of the Global Mission Centers is to equip members of the world church to understand people of other religious and cultural backgrounds, so that we may be more effective in our witness.

Rick McEdward, Director, Global Mission Centers
Silver Springs, MD, USA
February 2015

Introduction

When a death occurs, immediate family members suspend their normal routines and gather from far and wide to grieve the loss and plan the funeral. As word spreads that a relation has died, people—friends, foes, and those who were forgotten—come together to mark the passing of a life. There are no boundaries between religious and secular, Christian and Buddhist, rich or poor. All come with one focus—to grieve.

But underlying the emotions and decisions for the funeral are beliefs and assumptions that are widely divergent and conflict often arises. Christians want the funeral at the church. Buddhists want monks to bless the deceased. For some, singing is preferred while for others chanting the suttras is best. But all desire to do what little they can to pay honor to their parent, their leader, their child, their friend.

So what does an Adventist pastor say to a weeping woman who wants to place a bottle of soda and her niece's favorite sweets by the flower wreaths and casket at the front of the church sanctuary? What does the Adventist do when attending a former boss's Buddhist funeral and everyone is placing a bundle of incense, small candle and a flower on the casket before cremation? How does an only son show honor to his deceased Buddhist father when society expects him to take a lead in the funeral by being ordained as a monk to earn merit?

A simple "no" in each of these real–life scenarios can be the start of a major feud and cause significant damage to relationships. For anyone who has lived and worked among Buddhists, Taoists, and other East Asian religions it is a well–known fact that death marks the most important passage of life—akin to the importance of baptism for Christians. The Apostle Paul wrote in his epistle to the Romans, "Rejoice with those who rejoice, and weep with those who weep" (Rom 12:15, NKJV). How is it practically possible to do this? If weeping means you send your condolences by post or by staying aloof at a funeral, then it's possible. But I can't picture Christ staying aloof when people are hurting.

William Ury, in his very compelling book titled *The Power of a Positive No*, writes "…the more immediate and pressing need is for people to be able to say 'No' in a positive way that enables them to stand up for what they value without destroying their relationships" (2007:5). Ury then goes on to describe how a positive no is one that says 'Yes' to one's values, 'No' to anything that causes compromise, and then a 'Yes' to showing people that you are interested in their needs as much as you are to your own. The 2014 Mission Issues Leadership Conference hosted by Global Mission Center for East Asian Religions (CEAR) was not about changing or rethinking Adventist beliefs about death and how we should go about celebrating and mourning the passing of our loved ones. But rather the focus was on how we can ensure that we are adequately weeping with and ministering to our Buddhist and Taoist friends and family.

This volume presents the papers of church planters, pastors, professors, church members, and administrators that were presented at the three–day Mission Issues Leadership Conference hosted by the Global Mission Center for East Asian Religions in Bangkok, Thailand, May 20–22, 2014. The papers are presented here in three parts followed by a report on the recommendations voted by the delegates at the end of the three day meetings.

Part I establishes the Foundations for Ministering to Mourners in the Buddhist and Taoist context and looks at the nature of the problem and why learning how to minister to Asian mourners requires special prayer and attention (chapter 1 – Gregory Whitsett), the importance of understanding the beliefs and values of other cultures and religions as a starting place for ministry (chapter 2 – Danielle Koning), how people mourn and why mourning is important (chapter 3 – Amy Whitsett), Old Testament funeral rituals (chapter 4 – Wann Fanwar), Ellen White counsels and example on mourning (chapter 5 – Michael Kier), and finally a chapter looking at the role of rituals in Scripture and its implications for mission (chapter 6 – Gerald Klingbeil).

Part II then looks at specific Issues in Ministering to Mourners in Asia with eight papers giving recommendations for better ministry practices based on people's experiences in the following countries:

THAILAND	*Chris Sorensen (chapter 7),* *Surachet Insom (chapter 8), and* *Soontorn Thanteeraphan (chapter 9);*
LAOS	*Khamsay Phetchareun (chapter 10);*
CHINA	*Samuel Wang (chapter 11);*
TAIWAN	*Daniel M. Hung (chapter 12);*
INDIA	*Ramesh Chand (chapter 13);*
MADAGASCAR*	*Jacques Ratsimbason (chapter 14).*

Part III contains a very special feature—presentations by the two former CEAR directors: Elder Clifton Maberly who was the first CEAR director from 1992 to 2000, and Elder Scott Griswold, director from 2002 to 2012. Maberly's paper describes his work to open CEAR in Bangkok and the four contextualized, Lanna–style Thai paintings that depict the Second Advent, the Millennium, the Third Advent, and the New Earth. Griswold's paper emphasizes seven progressive but flexible steps of a Buddhist's faith development beginning with accepting Jesus as a worker of miracles and ending with accepting Jesus as their Savior.

It is the editors' prayer that all Christian disciples would find comfort in the scene of our Creator weeping before Lazarus' tomb. There Jesus was prepared to awaken Lazarus from the tomb but this expression of grief demonstrates that God is a victim of death with us and that His heart is grieved at the passing of each of his children on earth. May this volume challenge each of us to consider more deeply how to show compassion in our ministry to those who are mourning—whether Christian, Taoist, or Buddhist.

Gregory Whitsett, Director, CEAR
Bangkok, Thailand
February 2015

* *While this conference focuses on Asian contexts, Ratsimbason's paper from the African continent has some relevant parallels.*

Contributors

Gregory Whitsett is a pastor–missionary working currently in Thailand as the director of the Global Mission Center for East Asian Religions (a department of the Seventh–day Adventist General Conference Office of Adventist Missions).

Danielle Koning is a cultural anthropologist working in Thailand with Adventist Frontier Missions.

Amy Whitsett is a registered nurse with hospice care experience and is working in Thailand as Assistant for Special Projects at the Global Mission Center for East Asian Religions (a department of the Seventh–day Adventist General Conference Office of Adventist Missions).

Wann Fanwar is an Old Testament scholar teaching at Asia–Pacific International University in Thailand.

Michael Kier is a volunteer missionary working in Thailand.

Gerald Klingbeil is a biblical scholar and specialist in biblical rituals and works as Associate Editor of the Adventist Review and Adventist World.

Chris Sorensen is a church planting missionary working for Adventist Frontier Missions in Thailand.

Surachet Insom is regional director for Asia–Pacific at Adventist World Radio.

Soontorn Thanteeraphan is a pastor in Ubon Ratchatanee, Thailand.

Khamsay Phetchareun is lecturer of theology at Asia–Pacific International University in Thailand.

Samuel Wang is a missionary evangelist and developer of contextualized resources Chinese missions and is living in Thailand.

Daniel M. Hung was an Evangelical pastor in Taiwan at the time of writing in 1983.

Ramesh Chand was a doctoral student at Fuller Theological Seminary and a pastor in the Reformed Presbyterian Church at the time of writing in 2013.

Jacques Ratsimbason is Dean of Theology at Zurcher Adventist University in Madagascar.

Clifton Maberly was the founding director of the Global Mission Center for East Asian Religions and is currently serving at Nile Adventist Academy in Egypt.

Scott Griswold was the second director of the Global Mission Center for East Asian Religions and is currently serving Adventist Southeast Asian Projects based in the United States.

Section I

Foundations for Ministry to Mourners

CHAPTER 1

MINISTERING TO MOURNERS: ADVENTIST FUNERAL RITUALS THAT HONOR ALL ASIANS

Gregory P. Whitsett

INTRODUCTION

The Seventh–day Adventist Church holds that Scripture teaches two distinct beliefs that directly impacts how it mourns the passing of a loved one and conducts the funeral service, namely, the belief that the Christian Scriptures teach that when a person dies there is no conscious soul that survives (Genesis 2:17; 3:19; Ecclesiastes 9:5–6; Daniel 12:2; John 11:11–14; etc.); and, secondly, the belief that in the very near future this world will come to a climactic end which will usher in a series of events including the reunion of the righteous living and dead and culminating with the creation of a new heaven and a new earth where the righteous will live eternally in complete harmony, happiness, and health (1 Thessalonians 4:16–17; Revelation 21:1–4; etc.). Scripture identifies death as the enemy of humanity and our Creator and that one day it will be exterminated (Revelation 20:14).

Buddhist teachings are distinctly different. Death is the portal from this life to the next and the endless cycle of birth, death, and rebirth known as saṃsāra. Nirvana is the ultimate and permanent and mysterious condition that Buddhists intend to move toward through their myriad lives enslaved by the suffering of karma and impermanence. For Buddhists, the funeral rite is considered the most important rite of passage or event in a person's life and there are many details that must be attended to ensure an optimum rebirth and to prevent the spirit of the deceased from harassing their loved ones.

Because the Buddhist funeral is considered the most important ritual or rite of passage in a person's life, it is fitting that the Adventist Church make it a priority to ensure the funeral service addresses the needs of mourners who will most certainly include Buddhist loved ones and friends. Although Adventist funerals in many Buddhist societies across Asia have appropriately taken on certain local flavors, the Adventist funerals are still very much a foreign experience to Buddhists and most Adventists also feel out of place at Buddhist funerals. Of course this is grounded in the distinct differences of belief about death and death's solution. However, it is the presupposition of this paper that there is more that can and must be done to address the physical, emotional, and social needs of mourners.

The traditional focus of Adventist funerals is to minister to the bereaved and to bring to mind God's promises in a bodily reunion with their loved ones once again. The main objective of Buddhist funerals is to help the deceased 'soul' to successfully pass on to the next life and to earn merit for them which will in turn support them in better rebirth. We could say, then, that the Adventist funeral is focused on ministering to the survivors while the Buddhist funeral is primarily focused on the transition of the deceased into the next life existence. With these differences, controversy is only natural.

This paper seeks to highlight the biblical mandate that Christians are to live honorably in their multi–faith communities and to show sympathy and minister to those who are grieving their loss even in the face of distinct challenges caused by the very divergent beliefs. This paper then takes a look at what honorable living requires for Buddhists and specific problem areas for Adventists during funeral services. Last, several areas for further study are made for conducting a better ministry to mourners.

HONORABLE LIVING AS GOD'S IDEAL

Honor is one of three human qualities that were attacked when sin entered the world . After Adam and Eve had eaten the forbidden fruit, they heard Christ approaching and they experienced three negative emotions for the first time: (1) fear – in this case, fear of their Creator instead of the trust and confidence they had previously enjoyed in His presence, (2) shame – upon seeing their nakedness and how their Maker would be pained, and (3) guilt – the weight of responsibility and certain punishment for breaking the law and subsequent loss of innocence.

In the modern era, Christianity has had its greatest mission success among cultures where guilt–righteousness and fear–power are traditionally the major drivers of morality and social control. Inversely, Christian mission—including Seventh–day Adventist mission—has had its greatest difficulty demonstrating Jesus' preeminence in cultures where shame–honor is the primary driver of morality and social norms. This phenomena makes us ponder two possible reasons for this: (1) Is it possible that modern Christianity and the Seventh–day Adventist church have unknowingly contextualized the "Good News" and Christian life to Western values? or (2) Is it possible that Christianity is not contextualized but is by nature more attractive to some cultures than others? This author believes that the Gospel doesn't leave some cultures at a disadvantage but that any perceived challenges to sharing the Gospel in some societies is a reflection of the Church's inability or unwillingness to do the more difficult work of humbly adjusting its methods, models, and practice in appropriate ways to become relevant in those environments.

Mrs. White gave much instruction to cross–cultural missionaries and evangelists. In the book Evangelism, page 57, she wrote,

> *Christ drew the hearts of His hearers to him by the manifestation of His love, and then, little by little, as they were able to bear it, He unfolded to them the great truths of the kingdom. We also must learn to adapt our labors to the condition of the people–to meet men where they are. (White 1946. Emphasis added.)*

And, when sending a testimony to missionaries in Africa, Mrs. White penned,

> *Too many of the methods and habits and fashions have been transported from America to Africa, and the result is not favorable. (White 1977:97)*

In Gospel Workers page 468, we read,

> *The worker in foreign fields will come in contact with all classes of people and all varieties of minds, and he will find that different methods of labor are required to meet the needs of the people. A sense of his own inefficiency will drive him to God and to the Bible for light and strength and knowledge.*
>
> *The methods and means by which we reach certain ends are not always the same. The missionary must use reason and judgment. Experience will indicate the wisest choice to follow under existing circumstances. It is often the case that the customs and climate of a country make a condition of things that would not be tolerated in another country. Changes for the better must be made, but it is best not to be too abrupt.*
>
> *Let not controversy arise over trifles. (White 1905. Emphasis added.)*

What works in Boston, may fail miserably in Bangkok. Without prioritizing our energies and time to doing the difficult and uncomfortable work of research, study, reflection, and development of new methods that escape the faithful contextualization of Scriptural truths into Western traditions, we cannot expect that we will be met with open arms. Of course, the author is well aware that there will be opposition to the Gospel of Jesus Christ as enters new lands. But the acceptance of the Truth in Nineveh, Babylon, Samaria, and throughout the Roman world depicted in Scripture indicates that we can expect to find success in any land.

Not only has the Western version of the "Good News" seemingly deemphasizes the issues of shame and honor, but the social solidarity of Buddhist societies in Asia closely associates moral living with loyalty to one's family and community. A Christianity that teaches that individuals must love Christ more than their families and should separate from the customs and practices of their society is not going to have the same ring of "Good News" that it would in individualistic societies of the West.

Peter was one of Jesus' inner circle of three disciples but even he struggled to accept Jesus' openness to the nonJewish ethnic groups summarily labeled Gentiles. That all changed for Peter. The man who once recoiled at the thought of mingling among and ministering to Gentiles. In Peter's inspired letters we find a revolutionary ethic for Christians living in the real world of many cultures and many religions. In 1 Peter 2, Peter defines godliness as avoiding evil (1 Peter 2:11) and living honorably in contemporary society. On the surface, this hardly appears to be revolutionary but, when applied to real lives in the real world, it certainly is.

Peter exhorts Christians to conduct themselves honorably among the Gentiles (2:12); to submit to every ordinance of man for God's sake (2:13), to the king (2:13, 17), to governors (2:14); to fear God (2:17); to love the family of believers (2:17); to submit to masters—even the harsh masters (2:18), to husbands—even those who don't obey the Scriptures (3:1); for husbands to honor their wives (3:7); and to not return insults and evil to the wicked but rather bless them (3:8, 9). No relationship is left unaddressed, Peter is encouraging a lifestyle of righteous living in relationship to all people.

Very little is written in the Bible about Jesus' childhood, but what Luke writes in one sentence speaks volumes, "And Jesus increased in wisdom and stature, and in favour with God <u>and</u> [emphasis added] man" (Luke 2:52, KJV). Jesus' life and Peter's instruction complement each other. While Luke records two types of relationships—the vertical relationship with God and the horizontal relationship with people, Peter details the different types of honorable relationships we should have with people and can be summarized in four categories: God, believers, unbelievers, and those that abuse you. See Figure 1 below.

Figure 1.		
1 Peter 2:11-3:9		Luke 2:52
God	}	God
Believers Unbelievers Abusers	}	Man

The Peter's instruction and Christ's example from childhood onward teach that although Christians are suffer persecution they can still live honorably in the eyes of the world. And while the nature of the world is treat the inner circle of preferred people better than 'outsiders', honoring only those we prefer, Peter and Jesus' life instruct Christians to live honorably among all. Furthermore, rather than exhibiting the typical 'minority complex' of the typical minority groups that go against the flow of society, Christians are to maintain a respectful and honorable life within the society they live. Yes, God's people are 'called out' but they are not to live in isolation and thereby leave the world a dark place without a shining light. This principle is intended to be applied literally and directly in the Christian's life and should impact the decisions Christians make every day to show honor to civil and religious leaders, honestly pay one's full taxes, indiscriminately help the needy as it lies within your power to help regardless of social status, obey your parents, and remain respectful of one's employer when harshly treated.

HONORABLE CONDUCT IN THE BUDDHIST CONTEXT

Central to the cosmology of honor in the Theravada Buddhist

context is the family. The Aṅguttara Nikāya (numerical discourses), which contain 10,000 teachings of Buddha, record Buddha's teaching on filial (or family) piety. Buddha taught that parents are "worthy of offerings" (āhuṇeyya), an expression used in reference to the members of the Sangha, the monks. Buddha taught that the debt to one's parents is impossible to repay and can only be equalized by helping dishonorable parents seek refuge in the Triple Gem—the Buddha, the Dharmma (teachings), and the Sangha (monks)—and to instill in one's parents generosity in place of stinginess, wisdom in place of foolishness, and morality in place of wickedness (Saddhatissa 1997:97, 98).

In the Sigālovāda Sutta, a teaching found in the "long discourses" of Buddha, the story is told of Buddha meeting the young Sigāla (hence the name of the sutta) outside the city walls who was conducting his morning devotional exercises of worshipping the six cardinal directions of the earth and sky: east, south, west, north, nadir (downward), and zenith (upward). When Buddha questioned why Sigāla was doing this, he said that his father's dying wish was for him to carry out these devotions. But Buddha suggested that his worship was not correct, that the six cardinal directions represented six relations in which one is obliged to behave virtuously in a patron–client two–way relationship. These six relations are toward parents, teachers, wife and children, friends, servants and employees, and religious people and Brahmins (Sri Rahula 1990:119–123). In a sense, the Sigala Sutta parallels Peter's first epistle that we discussed earlier.

Parents, next to monks and Buddha himself, are considered one's greatest benefactors or patrons in life. There are five great sins in Buddhist thought, called ānantarika–kamma, that lead to a hellish destiny. These sins are causing a schism in the monks' order, wounding a Buddha, killing an arahat (Buddhist saint), patricide (killing one's father), and matricide (killing one's mother) (Nyanatiloka 2004:12). These are seen as heinous acts that only an 'incurably' evil person would commit.

The Sigālovāda Sutta records Buddha's teaching on five obligations parents have in caring for their children:

(1) Keeping children from a life of wickedness,

(2) Guiding children to do good and earn merit,

(3) Supporting children in their pursuit of knowledge and skills for life

(4) Helping children to find suitable spouses, and

(5) Providing goods to help them establish their own households.

In turn, children should demonstrate their gratitude to their parents through the following ways:

(1) Caring for aging parents,

(2) Assisting parents in the family occupation,

(3) Maintaining the honor of the household and clan,

(4) Behaving virtuously so as to be worthy of inheriting the parents' assets, and

(5) Making merit for one's parents after their death (Crawford 2010:84).

What we see in this mutual obligation of parents and children towards each other is a patron–client social system. The good patron acts out of generosity and genuine kindness for the good of others—or the client—in ways the client cannot do for themselves. The client, who is aware of the self–sacrificing and unmerited kindness will respond with gratitude, loyalty, and return favor while all the while giving public testimony of specific ways the patron has blessed them. The result is a relationship and flow of "generosity and gratitude" (Persons 2008:115).

David A. deSilva discusses the role of patron–client relationships in the Mediterranean society of the New Testament. He highlights that a key word in this social dynamic is charis, translated in Scripture as grace, favor, gift, blessing, thanks, etc., and is key concept in the patron–client social dynamic. The concept of grace in the West is primarily thought of in terms of God's saving grace of justifying sinful man (guilt–innocence language) but this word keyed a listeners mind in Bible times to the relationship between a benefactor (patron) and the subject being blessed (client). The same missiological impact these concepts had on the contemporary audience of Bible times is the same missiological impact it can have in the Buddhist cultures of the East.

The concept of charis was rooted in three contexts: (1) self–disinterested help toward someone in need, (2) the gift itself or results of the giving, and (3) the grateful response to the benefactor (deSilva 2000:104, 105). It is interesting to note that in our key text, Luke 2:52, the word favor in the phrase "in favor with God and man" is actually the word grace or charis. Jesus lived in grace with God and man, a role of blessing and responsibility with society.

Thai and Lao Buddhists commonly use the term boonkhoon to describe the grace of patron–client relationships. The compound word could be translated "virtuous kindness." In Theravada Buddhism, parents are patrons who demonstrate boonkhoon or charis through bearing children and raising them to adulthood. It is said that even if a mother deserted her child at birth, her *boonkhoon* is unpayable by the child who will forever be indebted. One saying states, "A mother's milk cannot be repaid." The gift of grace, the favor, or the honor the child receives is unmerited. And as we have already seen, the Buddha taught that the correct response of a child will be to respond with the graces of gratitude, service, and loyalty by caring for, giving material support, honoring, and earning merit for the parents. Inversely, if a child is unresponsive to their role as children, they are said to either "*bo hu boonkhoon,*" meaning the child does not know grace, or such a child is "*nelakhoon*", the child is devoid of grace or an ingrate.

Christians will readily agree with the Buddhist teaching that children are indebted to their parents and should care for them as needs arise. This is in harmony with the fifth commandment which commands children to honor their father and mother (Exo 20:12). However, difficulties arise when parents have a different belief system and expect that that children should earn merit for them after they die.

In the Buddhist cosmology of karma, earning merit is essential to improving the future status of a person. Making merit at the temple for one's dead parents is an essential act of love and honor in order to increase the position of the deceased in the coming life. Failure to earn merit through offerings and the son's temporary ordination to the monkhood is a major affront just as refusing to seek medical care in their behalf is when they are sick. For a Theravada Buddhist, a grateful, gracious, and honorable child will arrange and participate in merit making ceremonies for their parents when they die.

CASE STUDY: A LAO THERAVADA BUDDHIST FUNERAL

The author has had the privilege of working among a Theravada Buddhist cultures for twelve years and have attended many Buddhist and Adventist funerals. In this section, a Issan or Lao Buddhist funeral will be briefly summarized by highlighting six important phases of a Theravada Buddhist funeral ritual: the wake, ordination of monks and laypeople, the procession, the cremation, and the interment of the bones.

The Wake. Immediately following the death, family and friends quickly begin gathering for the several–day long wake. During this time, people will come to pay their last respects to the deceased by kneeling at the casket, greeting the deceased, and offering a white envelope containing money to help offset funeral expenses. Households and businesses that are close to the deceased will purchase wreaths of flowers decorated with a message written in silver or gold glitter stating something like, "May your soul (*vinyan*) fly to paradise, from (name of the family/donor)." The family of the deceased is expected to provide meals and refreshments for the guests. Every morning, and sometimes in the evening, the village monks will come and provide their services to earn merit for the deceased while the family and community members participate in the rituals.

Ordination of Monks and Lay People. The day before the cremation of the body, it is obligatory that the son/s, or grandsons of the deceased be ordained (*buad*) as monks to earn merit for the deceased parent or grandparent. As stated above, Buddha taught that this is one of five obligations of honorable children, and to fail in this area would be considered an extreme display of ingratitude. The morning of the cremation, female and male friends can also choose to be ordained as lay people, called *mae khao* (literally, white mother) who wear all white clothing as a sign of their ordination. However, they are not required to shave their heads as monks do. These rituals are all performed in order to earn merit for the deceased.

The Procession. After the morning ordination is over and the casket is loaded on the vehicle that will carry it to the temple, a procession is formed to usher the deceased to the temple grounds. If the home is a long way from the temple, the mourners will drive closer to the temple and form the procession line there. A white chord is tied to the front of the vehicle carrying the casket to lead it to the temple for cremation. Monks lead the procession, followed by the ordained laypeople, and then close family members. The rest of the community will follow the hearse. Mournful music is played over a loud speaker and the somber party moves toward the temple while passersby stop their activity to watch the impressive scene of orange robed monks, white clad laypeople, important community leaders and close family members, the multi–tiered casket reaching two or three meters high on the back of a flatbed truck, and the crowds of friends and community people parading to the temple.

The Cremation. At the temple, the multi–tiered casket is dismantled and transferred to the funeral pyre. During this process, fresh coconuts are cut open, the casket opened, and the clear juice ceremonially poured over the body in an act of ablutionary cleansing. The order of these events can vary from funeral to funeral as per preferences of the local leaders and the family of the deceased. The flower wreaths and belongings of the deceased will be stacked against the pyre to be burned with the body. The cord from the procession is taken and tied around the casket and strung to monks sitting in a pavilion.

After everything has been readied and the crowd seated either in the meeting hall (*sala*) or in the temple yard, the funeral proper commences. Various components of the funeral include reading a biography of the deceased, followed by a merit making ceremony led by the monks, a sermon preached on the impermanence of life and the cycle of life, death, and rebirth, and an offering collected to pay the monks for the services provided. When this has been completed, the crowd will pay their last respects by placing a small bundle of incense and candles on the casket while wishing the deceased a happy stay in paradise. The monks and male family members take all the belongings and set them on or next to the casket and then douse everything with diesel fuel. At this point, an honored person will light a small rocket strung to a wire that when lit, careens toward the pyre catching it on fire. It is popularly believed that a pyre that catches fire quickly and easily signifies that the deceased will enjoy a long stay in paradise. A failed attempt to light the casket is embarrassing and not a good sign. After the fire is lit, the crowd disperses—some heading home and others heading back to the deceased person's house for another meal.

Interment of Bones. The family will return to the cremation site the next day to retrieve the bones. The small container of bones will be placed in a stupa usually in the temple grounds or sometimes in a stand of trees outside town. A merit making ceremony is led by chanting monks here again.

Memorial or Anniversary Rituals. Even after the bones have been interred, this is not the end of rituals for the deceased. Depending on the Buddhist tradition which varies widely, subsequent merit–making and offering of food are done at intervals after the funeral. These can include ceremonies at 30 days, 90 days, and on the anniversary of the cremation. These can be expensive or simple and the anniversary rituals are voluntary.

In summary, a Lao Theravada Buddhist funeral has four principle functions.

First, the funeral performs the role of ushering the spirit of the deceased out of the current community of the living and sending it off to the next life. While the funeral has a practical function of respectfully disposing of the body, it is much more about sending the *vinyan* (soul) away to the next life and thereby preventing the spirit from troubling the home and community.

Second, the funeral provides an opportunity to teach the community the Buddhist doctrines of death, impermanence, and karma as a natural part of life that people would do well to remember.

Third, the funeral serves as a way for mourners to process their grief and prepare them for creating a new "normal" equilibrium. Emotional needs are met through the rituals which simultaneously guide mourners through the process of letting go and moving forward emotionally while providing an event where loved ones and community have a venue to support each other in their grief.

Fourth, the funeral serves a social function that promotes solidarity through the participatory and days–long process required. As a ritual that involves the whole community, it reestablishes community roles and promotes community unity. Those who may have been estranged and in conflict with each other have an opportunity to forget old wrongs and reset relationships. There is not space here to investigate further into the nature of rituals and their importance other than to say that they are able to communicate where words fall short.

Theravada Buddhist funerals are crucial rituals that are necessary parts of the community. However, when some community members become Christians, discomfort and crisis are inevitable.

RECOMMENDATIONS FOR MINISTRY TO MOURNERS

Regardless of how tactful a Christian might be, Buddhist funerals are at best awkward social events for Christians. While some may opt to skip a funeral, arrive late, leave early, or keep to the back of the crowd, this type of position sends a callous and unsympathetic message that misrepresents the loving character of God. In a word, it is dishonorable. Furthermore, this prevents a Christian converts from reestablishing solidarity with his community and can be seen as threat to social order. Such behavior would be viewed by the community as insubordination to the family and downright shameful. On the other hand, some Christians may wish to join with the community and their family and focus on maintaining mutually honorable relations in order to avoid creating conflict and in the process participate fully in all aspects of the Buddhist funeral. While the local community might be pleased with such a response, the Christian experiences compromise of Truth and disloyalty to God.

In both of the above cases, the Christian is failing to live in favor with both God and man—God's ideal for His followers. So the question is this, is it possible to live in favor with both God and man in the Theravada Buddhist context, or are Christians living in those environments exempt from that requirement? It is safe to conclude that it must be possible or God wouldn't instruct His followers to do it. What he requires is attainable through the Holy Spirit's guidance. In order to achieve the correct balance of honorable living the following principles are proposed.

MAKE CHRIST'S HONOR PREEMINENT

Followers of Christ must determine to honor their Creator and Savior first and foremost. Nothing should compromise this priority. Great care must be taken by Christians to avoid activities that share God's honor, promote teachings that are in opposition to God's plan of redemption, and mislead others.

SHARE IN THE LIFE OF THERAVADA BUDDHISTS

Christians must avoid the temptation to believe doing nothing is safer than trying to participate in Buddhist funerals. Failure to mingle and minister to people and live honorably within the local community is just as dishonorable to God as failure to form clear boundaries. In the book, Ministry of Healing, Ellen White writes,

> *Christ's method alone will give true success in reaching the people. The Savior mingled with men as one who desired their good. He showed His sympathy for them, ministered to their needs, and won their confidence. Then He bade them, "Follow Me."*

There is need of coming close to the people by personal effort. If less time were given to sermonizing, and more time were spent in personal ministry, greater results would be seen. The poor are to be relieved, the sick cared

> for, the sorrowing and the bereaved comforted, the ignorant instructed, the inexperienced counseled. We are to weep with those that weep, and rejoice with those that rejoice. Accompanied by the power of persuasion, the power of prayer, the power of the love of God, this work will not, cannot, be without fruit. (1905:143, 144)

Christ's ministry not only includes sharing Truth but sharing our lives with others as expression of God's presence and love. We are to join in with people in their cultural traditions whether at times of celebration or during their darkest hours. But we are not to simply be with people, we are to gain their confidence and share our walk with Jesus with them.

FORMULATE CHRISTIAN FUNCTIONAL SUBSTITUTES

This is where the mission challenges become real. Solving real problems is never neat and clean; inherently it's a messy and difficult process. But with grace, Christians can learn to debate issues respectfully and look for solutions in council with the Bible, Ellen White's writings, and the guidance of the Holy Spirit.

Seventh–day Adventists living in Buddhist contexts need not only to participate in funerals for their own dead but also to honorably participate in funerals for their loved ones at Buddhist funerals. It is easy to focus just on how to modify Adventist funerals but special attention to the topic of minister to mourners must include formulation of plans for Adventists attending local Buddhists funerals. This must be done in such a way that does not violate Christian beliefs and practices. Typically the two biggest concerns for Adventists are concerns of idolatry and the popular belief of the consciousness of a human soul separate from the body. While the risks of are serious when developing new ritual forms, total avoidance of this work carries serious risks as well. Wholesale rejection of the local community and refusal to participate in any degree at Buddhist funerals will mark Christianity as a foreign religion and in opposition to the people. In turn this can drive some Christians 'underground' in their decision to participate in Buddhist funerals without proper study and council. In either case, the mission of God and His honor is undermined.

Paul Hiebert's critical contextualization model prescribes a way for sorting out whether the local Christian community should keep, reject, modify or substitute the old belief or practice. In his model, he outlines a four–step process. First, Christian leaders must recognize the need to deal biblically with all areas of life in the local community. Second, Christian leaders must guide the local church in respectfully and uncritically gathering and analyzing the customs associated with the matter being studied. Third, the pastor or missionary will next guide the local church in a Bible study related to the matter at hand in order for them to clearly understand and accept the biblical teachings and principles that apply to the cultural situation. The final step is for "the congregation to evaluate critically their own past customs in the light of their new biblical understandings and to make a decision regarding their use" (1985:186–187).

In the Theravada Buddhist funeral ritual there are several areas that will need to be addressed. Below are some examples of what local Adventist congregations need to prayerfully process. For the sake of the reader's understanding, examples of possible solutions are given.

Paying Respects: Christians, like Buddhists, need to be able to approach the casket to process their grief. Adventist instructions should include a reminder that because the deceased is completely unaware of anything until Christ raises them to life at the end of time, their communication with the deceased is a conversation is only for their benefit. Additionally, words spoken to Christ to forgive the wrongs between the deceased and the bereaved can be an act of reconciliation and hope. The act of filing past the casket set on the funeral pier, bowing, speaking some heartfelt words to the deceased, and placing a small bouquet of flowers, incense, and candles isn't necessarily opposed to Scripture when done in other contexts. A bow is a typical Asian greeting and show of respect for authority. Speaking to the deceased or to God can simply be an expression of grief, the placing of the small bundle of flowers can be an act of saying goodbye. The local Adventist congregation will need to determine how best to carry out this responsibility. Teaching on these matters will be important to taught and reviewed after the decision in order to help members and new comers understand the dynamics involved. When ordering flowers, the accompanying message with the flowers should reflect the donor's beliefs while at the same time not offensively inserting new teaching into a Buddhist funeral. For example, instead of the placard stating the typical wish for the soul to enjoy paradise, one could write: "May you receive your reward in paradise." This is a small edit but at the same time does not highlight the fact that the donor is different and separate from the community.

Ordination of Male Descendent(s): it is expected that a son or grandson will become a monk to earn merit for the deceased. Failure to do so could shame oneself as well as potentially shame the surviving family and insult the community. Again, the local congregation will need to prayerfully determine how best to address the issues of honor while not compromising faith in Christ's merit for sinners.

Is it possible to form a Christian ceremony for the descendants of the deceased to dedicate their service and funds in honor of the deceased for the benefit of Christ and the community? Such a ceremony could be an ordination to become a deacon (or deaconess for women). The ordination could include (1) shaving the head to denote mourning and as a sign of being an ordained religious person, (2) wearing special clothing (perhaps similar to what would normally be worn at the Buddhist funeral by lay people—a white shirt and black pants) during the entire period of a person's service to Christ and the community to identify their role in the mourning process, (3) walking in the procession with mourners to the cremation, and (4) serving the community in acts of charity and service away from the normal career responsibilities of life for a self–designated period of time. Careful and sensitive effort will need to be taken to fully explain the meaning of the "ordination" to the gathered community by the officiating pastor.

Bowing to Monks: It is a particularly sensitive issue for Christians to know how to address monks. Should Christians avoid monks to avoid conflict. Should Christians adopt a foreign greeting of handshake or wave when approaching a monk? Is it possible for Christians to bow to monks—once—with the understanding that this is both a common greeting among peers as well as a show of honor toward those older than oneself and to those in leadership positions? Many Christians have concluded that this social decency.

Merit–Making Through the Chanting of Suttas: On the one hand suttas recited during a funeral focus on the ultimate reality that death comes to everyone and is no respecter of persons. We certainly wouldn't disagree with this teaching. However, the act includes bowing three times to show reverence to the Triple Gem (Buddha, Dhamma, and Sangha) and this is clearly in opposition to Christian teaching. Also, while these suttas are being chanted, the posture of the audience is to sit respectfully on the floor and bow respectfully in a show of deference and reception of the Dhamma being recited. This also creates opposition. Most have encouraged that the Christian should sit quietly and respectfully in the back of the room during this part of the service. That is less convenient for a person who is a direct relative of the deceased as they are expected to be at the center of attention. If a Christian ordination has been adopted, it is possible for that person to sit to one side, perpendicular to the monks sitting across from the lay audience. It might even be possible for Christians to have some Scripture texts that can be recited responsively reflecting on the subject of death and deliverance from its grip along with a prayer with posture similar to Buddhists.

Functional substitutes are meant to fill gaps that would naturally form if the Christian community fails to carefully address the holes created by converting from Buddhism. Such holes, if ignored, will cause unnecessary harm to both the individual and the community.

IMPLEMENT LOCAL DECISION MAKING

While the pastor, missionary, or field administrator may be tempted to tell local congregations what they can and cannot due in contextualization, the leader's task is to make sure that the Scriptures are faithfully understood and that the process of study and application of truth has followed the proper steps as discussed earlier in this paper. Good Christian leaders will guide local believers to faithfully address the issues with the guidance from the Holy Spirit (John 16:13). Controversy is bound to arise in cases where outsiders to the local community do not trust a local congregation or region to make decisions over the application of spiritual truths. This breeds unhealthy and dependent Christians. While this is scary for leaders, this must be our practice. It is possible that the leader would encourage a congregation to adapt more or less to local customs but ultimately it are the cultural insiders, in community, that need to make these decisions.

DISSEMINATE LESSONS LEARNED

As Christian functional substitutes are implemented and refined, reports on what has been tried, what is working, and what has not fared well needs to be disseminated through published case studies and constituency meeting reports where minutes and archives will record the activities. By doing so, the project work loop is closed and the information shared then aids the development of expertise in the Church and builds synergies with work in other areas.

PROVIDE STRATEGIC SUPPORT

Unfortunately, few pastors, church administrators, and college professors have formal training in cultural anthropology and missiology. However, special attention needs to be given to the missiological challenge to make sense of Christianity for those coming from and living in Buddhist contexts. Missiologists and leaders who have this type of training need to be invited to consult with colleges to design courses for ministerial training and coach local leaders and pastors in acquiring the tools for developing contextualized practices. These types of leaders can sometimes be found in the local field, church administration, at some universities, at seminaries, and specifically working with church and parachurch mission organizations such as the Global Mission Center for East Asian Religions. These workers need to be called upon to provide the strategic support so critically needed in areas where the Church is struggling to establish itself honorably in the community such as among Theravada Buddhists.

SUMMARY

The Christian's dual obligation to both God and fellow human beings is founded on Scripture. While principles are universal, their application may look contradictory in different contexts. Each Christian has the obligation to honor God and man and therefore, these issues are extremely relevant to all Christians. It is important that Christians living in Buddhist communities understand that failure to develop guidelines and theologies detailing honorable living and ministry will fail to fulfill God's ideal. It is vital that we as a world Church encourage and support local churches and mission leaders in the Buddhist world in developing Bible–based customs, rituals, and theologies to satisfactorily address human and community needs. This is especially needed in times of loss. When we have done this, we will begin to live as Christ lived—in favor with God and man. This is not an extra–curricular program—it is essential Christianity.

REFERENCES

Crawford, Christa Foster. 2010. Duty, Obligation and Prostitution: How Family Matters in Entry into and Exit from Prostitution in Thailand. In Family and Faith in Asia: The Missional Impact of Social Networks, ed. Paul DeNeui, 77–99. Pasadena, CA: William Carey Library.

deSilva, David A. 2000. Honor, Patronage, Kinship and Purity: Unlocking New Testament Culture. Downers Grove, IL: InterVarsity Press.

Hiebert, Paul G. 1985. Anthropological Insights for Missionaries. Grand Rapids, MI: Baker Book House Company.

Nyanatiloka, Bhikku. 2004. Buddhist Dictionary: A Manual of Buddhist Terms and Doctrines. Chiang Mai, Thailand: Silkworm Books.

Persons, Larry Scott. 2008. The Anatomy of Thai Face. MNUYSA: Journal of Humanities 11, no. 1:53–75. http://www.manusya.journals.chula.ac.th/files/essay/Persons_p53–75.pdf (accessed 19 August 2013).

Saddhatissa, Hammalawa. 1997. Buddhist Ethics. Boston, MA: Wisdom Publications.

Sri Rahula, Walpola. 1990. What the Buddha Taught: Tripitakavāgīśvarāchārya (Revised edition). Bangkok, Thailand: Haw Trai Foundation.

White, Ellen G. 1905. Ministry of Healing. Mountain View, CA: Pacific Press.

_____. 1915. Gospel Workers. Washington, D.C.: Review & Herald Publishing Association.

_____. 1946. Evangelism. Washington, D.C.: Review & Herald Publishing Association.

_____. 1977. Testimonies to Southern Africa. Cape Town, South Africa: South African Union Conference of Seventh–day Adventists.

Chapter 2

Towards an Educated Ministry to Mourners:

Research Tools for Understanding Funeral Practices in Southeast Asian Mission Contexts

Danielle Koning

INTRODUCTION

Before dawn we gather at the Thai Buddhist forest temple shrine. One of the relatives pulls out a plate from the crematory – the ashes of the family's beloved father who was cremated yesterday. Within moments the entire family crowds around, eagerly looking for remains. They pick out pieces of bone and fill pretty little boxes with them. A young girl shouts and jumps up in exhilaration when she finds father's ring. She is the luckiest of all and everyone talks about her treasure on the way back home.

Death is an intrinsic part of the human experience. Yet in its universality, cultures around the globe produce vastly different ways of understanding and ritualizing, grieving and celebrating, embracing and resisting death. Being from the secular, modernistic country of the Netherlands, I grew up with a detached understanding of death – that death belongs to a different realm than life, and therefore we should not get close to it – we should tuck it away in a hospital, a coffin, a cemetery. So, for me, the Thai Buddhist–animistic practice of sorting through a loved one's ashes was quite a new experience and somewhat provocative.

In the context of death, Christian ministers want to serve. We want to cry with those who weep. We want to care for those who have lost a loved one. We want to share Christ as opportunity affords during funeral ceremonies. In this paper, I will argue that to reach these important objectives, it is pivotal for us to understand those whom we are crying with – precisely because of the great cultural diversity in framing and ritualizing death. Secondly, I will provide tools for how we can reach this understanding in the best way in order to be the best servants we can be. My ultimate goal in this paper is to support the church in Asia in moving towards an 'educated ministry to mourners'.

WHY RESEARCH IS IMPORTANT IN MINISTRY TO MOURNERS: LESSONS FROM FUNERAL RESEARCH

Since the understanding, ritualizing and grieving of death are so different across cultural contexts, there is a profound need to research funeral practices wherever we minister. When we neglect to study local concepts, values and customs in regard to death, we will tend to approach mourners with our own (personal and cultural) understandings and practices that may or may not be appropriate for those we minister to. We then run the risk of answering questions that are not being asked, offering help that is irrelevant, and, even worse, misrepresenting the Christian message because we fail to know how it is understood.

It is important to note here that cultural research is not only important for cross–cultural workers, but also for those who are working within the country or region they grew up in. Anthropologists have consistently found that 'being native' does not necessarily equal 'complete cultural understanding'. Natives, for example, are likely to understand their society through the lens of particular subgroups they are part of – such as a Christian or ethnic subgroup – and miss or misunderstand the perspectives of other subcultures. Some Christian subgroups have lost touch with the cultural lives of their non–Christian country mates. Further, natives naturally understand 'what' happens in a culture on a surface level (e.g. the practice that male relatives become monks at a funeral), but don't necessarily have a conscious grasp of the deeper issues that the practice is rooted in (e.g. the worldview underpinnings of the idea of merit transfer). Deeper cultural understanding requires that one takes a mental distance from one's own culture and intentionally reflects on it. Engaging in research helps to accomplish just that.

In this section, I will illustrate why research is important in ministry to mourners by sharing how my small–scale study on Thai Buddhist funerals delivered insights that should have implications for our ministry practice. What these implications will look like exactly is the task of Asian church communities to answer. Here I simply wish to make the point that it is only through studying those we minister to that we uncover the critical issues that must be missiologically thought through in order to develop ministry practices that are relevant, appropriate and effective. I will discuss three issues by sharing the insights gained through research and the missiological questions that are implied in them.

ISSUE 1: SENSES AND RITUALS

Mainstream Thai Buddhist practice is highly sensory and ritualistic. Its lay emphasis is not so much on understanding as it is on doing and experiencing. This is no different for funerals, which are a highly significant social and ritual event in Thai culture. That is, Thai Buddhist funerals do not emphasize cognitive reflection or verbal meaning making, but focus on the performance of proper ritual. Lay people do not usually reflect on such ritual acts beyond the general knowledge that their performance will benefit the soul of the deceased. Here are some illustrations of the deeply sensory nature of these rituals: lighting incense and candles (smell, sight), changing dress and undergoing initiation to become nuns and monks (touch, sight), cooking and eating every meal together for several days (touch, taste), listening to monk's chanting and drum beating (sound), praying together before the coffin (sound, sight), offering money and food (touch), shaping a personal figure out of the deceased's ashes (touch and sight), raising a flag (sight), dancing (touch), erecting a minihouse for the deceased (touch, sight), and smearing the deceased's ashes on the temple wall (touch, sight).

The significance of learning about the sense–oriented nature of Thai funerals lies in its stark contrast with mainstream Seventh–day Adventist religious practice. SDA church culture builds on a Protestant heritage that is at best reserved and at worst suspicious about including materials, rituals and the senses as a major part of the Christian experience. In the (legitimate) quest to avoid idolatry and mystical deceptions, SDA's have de–materialized, de–ritualized and de–sensitized Christian practice. Our focus is on mind and character development, on preaching and discussing, on Bible understanding and theology. Our funerals, as well as most of our evangelistic strategies, are therefore teaching– rather than ritual–oriented.

Could it be that the church in Asia needs to develop a stronger ritual repertoire and appeal more to the senses in order to effectively minister to mourners? During funeral observations and in conversations with people, it was evident that one of the intentions and effects of ritual practices was to serve as bodily aids in processing grief. At one funeral, after the main cremation ceremony was done, one of the participants expressed that he felt very happy. He said: "We have done everything we could, there's nothing else for us to do. So now we can lay down our monk robes, drink, dance, and feel good". At another, Thai–Chinese funeral, participants exchanged their black and white clothing for the most colorful clothing when all rituals were done, by which they intentionally expressed a new beginning – "we leave our sadness behind at the burial site", one relative said.

The missiological questions that walk away from these findings are: could it be that the most meaningful form of ministry to mourners in Asia is not a sermon but a ritual – not to reflect but to sense – not an invitation to listen but a call to participate? Could it be that teaching Christian views on death and the afterlife should flow less through words and more through experience? How can we include the senses in our Christian funeral practices and ministry to Buddhist mourners?

ISSUE 2: IMPLICIT SOCIAL SUPPORT

In many Asian contexts, support during times of grief is not so much expressed through explicit addressing, but through 'implicit social support'. Pearson, Kim and Shearman (2009) define this as "the emotional comfort one can obtain from social networks without disclosing or discussing one's problems vis à vis specific stressful events. Implicit support can take the form of reminding oneself of close others or being in the company of close others without discussing one's problems. The conceptualization of implicit support particularly emphasizes the absence of explicit disclosure and sharing of stressful events. Thus, in relying on it, people do not have to risk disturbing relationships" (Pearson, Kim, and Sherman 2009: 7).

My research in Thailand affirmed these ideas. At one funeral, I talked with the siblings of the deceased. The talk was set in a cheerful tone and the siblings did not refer much to the immediate context of the funeral. After the cremation ritual, I could tell the siblings were emotional, but they did not draw attention to that and instead focused our conversation on other topics. After another funeral, it took two months of regular visits before the wife who lost her husband opened up to me about her feelings in regard to her beloved's death. The sister of this husband, who was clearly Americanized after having lived there for more than 30 years, confided to me that she had terrible guilt feelings regarding her brother's death but that there was no way she could address these in her Thai–Lao family, because "we don't talk about such things".

Instead of verbally expressing their inner worlds, the Thai mourners I spoke with were comforted by their loved ones in other ways. While a man was on his death bed in the final stage of cancer, lots of neighbors came to visit – his wife recalled that they were very loud and laughed a lot – their 'implicit social support' in the form of their presence was more important than explicitly addressing the sadness of the circumstances. After showing up at the funeral and helping with all its practical needs (such as cooking food for lots of people for several days; sharing plates and chairs, etc.), friends, family and neighbors still came to visit regularly after the ceremonies were done.

A brother of the widow mentioned: "We go and eat at my sister's house frequently now, so she doesn't feel alone".

There are several implications to consider here for ministry. First, the importance of 'implicit social support' demonstrates the need for our presence. In practice, this may not be as easy as it sounds, one reason being that Christians don't always feel comfortable in non–Christian settings. At one Buddhist funeral I attended I observed that a pastor who had known the deceased in the past didn't seem to know what to do. He introduced me and another researcher to the family, said a few short words to them, and then quietly left after sitting at the back for a short time. There are many things that are uncomfortable for a Seventh–day Adventist at a Thai Buddhist funeral – we are the only ones not 'wai'–ing during the monks' chanting, we stand out by not talking to the deceased, and we feel awkward when we refuse the pork noodle soup offered us following the service. But if implicit social support is the most important form of support, then we have to be present. The missiological questions here are: how can SDA's (both ministers and lay people) be encouraged to be more present at Buddhist funerals? In what ways should SDA's participate in Buddhist funerals? How can they be a true blessing there? What would constitute compromising behavior at a funeral?

The second implication is that ministry in Asia would do well to avoid explicit forms of social support, such as emphasizing the expression of feelings or centralizing the bereaved persons and their grief. The missiological question here is: in what ways do our current SDA styles of ministry to mourners in Asia live up to this principle of avoiding explicit forms of social support? What could be improved?

ISSUE 3: THE SOUL'S JOURNEY AFTER DEATH

One of the key objectives of Thai Buddhist funerals is to make sure that the spirit of the deceased does not remain attached to this world so that it will not bother its relatives and can move into the best possible place in heaven. At one funeral, a young lady told me that Thai people try not to cry during the ceremonies in the temple as it will make the spirit of the deceased concerned and not want to leave. The proper execution of all rituals over a period of several days is aimed at encouraging the spirit to leave and to leave well. Loved ones tell the deceased that he/she doesn't need to worry or stay close, so that the spirit feels comfortable to depart. Forgiveness is asked for wrongs done and gifts, money and food are given to increase the deceased's merit. The deceased is provided a house and basic survival tools for the afterlife.[1]

As Seventh–day Adventists, we may tend to respond to such findings with the urge to correct: people need to know that there is no such thing as an immortal soul! However, before we hurry into a corrective mode, we must understand how central the belief in spirits is to Thai people and how many needs and understandings are implicated in it.

First, the belief that one can still interact with the soul of the deceased gives comfort by providing a basis for various emotional coping mechanisms. The need to process grief and to bring about a sense of closure is met by chanting for forgiveness as well as by expressing care through a good and generous execution of all necessary rituals. The missiological questions here are: when people learn that the spirit of their loved one is not accessible after death, how will they deal with the weight of grief, the need for closure and the desire to continue to care for their loved one? What Christian alternatives can the Asian church offer? For example, could we develop rituals of family and community care (serving the living rather than the dead) as a part of funeral ceremonies?

Second, if we consider how deeply ingrained the belief in an immortal soul is in Asian psyches and cultures, it will not be hard for us to recognize that a mere theological treatise on why the belief is not true will not suffice to make people 'unlearn' it. We must again realize that people don't learn beliefs by hearing them, but by experiencing them – which is what ritualistic folk Buddhism is so good at. The missiological question here is: how can we ritualize our belief in the mortality of the soul? If Thai Buddhists constantly enact the belief that the soul lives on after the body dies, could Seventh–day Adventists dramatize the breath's return to God and the body's return to dust

– as well as the whole man's resurrection at the second coming?

HOW TO DO RESEARCH ON FUNERAL PRACTICES: MISSIONARY–ANTHROPOLOGICAL PRINCIPLES

In this section, I will outline some basic principles to guide Christians in doing research on funerals and other cultural practices.

EXPERIENCE – DON'T JUST READ

Participating in rituals and social groups that are non–Christian and culturally different than one's own can be uncomfortable. There is therefore always the temptation to learn about other cultures via books. In terms of learning and understanding, however, there is no substitute for spending lots of time with actual people. Only when we spend time, we discover how local people perceive things (which may be different from what generalizing, formal book studies have to say!). Only when we spend time can we develop an intuition for knowing how to relate to people and what works and doesn't work in ministering to them. Only when we spend time can we 'shake' our own assumptions of how things work, what people need, and what's important to people. We need to be willing to go through the discomfort in order to find these treasures. It would have never hit me, for example, how deeply sensory Thai funerals are if I had only read a book in the privacy of my own home, remove form and deprived of all the rich sounds, smells, tastes, touches and sights!

DETERMINE WHAT YOU WANT TO LEARN

Doing research is only effective when it is guided by a set of questions. You will need to determine what kind of information you are looking for before you do any research. The information you are looking for may be problem–driven: emerging from specific problems or questions that arise in ministry to mourners in your context. But you may also be interested in exploratory research – having your 'eyes wide open' to learn about your research group on issues that you did not know about beforehand but that may be extremely relevant to your ministry. Both types of research are important – and both require guidance by questions. Generally it is helpful to determine one main question and then develop that question into sub–questions. For example, let's say your main question is "What are the needs of my research group in case of a death?" Your sub–questions could then be: "What are their spiritual needs?", "What are their relational needs?", "What are their practical needs?" etc.

LOCATE YOUR RESEARCH SITE

Doing research needs a context – where will you do your study? There are both pragmatic and substantial considerations here. Often a research site is chosen because of convenience – the researcher already has connections or lives close, or the site is easy to travel to and stay at. Such considerations are important as they make it easier for us to frequently follow up on our research. More substantial considerations concern the nature of what we want to understand. Let's say I would like to better understand how Thai teenagers experience Buddhist funerals. In that case, it wouldn't make sense for me to go to a sleepy village that mostly consists of elderly people and young children. I'd probably want to choose a somewhat sizable city and try to get connected to schools and youth centers there.

GETTING ACCESS AND FINDING A ROLE

To visit funeral ceremonies and interview community members requires what anthropologists call 'access' to the field. Every field or research location has 'gate–keepers' who control who has access to what within that territory. When we enter communities as researchers, we need to be particularly sensitive to having permission from those gate–keepers (which, depending on the context, may be community leaders, the elderly, monks, state officials etc.)

To gate–keepers and to all who we encounter during our study, we need to have a role that is understandable and acceptable. In Thailand I often present myself as a 'student of Thai culture', which is sufficient for people to both make sense of my presence and appreciate me for my interest in them. In other contexts, the idea of being a researcher or student may not be as acceptable and could even raise suspicion. Roles can alternatively be connected to particular tasks – I 'legitimized' my presence at one funeral, where I did not know anybody, by helping to cook and wash dishes. Having a contact to introduce you in a new setting, allowing you to take the role of 'friend of…' is also very effective.

LISTEN AND OBSERVE – DON'T PREACH

When we're in the field, as ministry–minded people we may find it easy to seize every opportunity to share our Christian message with others. There are however few things as interruptive to researching people and building trust relationships as acting as 'the teacher'. We need to become like novices – irrespective of our professional or educational status, we have to become like children who are to be introduced to a new world. We need to see our research group as the experts and have a receptive attitude to learning from them. When we conduct research, it is our place to listen, not to talk – to observe, not to intervene – to ask, not to provide answers. Be as unobtrusive as possible. Intentionally choose to postpone any judgments. I have consistently found in divergent cultural contexts that a humble, quiet approach makes people comfortable to open up and encourages them to share intimately.

RESEARCH METHOD 1: PARTICIPANT–OBSERVATION

Anthropologists use the unique research method of 'participant–observation'. It means to do two apparently contradictory things at the same time in order to get an up close understanding: to participate and to observe. Our discussion about the need to find a role already pointed to the need to participate. Another rea–son why participation is important is that it may provide understanding that simply observing or interviewing could not. For example, when I participated in the popular Thai Loy Krathong festival and released a lantern and saw it fly away high into the sky, I felt a joyful release inside and experientially understood how powerful this act is in evoking the idea of leaving sins and evil behind. I would have never understood this by just watching other people releasing their lanterns.

For Christians, the concept of 'participation' naturally brings us into an area of tension. We want to understand those we serve, but we don't want to compromise our allegiance to God or be a stumbling block to fellow believers. This is a complex and vast field of decision making. Here I can only acknowledge this tension and briefly share a few principles to keep in mind as you personally engage your people group. First, we need to distinguish non–negotiables from negotiables as we find them in the Scriptures. For example, I will not bow down to a Buddha image – but I might eat the food that's been offered to monks. I will not chant along with Buddhist prayers – but I can sit in the temple and listen to them. I will not eat pork – but I will eat clean meat.

Second, before joining any event, pray for God's guidance. Pray that God will make it clear which practices to engage and which not. Pray that God will help you to stay aloof from certain practices without being offensive. I have found that with prayer, a smile and polite behavior, people accept me when I am the only one not bowing to an important monk, or the only one not tying white thread around the wrists of a newly married couple.

Third, we need to remember that we cannot only err in participating, but also in not participating. Because we want to be 'on the safe side', we may stay at a distance from most cultural events. But in doing this we may develop ministry practices that are misinformed or even misguided because we lack understanding. We are rightfully concerned about avoiding idolatry – but are we equally concerned that the people we minister to will have a chance to hear a meaningful gospel presentation?

In the method of participant–observation, observation is as important as participation. Observing allows us to begin to form an idea of how things relate and what is important and what not. Interviewing and asking direct questions can sometimes give us a wrong idea of proportions. For example, I once interviewed a pastor about the evangelistic activities in his church. Because I emphasized this topic, we talked about evangelism for a long time and it seemed that his church was very active in this area. But when I went to observe his church, I realized that, actually, the church did not do much evangelism at all. It wasn't that the pastor had lied. Rather, it is just the nature of interviewing. It allows us to explore ideas, ideals, exceptions and possibilities that may not represent mainstream, day–to–day experience. It is therefore very important to always include observation in our research tool kit and not rely solely on interviews.

RESEARCH METHOD 2: INTERVIEWING

Interviewing is a technique used to ask questions that mere observation cannot answer. There are a few principles for good, reliable interviewing:

Be bonded: Make sure that you have established a good level of rapport with someone before you interview them. They need to understand your intentions and feel as comfortable as possible in order to truly open up and speak beyond stereotypes or what they think you would like to hear.

Be neutral: Ask open questions. For example, "Funerals take a really long time, right?" is a closed question, and even a little judgmental. Closed questions are especially problematic in Asian 'face–saving cultures', where it is considered impolite to bluntly disagree with a suggestion, and can be embarrassing to admit that you do not understand something. An open question, on the contrary, cannot be answered with 'yes' or 'no', and does not suggest anything about the possible answer. Examples of good open questions are: "What is important to you when you go to a funeral?" or "Why do male relatives become monks during a funeral?"

Be understandable: Ask simple, clear, short, singular questions. This is harder than we may think but it is very important. Often people feel like they are not 'knowledgeable' enough to be our informants, and we want to make them feel as comfortable as possible by asking easy–to–understand questions.

Be sympathetic: Culturally appropriate, affirming, non–verbal behavior can go a long way in helping interviewees open up. Nod, make agreeing sounds, do whatever is appropriate in your context to let your interviewee know that you are understanding them and are valuing everything that they are sharing with you.

Be deep: Make sure you really understand what people are saying. Here are some suggestions to achieve that:

- Rephrase your informants' answers back to them and get their response.
- Ask the same question in different ways and at different times and places (you'll be surprised at how much this will add to what you already heard!).
- Ask follow–up questions.
- Don't assume you already understand things that you have not yet researched. When people say something like: "You know what that's like, right?" be humble enough to say: "No, I don't. Could you explain it to me?"
- Make sure you interview people of various backgrounds in terms of gender, age, ethnicity, socio–economic status and religion. Interview men & women, children & the elderly, people of high rank & people of low rank, leaders & followers, etc. Different people may have very different understandings to share with you!
- Check your findings and conclusions with community members and experts. A great tool is hosting a 'focus group' where you invite a diversity of community members to discuss your findings.

ETHICS

There are several important ethical principles for us to keep in mind when doing research as Christians for ministry purposes. First, treat people like human beings – as children of God. Don't reduce them to tools for getting information. This may sound obvious, but when you are 'on a mission' and pressured for time to get data and information, it's not that hard to slip into this kind of thought! Second, be sensitive with the information you gain. Make sure you process it in a way that ensures the anonymity of your informants and does not endanger them.

PASSING IT ON

The knowledge and insights you gain are to benefit your ministry. For this purpose, you will need to document them. Methods of doing this range from listing simple bullet–point notes in a Microsoft Word document, to writing more complete papers. Whatever form you choose, the important thing is to just write the information down. There is an awful lot of information that you forget if you wait a day before writing things down.

Aside from documenting, the implications of your insights need to be presented and discussed in your church community. The church must decide how your findings should impact its ministry strategies.

Finally, when you have gained some experience with the process of doing research and applying it to ministry, you can become a trainer and equip others in your church to do research and know how to apply what they learn to ministry.

MAKING IT HAPPEN: GUIDANCE FROM CHURCH LEADERSHIP

If research is to become an integral part of ministry, the encouragement, guidance and support of mission leaders, ministerial directors, etc. is vital. There will be a need for church leadership to help establish the needed organizational infrastructure, such as:

- Research training for local workers
- Supervision or organized peer support in the cycle of research and ministry

- A national or international church wide (online) platform for sharing and discussing:
    - Research findings and their implications for ministry
    - Research methods, including questions of ethics

With this support of church leadership, we will be able to build a movement 'towards an educated ministry to mourners', and, ultimately, an educated ministry at large.

NOTES

1. *According to Pearson, Kim and Shearman (2009), the focus on the journey and well–being of the deceased rather than the emotional experience of the bereaved is another expression of 'implicit social support'.*

REFERENCE LIST

Pearson, Dairine M., Kim, Heejung S., and Sherman, David K. 2009. Culture, Social Support and Coping with Bereavement for Asians and Asian Americans. The Forum 35, no. 2: 7–8.

Chapter 3

Good Grief:

Understanding Grief to Better Support Those Who Are Bereaved

Amy Whitsett

Experience – Pa Ying

Two weeks ago I stood in the doorway of Pa Ying's tiny house. The one–room home was lit by a bare bulb hanging from the ceiling which cast sharp shadows in the corners. At the far end of the room sat two adult sons, red–eyed and in a daze. The other half of the room closest to the door was filled by two small mattresses, leaving a narrow walk space. The village chief sat cross–legged on one mattress next to an also red–eyed and equally dazed old man. On the mattress behind them lay Pa Ying's body – still, silent, covered by a mosquito net and cooled by a fan. The church planter and I had come to pay our respects and see what we could do to help the family.

I watched the old man, Pa Ying's husband, as he struggled between feelings of despair and unbelief. He was so overwhelmed that he couldn't concentrate on anything, much less on answering our questions. When he did answer, his answers were disjointed, out of order, incomplete and always returned to telling bits and pieces of the story of Pa Ying's sudden death. I don't think he even answered one question appropriately. Instead, he defaulted to the village chief.

As he sat, he kept changing position and looking around the room, as if needing to do something but not knowing what. Though he was visibly exhausted, he said he planned to stay awake all night. How could he sleep anyway – he was in shock. I felt sorry for him. I knew it would be a very long night, and I wished more than anything that I could do something, say something that would allow him to rest his mind and body even for a few hours.

This wasn't the first time I had seen death. In fact, as a nurse in the United States, my specialty was working with terminally ill patients and their families, and I walked with hundreds of patients and their families through the grief process. While many find such nursing difficult and depressing, I found that ministering to those who were dying and/or mourning the loss of a loved one was the most fulfilling nursing position I ever held. Not only was I a nurse attending to the physical needs of the patient, I was also serving as a counselor and pastor ministering to the emotional and spiritual needs of the dying as well as their family and care givers.

But as I left Pa Ying's house, I felt useless. The church planter tried to comfort the family, assuring them that their wife and mother was at peace – sleeping, resting. But Pa Ying was the only Christian in her family – and a new one at that. So what the church planter shared, while true, was far outside of the family's beliefs and understanding, outside their worldview. While they nodded their heads, I'm not sure that any of it made sense to them. But more than sharing words, I felt an intense need to do something to help the family, to support them in their sadness, to love them for Jesus, but I didn't know what to do. Instead, the family was surrounded by their Buddhist friends and community, supporting and guiding them through the next six days of funeral ceremonies.

As I drove home that night, I mourned the loss of Pa Ying. But I also mourned the loss of opportunity – the opportunity to honor Pa Ying and her newfound faith with a Christian funeral, the opportunity to just be present with her family as they grieved, the opportunity to surround them with so much love and support that they couldn't deny the life–changing and life–giving love and power of Pa Ying's

Jesus. And I wondered why it had to be that way. As I thought more about what I had experienced, I realized once again what a wonderful opportunity and what a heavy responsibility we as a church have to minister to those who are mourning.

Understanding Grief

In order to understand the opportunity and recognize our responsibility, one first must understand grief and how it works. Grief is a natural and normal response to loss (Howarth 2011:9). According to Miriam–Webster's dictionary the definition of grief is rather simple: grief is "deep sadness caused especially by someone's death". Similarly, the Oxford dictionary identifies it as, "intense sorrow, especially caused by someone's death". In reality, however, grief can be felt as a reaction to any loss and can be experienced in varying degrees. For example, if a student fails a test in school, he may feel grief. But he won't experience grief to the same degree or for the same length of time as he would if he failed his entire class and could not graduate as a result. Both experiences elicit a grief response but in different ways and to different degrees. But when loss involves a life, the grief is much more intense and extreme. So in reality, it seems that grief is much more complicated than its simple definition implies. In fact, more than just being a feeling of "deep sadness" as Miriam–Webster defines it, grief is experienced as all–inclusive, complex package of physical, emotional, cognitive, behavioral, sexual and spiritual responses (Dent 2005:22). The most common emotions one can feel include but are not limited to sadness, depression, despair, anger, guilt, and denial (National Cancer Institute 2011:6). And as if emotional stress wasn't enough, grief also elicits physiological reactions including crying, fatigue, insomnia (inability to sleep), anorexia (loss of appetite), lost interest in life, disorganization, and sometimes dreams or illusions of the one who died (National Cancer Institute 2011:6; LifeCare 2001:4). Grief also weakens the immune system, which can lead to frequent illness (LifeCare 2001:4). To complicate grief even more, these emotional and physiological reactions can be unpredictable and strike when one least expects them (National Cancer Institute 2011:6). Grief can also be so powerful that it demands ones complete focus and energy, often making even the simplest tasks of life overwhelming (LifeCare 2001:2).

Interestingly, grief knows no cultural boundaries (Pearson, Kim and Sherman 2009:7; National Cancer Institute 2011:24). Studies have shown that these responses, while sometimes expressed in a uniquely cultural way, are present in all cultures. So whether one is African, American or Asian, if one experiences a significant loss, he or she will also experience any or all of these and other grief–related reactions.

Grief – A Recent Field of Study

Throughout history there are stories of those who have successfully readapted their lives and moved on successfully in spite of great loss. But there are also stories of those who have never recovered from their pain and grief. Based on our Christian belief that grief has been a part of life since Adam and Eve's sin, it is a bit surprising to discover that it has only been in the past forty years that there has been a focus on trying to understand grief and bereavement. Only recently have attempts been made to identify what key elements ensure a successful recovery versus prolonged and painful grief (Dent 2005:22). The resulting theories are as varied as are the types of grief symptoms one experiences, again suggesting the complex nature of grief.

Perhaps the best known theory of grief was suggested by Kubler–Ross in her book, *Death and Dying*, published in 1970. Kubler–Ross' theory suggests that grief is a complex process of moving through five emotional stages: denial, anger, bargaining, depression and finally acceptance (Mallon 2008:8). Other researchers and practitioners argue with her theory – either with the stages themselves, or with the order in which they are experienced. In another study, Worden focused on the emotional stages being tasks that the bereaved have to process through in order to make a complete adjustment (Mallon 2008:9; Dent 2005:22). Stroebe and Schut looked at the free expression of grief in contrast to limiting expression through self–control. They concluded that both are important, forming what they termed a dual–process of grief (Mallon 2008:9; Dent 2005:22). Klass and a group of colleagues studied the purpose of grief in relation to the deceased and suggested that the ultimate purpose of grief is to adjust one's relationship from one with the living to one with the dead. They theorized that the goal is to have some form of continued relationship with the deceased (Mallon 2008:10; Dent 2005:23). The list of research could go on.

However, one author observed that the weakness with the majority of grief theories is that they tend to focus on the grief of individuals. Yet death rarely affects just one individual. Instead, death affects groups of people, with each individual reacting and interacting in different ways. This is a significant observation because the emotional and social health of the group has a direct effect on how well the individuals in the group grieve and adapt to loss (Dent 2005: 23; Mallon 2008:12). Perhaps this is part of the answer science is looking for.

How Do We Help?

With the complexity of grief, and science still searching for the golden key to successfully coping with and recovering from grief, it would seem that one would need a clinical psychology or professional counseling degree in order to adequately and successfully support people through their grief. And yet that is what pastors and church leaders are called on to do – but without the benefit of much if any professional training. The good news is that there are things that pastors and lay people can do to support and minister to church members, their families, friends and communities as they grieve.

First, when a death occurs, we must stop and pay attention (Veldt 2010:270). Death is a tragic event, even when it is anticipated. Because of its life–altering effects, we must not treat it as just another task to deal with so we can get on with our work. We must never forget that our business of the Great Commission is about people – not to–do lists! We must stop and acknowledge what has happened. We need to keep in mind that while our lives may be affected for just a few hours or days, the lives of the family members are permanently changed. There is no 'normal' for them to return to and so they must adapt and create a new normal (Mallon 2008:13). The grieving need to know that we understand this reality.

Second, we need to be ready and willing to provide physical support (LifeCare 2001:2). One of the easiest types of support to give is physical support. In the first few hours after the death of a loved one, the family is in a state of shock and disbelief. Life comes to a standstill and all focus is on the death and funeral preparations. Due to the emotional stress, sometimes it can be difficult for the family to take care of their personal needs such as eating, sleeping, bathing, etc. They may not have time to go to the market to purchase household necessities such as toothpaste or toilet paper. Or maybe they need help with child care or making sure laundry is washed.

Helping to provide such physical support has a double blessing. Many church members feel uncomfortable and out of place especially at non–Christian funerals. What rituals can they safely participate in without compromising their commitment to Christ? Which ceremonies should they join in and which ones should they just be spectators at? There is also great social pressure on them to participate in honor– and merit–making ceremonies, particularly if they are a relative of the deceased. Do they participate and then try to live with a tormented conscience? Or do they refrain and endure the resulting social and familial criticism? Rather than having to choose between these two difficult options, what if there was a third option? What if our church members were encouraged to identify areas of need and help provide tangible physical support to the grieving family as way of showing support and respecting and honoring the deceased? What would that do for our members? What impact would it have on the local community's impression of our church?

In our early years in the mission field our family participated in the funeral of our neighbor. Each day of the five–day wake and funeral period, the neighbor family hosted large numbers of friends and family as they came to pay their respects to the deceased. Part of the hosting included feeding the guests three meals a day. While I didn't know how to cook the food, I did know how to wash dishes. So I made that my task. The family didn't like it at first as they couldn't allow a foreigner, someone of higher status, to sit on a low stool, washing dishes. I gently yet passionately explained that I wanted to help them and that was one way I knew how – we foreigners do know how to do a few things after all! It took a little convincing but the family relented and I became the official dish washer. We found other ways to show our care and concern. My husband stayed up with the family all night for the five nights (the cultural practice) even though he was working full time. Instead of taking money gifts we took bags of fruit. Rather than playing cards and gambling, we taught them how to play dominoes. We even gave them our 'veggie' coffee when they ran out and the honored guest, the village chief, was falling asleep and requesting something to keep him awake! As a result, the family accepted us as a full brother and sister in their family. More importantly, the community embraced us. After the funeral, everywhere we went in the community, people knew us and treated us as one of them. No one was offended that we didn't participate in some of the rituals and ceremonies. Instead, they were honored that we wanted to be with them, that we would put our busy lives on hold to participate in their grief.

Intrinsic vs Extrinsic Support An interesting study recently compared Asians/Asian Americans and European Americans and how they obtained support from their friends, families and communities in times of need – also known as social support. The study revealed that there are two patterns of social support: intrinsic and extrinsic.

Intrinsic support is support received without specifically asking for it and without revealing one's need. It assumes one of two things. First, that either those around will identify the needs of the individual and meet them. Or second, that the emotional support and comfort of knowing that one belongs to a group is enough to help one face difficulties and challenges on his or her own (Pearson, Kim and Sherman 2009:7–8; Kim 2008:522).

Extrinsic support, on the other hand, is support that is specifically solicited or asked for. It assumes that one must present his or her need in order to receive the support needed. It also leads to the assumption that if help is not asked for, help is not needed (Pearson, Kim and Sherman 2009:7–8; Kim 2008:522).

The study revealed that the type of support one prefers, i.e. intrinsic vs. extrinsic, varies from person to person. However, the study also found that culture plays a significant role in determining how needed support is solicited and how it is given. The study noted that when one receives intrinsic support when he or she is expecting extrinsic support, and vice versa, he or she feels unsupported and alone. Therefore, those ministering to the needs of mourners must keep this in mind. Even though culturally, Asians tend to prefer intrinsic support, it is very possible that individually they have a need for extrinsic support. So we must intentionally offer help and support in different ways, otherwise what we do may not be interpreted as meaningful support (Pearson, Kim and Sherman 2009:7–8; Kim 2008:522).

Third, we need to be able to help the family plan the funeral. Because of the overwhelming and debilitating nature of the initial shock and grief, the family of the deceased often relies on others to guide them through the process of caring for the body and planning the funeral. Unfortunately, in Southeast Asia, few church members have seen a Christian funeral so have no idea how to plan one (Green 2014). And few church members are living in community with other Adventists who, given they were trained, could give them that guidance. The result is that the family often has to default to a Buddhist funeral simply because those surrounding them and supporting them through the immediate period of shock are Buddhist – and Buddhists know how to do Buddhist funerals. If Adventist church members are going to have Adventist funerals, we must be present immediately after the death.

Fourth, we must realize that dealing with grief and supporting those who are grieving can be a long and sometimes difficult process (LifeCare 2001:3). Mourners need a great deal of emotional support, especially after the initial shock of the death has passed. They often need someone to talk to, someone who will just listen as they verbally process their pain and confused emotions and try to make sense of everything (Mallon 2008:12). This can be intimidating to those who are listening. What should one say? What if a question is asked that can't be answered?

One cannot spend an hour, or even a day with someone who is mourning and expect to fully relieve their suffering, regardless of what is said or done. While not everyone agrees just how long grief can last and still be considered normal, one should expect grief to last for several months up to a couple of years, though the intensity of the grief should decrease as time goes by (National Cancer Institute 2011:6).

Last year a friend of ours visited us several months after the death of her six–year old granddaughter whom she was raising. I was intimidated because I didn't know what to say. But as we spent the next couple of weeks together, I realized that the most important thing was for me to just listen. I listened as she told stories and shared memories of the fun times they had together. I listened as she recounted the drama of the death and funeral over and over again. And I listened to all the 'What ifs'. What if she had taken her to the doctor sooner? What if she had taken her to a different hospital? What if the granddaughter was living with someone else? What if we hadn't moved away? What if? What if? What if? And as the days went by she did less talking and more listening. Eventually, God gave me words and scripture verses that gave her comfort. But it didn't happen without listening first – to her and to God.

Sometimes as Christians we fear that others expect us to have the answers that will miraculously take away their pain and make sense of the death. But I discovered that that wasn't what my friend expected – or needed. There is nothing that can be said that will take the pain away, and those grieving know that. Instead, they just need a listening ear, someone they can count on to hear them tell their stories over and over again, and to not cast judgment when they ask the hard questions that have no answers. And I believe that God wants to use us to support them as they grieve. By being present physically and emotionally, God has the opportunity to touch them and heal them where they hurt.

Lastly, we must understand that grief is extremely personal and is unique to each person and each situation (Mallon 2008:13; Dent 2005:23)**.** Grief is an internal journey of processing ones emotions and feelings, of creating meaning and adjusting to life without their loved one. It is a process that the one grieving <u>must</u> go through, and he has to go through it at his own pace and in his own way.

CALL TO ACTION

Providing care for those who are mourning is a vital ministry that must be taken seriously. Below are a number of suggestions on how the Adventist Church should demonstrate our commitment to supporting people in their grief.

A Plan of Action. Caring for people who are grieving a loss requires preparation. The Adventist church in Asia must have a plan of action. Here in Thailand when there is a death, the community rallies around the family with individual members fitting into predetermined, culturally dictated roles. Everyone knows what to do and fill those roles automatically. Likewise, our church needs a funeral plan so that when a death occurs, pastors and church members know what to do in order to support the grieving family and community (Green 2014). I believe that the Adventist church should strive to be the funeral experts! We need to be known as the church that knows how to care for those who are mourning. But it can't happen without a plan. Planning everything after the death is too late.

Cemetery or Crematory Plan. The church needs to develop a plan for respectfully disposing of the body. The following questions need to be addressed: Is it appropriate for Christians to cremate? If so, where should the cremation take place? Is it acceptable to rent the crematory facilities at a local temple? Or should Christians only bury? If so, how should the local church go about acquiring a piece of property for use as a cemetery? Or should the local missions purchase and develop properties for regional use? These questions need to be addressed at both the Union and local mission/field levels.

But it's not only the unions and missions that need a plan, individual churches do as well. Some churches may have a cemetery they can use but others may not have that luxury and need to have an alternate plan. If cremation at a local temple is an accepted option, pastors, local church elders and deacons need to develop a cooperative relationship with the local temple and village leaders and know how to interact with the temple staff in a way that demonstrates respect and builds the Adventist reputation in the community.

Memorials & Anniversaries. The other area that needs urgent attention is that of remembering and honoring the dead. One of the grief theories mentioned earlier in this paper indicated that one of the goals of grief is to establish a new relationship with the deceased, not just forget and move on. Buddhists do this quite well. They participate in certain rituals to earn merit for their loved ones and perform specific ceremonies to provide for the physical needs of spirit of the deceased. Some set up small shrines in their homes with photos, candles and flowers, while others leave offerings at temple stupas containing the bones of their loved ones. Buddhists are good at keeping the connection and relationship alive – primarily because they believe that the soul lives on. While Adventist Christians believe differently, there is still need to remember the dead, to keep their memories alive, not for their sakes, but for the sakes of those still living. Being able to remember loved ones reminds us that their lives were not lived in vain, they had purpose and meaning, they added to our own lives and will be missed. Perhaps part of the Sabbath service following a funeral can be dedicated to remembering the one who died. Tell stories, share memories, celebrate the life lived and encourage each other with the hope of New Life. Maybe the church can designate special yearly "Memorial Sabbaths" dedicated to remembering the lives those we loved. On those Sabbaths members could each bring flowers and together make a large bouquet for the front of the church to symbolize the place deceased loved ones still hold in our hearts. Singing songs and recalling promises of Heaven and new life would provide comfort for those still mourning, while at the same time reinforcing our unique Adventist beliefs. Such a service would provide an opportunity for the church to come together to laugh and cry and support each other, to recognize and validate the pain that still remains, and for members to realize that they are part of a community who understands and cares, a community who will be there for them in their time of need.

Conclusion

The grief process will never be painless. No matter how many studies are done or theories are posed, there will never be shortcuts or alternate paths to follow. Grief is a part of life. But we can make the journey a bit easier, a bit lighter, a bit more bearable, by learning how to better help and support those going through it. We must take the issue of ministering to mourners seriously by understanding grief and how it works, understanding the needs of the bereaved and how we can provide the support they need, and creating a complete funeral plan so each pastor and church member is equipped and prepared take advantage of one of the greatest opportunities we have to love people for Jesus.

Reference List

Dent, Ann. 2005. Supporting the Bereaved: Theory and Practice. Counselling at Work (Autumn): 22–23. [Electronic form]

Green, Shannon. 2014. Ministry to Mourners in Thailand: Assessing the Needs. [Motion picture]. Thailand: Global Mission Center for East Asian Religions.

Howarth, Robyn A. 2011. Concepts and Controversies in Grief and Loss. Journal of Mental Health Counseling 33, no.1 (January):4–10. [Electronic form]

Kim, Heejung S., David K. Sherman, and Shelley E. Taylor. 2008. Culture and Social Support. American Psychologist 63, no. 6 (September): 518–526. [Electronic form]

LifeCare. 2001. A LifeCare Guide to Helping Others Cope with Grief. LifeCare.com. www.foh.dhhs.gov/NYCU/copingtips.pdf (accessed 23 January 2014).

Mallon, B. 2008. Attachment and Loss, Death and Dying: Theoretical Foundations for Bereavement Counselling. In Dying, Death and Grief: Working with Adult Bereavement. London, England: Sage Publications. [Electronic form]

National Cancer Institute. 2011. Grief, Bereavement, and Coping with Loss. Cancer.gov. http://www.cancer.gov/cancertopics/pdq/supportivecare/bereavement/HealthProfessional (accessed 23 January 2014).

Pearson, Dairine M., Heejung S. Kim, and David K. Sherman. 2009. Culture, Social Support, and Coping with Bereavement for Asians and Asian Americans. The Forum 35, no. 2 (April): 7–8. [Electronic form]

Veldt, Luke. 2010. After the Funeral: Helping Mission Leaders Care for Those Under Their Care. EMQ 46, no. 3 (July):270–275. [Electronic form]

CHAPTER 4

DEATH AND BURIAL IN THE HEBREW BIBLE

Wann Fanwar

INTRODUCTION

The most significant questions of life inevitably pertain to life and death. These are questions unbound by cultural considerations, time restrictions or intellectual explorations. Without appearing hyperbolic, it may be safe to say that everyone, everywhere, will, at some point in their lives, raise these questions.

The Hebrew Bible (HB), also known to Christians as the Old Testament (OT), does not stand disconnected from these questions. It tackles them head on and provides its own take on what life is, what death is and the significance of where the dead are.

The biblical concept of life, human and non–human, originates in the creation story. The first statement of the Bible asserts that 'God created' everything (Gen 1:1). This creation involved all life forms on planet earth (cf. Gen 1:1–31). The crowning work of this process was the creation of humanity in the form of the first human couple, Adam and Eve (Gen 1:28; 2:1ff.). Humanity was accorded the responsibility of rulership over this newly created world and Adam and Eve were placed in a category different from the other life forms on the planet (Wenham, 1987:33).

The distinctive feature of the biblical material is its insistence that human life resides in the very thought of God. In HB, God is portrayed as the originator of life, the very essence of its intentionality. To put this differently, human life is virtually an extension of God himself. Gen 1:26–27 portrays this intentionality by speaking of human existence as a two part reality comprised of male and female halves which combine to form God's image (see discussion by Wenham, 1987:32–33).

So God created man in His own image;

He created him in the image of God;

He created them male and female

(Gen 1:27; cf. 5:1; HCSB).

The parallelism between the second and third lines implies that the image of God consists of maleness and femaleness (Sailhamer, 1992:95; cf. Sarna, 1989:13). In the customized creations of Adam and Eve recorded in Gen 2, we glimpse other components of this divine intentionality. The following translations intersperses Hebrew and English words so as to highlight the wordplay embedded in the narrative (see Alter, 1996:8).

Then Yahweh formed the 'adam (man) from the dust ('apar) of the 'adamah (ground or soil) and breathed nishmat khayyim (living breath) into his nostrils and the 'adam became a nepesh khayyah (living being) (Gen 2:7; personal).

This type of wordplay, called paronomasia or pun, is a favorite literary technique of writers in HB (Wenham, 1987:59). Adam's words, when he first sighted Eve, are equally revealing and display similar wordplay.

This at last is bone of my bones and flesh of my flesh; she (lit. 'to this') shall be called 'ishah (woman, wife) because from 'ish (man, husband) she was taken (lit. 'was taken this') (Gen 2:23; personal).

The texts play on similar sounding words to connote the integration of creation but also draw attention to the uniqueness of humans (Sailhamer, 1992:98). He (the male) is the possessor of 'living breath' which makes him a 'living being'. Without this 'living breath', he would be nothing more than *'adamah*. She is as much a part of him as he is a part of the earth. All these realities are the creative handiwork of God (Sarna, 1989:17). The possession of this living breath is the very essence of being human (cf. Josh 11:11; Isa 2:22; Wenham, 1987:60; Knibb, 1989:398).

The convergence of human existence in the very mind of God is augmented in two passages which appear much later in HB. Psalm 139 delves into the unbreakable bond between divine and human which transcends time, space and any other reality. It distinctly places human life as recorded in God's book even before the reality of it unfolded (Ps 139:16). In the call to Jeremiah, God insisted that Jeremiah had been chosen prior to his conception (Jer 1:5). The evidence suggests that human life is irrevocably bound to God's intentionality (Kidner, 1987:25).

The phrase *nishmat khayyim* roughly parallels *ruakh khayyim* ('spirit of life'; cf. Gen 2:19; 6:17; 7:15, 22; 9:9; Isa 42:5; Zech 21:1; cf. Knibb, 1989:398) and is applied to all living things (Wenham, 1987:60). However, there seems to be a stronger relationship between *nishmat/ruakh khayyim* and human life as evidenced in passages such as Gen 2:7; Job 27:3; 33:4; Isa 2:22; and Lam 4:20. Death then is the disappearance or removal of this living breath (Ps 104:29–30; cf. Knibb; 1989:398). The subsequent determination of death is relatively simple in Hebrew thought. If life is the connectedness between God and man, death is its disjunction. This biblical perspective of death is best encapsulated in the words of Qohelet via a broken chiasm: a–b–c–d–b–a–c–d.

returns . . .

the dust (*'apar*) . . .

to the earth . . .

as it was . . .

the spirit (*ruakh*) . . .

returns . . .

to God . . .

who gave it.

(Eccl 12:7; personal)

The parallel lines in the verse clearly indicate that death is the reversal of the created order expressed in Gen 2:7 (Fox, 1999:332).

> *. . . death is a cruel reversal of God's intentions. God formed man from the dust of the ground (Gen 2:7), and gave him life, personality, intellect, capabilities, moral responsibility, and powers of creativity. Death reverses the process and turns us all into dust again, colorless and lifeless (Tidball, 1989: 183).*

The reference to 'dust' and 'spirit', the connection of dust with earth (a synonym of ground) and the divine source of life all highlight this reversal of life, called death. Essentially, death ends in nothing (Loader, 1986:132).

A more dominant question for people in biblical times was, 'Where do the dead go?' The answer to this question is encapsulated in the Hebrew word *sh'ol*. While the word itself has a rather extensive semantic range, its basic concept is akin to our modern English word 'grave'. Knibb argues that while *sh'ol* is the 'land of no return' it should also be differentiated from 'grave' as it connotes 'the realm of the dead' where the dead continue to live 'in a very weak and reduced state' (1989:407, 405).

The most telling evidence is recorded in Ezekiel 31 and 32. In these chapters, *sh'ol* (31:15, 16, 17; 32:21, 27) parallels two other words, *qeber* (32:22, 23, 25, 26) and *bor* (31:14, 16; 32:18, 23, 24, 25, 29). The word *qeber* is derived from the verbal root q–b–r which always implies burial or grave, whereas *bor* nearly always means a pit or hole in the ground. The parallel between the three words clearly points to *sh'ol* as grave rather than some place where the souls of the dead go to (Harris, 1980:892–893). Fox argues emphatically, 'Thus Qoh 12:7 does not imply continued existence of the sort that would overcome death and compensate for the miseries of life' and discounts 'the possibility of an enduring soul as unknowable and irrelevant' (1999:331, 332).

BURIAL IN HB

With the concept of life and death as background canvass, we discover that burial was extremely important in OT times. Abraham's purchase of the cave of Macpelah to bury Sarah in (Gen 23) illustrates this point. Further, the OT regularly records the burial of famous characters even when little else is known about them (cf. Jdgs 10:1–2; 10:3–5; 12:8–10; 12:11–12 and 12:13–15). By contrast, if a person did not receive a proper burial, this was considered very disgraceful (Isa 14:18–20; Jer 16:4; Trafton, 1996).

PATRIARCHAL PERIOD

The patriarchal narratives of Genesis reveal that several generations were often buried in the same family tomb as was the case with Abraham's family. Sarah (Gen 23:19), Abraham (Gen 25:9), Isaac, Rebekah, Leah (Gen 49:31) and Jacob (Gen 50:13) were all buried in the cave of Macpelah (Motyer, 1980:211).

Sometimes circumstances prevented a family member from being buried in the family tomb as was the case with Deborah (Gen 35:8) and Rachel (Gen 35:19–20). In both instances, the tombs were marked by a tree and a pillar or *stele* respectively (Thompson, 1986:92). Coffins were not part of the norm either and the reference to a coffin for Joseph (Gen 50:2–3, 26) is an exceptional case (Motyer, 1980:211; Thompson, 1986:93).

BURIAL LEGISLATION

The Torah provided certain instructions with regards to death and burial which would suggest the start of Israelite tradition. The Torah set out prompt burial as the norm for Israel (Deut 21:22–23) unless a Sabbath or feast day was involved (Gower, 1987:72). Moreover, contact with the dead rendered a person ceremonially unclean and therefore a period of ritual cleansing was required immediately after the burial. The cultural practices of mourning, lamenting and tearing of clothes were forbidden for the high priest (Lev 21:1–11) and those under the Nazarite vow (Num 6:7). Other cultural customs such as body lacerations, shaving or balding were prohibited for every Israelite (Lev 19:27–28; 21:5; Deut 14:1). Other Canaanite practices such as 'eating of tithe in mourning or offering them to the dead' (Deut 26:14) were also prohibited (Motyer, 1980:211).

The Torah allowed for longer periods of mourning for certain situations. The death of a national leader like Moses (Deut 34:5–8) and Aaron (Num 20:28–29) could occasion a 30–day mourning. The same length of mourning was also prescribed for women who were captured during war and forced to marry their captors. The mourning apparently was for their parents who may now be lost to them (Motyer, 1980:211).

Excursus on Cremation

Cremation was not the normal practice among the Israelites (Alter, 1999:191), but there are several examples of cremation in the OT, for example, Achan (Josh 7:25–26), Saul (1 Sam 31:12) and the King of Edom (Amos 2:1). However, in several of them God's judgment (cf. Amos 2:1; 6:10) and curse are involved (Josh 7:25–26).It should be noted that when Paul offered his body to be burned (1 Cor. 13:3), he was speaking about martyrdom rather than cremation (George, 2002:1). A brief glance at certain cremation stories may enable us to clarify the stories.

In 1 Samuel 31:12–13, the people of Jabesh–gilead went to Bethshan (about 16kms distance) to retrieve the mutilated remains of King Saul and his son. Then they burnt the bodies and buried the bones. The reason for burning the bodies is not spelled out but in this episode it may have been done to keep the bodies from greater dishonor or because the corpses 'had already begun to rot' (Alter, 1999:191).

2 Chronicles 16:14 records Asa's funeral which apparently included burial and burning. It may be argued that the fire here refers to cremation. There are three clauses in this verse: 'they buried him . . .', 'they laid him out in a coffin . . .' and 'they made a great fire . . .' The verse seems to suggest cremation as the third act in the burial. However, the Hebrew reads 'they made a great fire to/for him', that is in his honor. This is the reading of several translations (HCSB, ESV, NKJV, NET, JPS, NLT, NIV, CEV, etc.). In fact the Septuagint (LXX) translates the last clause as 'they made a great funeral for him'. In the case of King Jehoram (2 Chron 21:19), the text specifically states that no great fire was 'made to/for him'. The same context is used here as in the Asa story – Jehoram was not honored by his people. The reference to such ceremonial fires also appears in relation to King Zedekiah (Jer 34:4–5). In these stories, the fire does not indicate cremation but some sort of ceremony for the deceased king (Payne, 1994:650).

While the biblical data on cremation is inconclusive at best, there are certain reasons for arguing against cremation. Most of the biblical stories involve burial rather than cremation, whereas most of the cremation cases involve some divine judgment (see above). There are also practical considerations against cremation. The biblical narratives often involve a burial marker but this would be impossible if the body is not buried. There is also the question of who would keep the ash urn usually given to the family after a cremation.

At the same time, there are arguments in favor of cremation. The biblical resurrection concept does not require burial or cremation since God will raise the dead regardless of burial type. Moreover, even buried bodies will eventually decompose and become dust, and cremation simply speeds up the process. From a practical point of view, cremation is normally cheaper, allows for flexibility in organizing memorial services, is preferred in certain instances (when land is unavailable) and if it involves a pre–death wish of the person (cf. Fairchild, 2014:2).

Perhaps, in the absence of definite biblical teaching, the issue is as much a matter of choice. However, questions about a marker to remember the deceased and place for keeping the urn should be carefully thought through. The suggestion by Fairchild is a balanced way to approach the subject.

How you want to be laid to rest is a personal decision. It is important to discuss your wishes with your family, and also know the preferences of your family members. This will make funeral preparations a little easier for everyone involved. (Fairchild, 2014:2)

Burial Steps

As Thompson put it, 'Death, in Bible times, was never hushed. When a person died there was an open and public demonstration of grief . . .' (1986:92). This sentiment gave birth to the first major step of burial – lamentation.

Wail and Lamentation

The 'wail was an announcement to the neighborhood that a death has taken place' (Gower, 1987:71). Perhaps the most dramatic demonstration of the wail and lamentation which accompany death is seen in the narrative about the death of the firstborn of Egypt. As Gower describes it, 'that wail could be heard through the whole country' (1987:71). Micah 1:8–9 speaks of the prophet's wail and lamentation over the impending doom (death) of the nation and compares wailing to the sounds of jackals and owls (Gower, 1987:71).

> *Therefore I will wail and howl,*
>
> *I will go stripped and naked;*
>
> *I will make a wailing like the jackals. And a mourning like the ostriches,*
>
> *For her wounds are incurable. For it has come to Judah;*
>
> *It has come to the gate of My people—To Jerusalem. (Micah 1:8–9, NKJV)*

Similarly, David mourned over the deaths of his son Absalom (2 Sam 18:33–19:4) and Abner (2 Sam 3:31–34).

The mourning period usually lasted for seven days (Motyer,

1980:211; Thompson, 1986:92). This was certainly the case with the burial of King Saul and his sons (1 Sam 31:13). However, the days of mourning could be longer than a week. In the national mourning for Moses, the period lasted for 30 days (Deut 34:8). Genesis 50:1–5 states that the Egyptians mourned the death of Jacob for 70 days, but clarifies this by explaining that the embalming process took longer than expected. It should also be noted that the death and burial of some leading characters, for instance, Elisha (2 Kgs 13:20–21), involved minimal fanfare. The account of Abraham mourning over Sarah states no time period (Gen 23:2).

The activities associated with this funeral lamentation involved mourning, crying, beating one's chest, tearing clothes (2 Sam 3:31), wearing sackcloth and covering with ash (Thompson, 1986:92). Laments were even composed and sung at such times by professional mourners or hired wailers (Jer 9:17–18; Amos 5:16) making the funeral procession a rather noisy affair (Thompson, 1986:92–93). Everyone participated in the mourning wails as this provided a legitimate outlet for grief and may have been viewed as a duty for the relatives of the dead person (Thompson, 1986:93).

The funeral for Abner (2 Sam 3:31–34) underscores the most essential elements of mourning: (1) mourning was required (v31); (2) it involved tearing of clothes (v31); (3) wearing of sackcloth was deemed appropriate (v31); (4) a procession was held (v31); (5) wailing was described (vv2, 34); and (5) a lament was composed and sung (vv33–34).

Burial Proper

Israelites valued a proper burial (Eccl 6:3) and considered not being buried as divine judgment (Deut 28:26; 2 Kgs 9:10; Jer 7:33; Horn, 1979). Quick burials were held, often within 24 hours (Horn, 1979:167), partially driven by the hot climate which led to rapid decomposition (Gower, 1987:72). The body was normally washed, wrapped in cloth and carried on a bier or wooden stretcher to the burial site (Gower, 1987:72; Horn, 1979:167). Burial sites could be natural caves or artificially–made ones (Gen 49:29–32; Jdgs 8:32). Inside the cave, niches or shelves were carved out where the corpse would be placed. Decomposed bones were then placed in ossuaries, stone jars or bone boxes, to allow reuse of the tomb. After the burial, the tomb was sealed with stone. Alternatively, the body was surrounded by boulders in a rough oblong shape about 50 cms in diameter. The body was then covered by earth (Gower, 1987:72–73). Because of the hardness of the ground, burial was actually not common in Israel and the burial sites described above were normally kept outside the village except for royalty (1 Kgs 2:10; Gower, 1987:73). The Egyptian burial rite of embalming was not practiced, though there is some evidence of embalming as in the story of Joseph (Gen 50:2, 26).

Funeral Meal

In the lengthy job description God gave to Jeremiah, several events are listed that Jeremiah was or was not allowed to participate in. Included in the list is a prohibition from entering any 'house where a mourning feast is taking place' (Jer 16:5; HCSB). Literally, the verse reads 'a house of mourning (*marzeakh*)'. However, the parallel with Amos 6:7, 'mourning (*marzeakh*) of revelry' and the mention of food in verse 7, implies that this is a meal or feast (Brown, 1979:931). This action of the prophet served to highlight the fact that Judah's demise would be similar to a funeral but without the funeral meal (Jer 16:7).

Conclusion

The burial customs recorded in HB reflect both the theological view of the Scriptures on life and death, and the cultural milieu of Israel's world. The conceptualization of life and death are tied in closely to the teachings of the Torah and the prophets. Life is created by God and God's intentionality differentiates humans from other living things. The 'living breath' is the symbol which denotes this humanness that we all share.

The presence of sin precipitates the reversal of life and this is referred to as death. In HB, death is the dissolution of the creation intentionality of God. If life is the combination of material (the dust of the ground) and divine (the living breath), then death is the reversal of this. A dead person is one whose material components return to their source and whose breath of life also returns to its source, that is God. While the dead are depicted as going to *sh'ol*, this does not connote a place where some version of life continues to exist. Rather, *sh'ol* is the grave, the pit in the ground where the dead are buried.

Further, it has been observed that burial customs reflect the cultural norms of Israel's neighbors but exhibit clear distinctions. Like many of the tribes around them, the patriarchs and Israel buried their dead in tombs or marked graves. In some instances, the cultural practices of other nations are copied, as in the embalming of Joseph's body and the practice of wailing. At the same time, certain Canaanite rituals such as body lacerations were expressly forbidden by God. To use terminology from today's world, genuine contextualization occurred in HB. On the one hand, certain cultural practices within Israel's milieu were adhered to, while, on the other hand, other cultural practices were rejected.

It appears that following this double–edged contextualization method of considering biblical principle as well as cultural norms is the way forward in this discussion concerning life, death and burial practices. Customs which do not conflict with any specific biblical teaching should be embraced, while those that may contradict Scripture or foster a degree of ambivalence should be very carefully thought through. This is not to say that any particular practice should be rejected outright. Before we reject any cultural practice, we ought to consider the complete ramifications of acceptance or rejection. A double–edged contextualization is perhaps the safest way forward.

I contend that double–edged contextualization involves accommodation, adjustment and restructuring in both directions. Another way of putting this is that genuine contextualization results in gospel methodology transforming culture while also enculturating itself so as to be considered less foreign. The HB underscores this idea rather profoundly and implies that this is the way God's church should live today. This is especially significant when applied to the subject at hand.

Funerals are as significant today as they were in biblical times. The also afford the church with great opportunities for ministry and pastoral care. Through careful application of the double–edged contextualization practiced in HB, we may benefit in ways we have not yet considered possible. At the very least we ought to view funeral practices as missional opportunities, not merely to minister to the bereaved but also to grow God's kingdom. Exerting the proper effort to accomplish these goals may uncover quantum leap possibilities for the Church.

Reference List

Alter, Robert. 1996. Genesis. New York: W. W. Norton.

Alter, Robert. 1999. The David Story. New York. W. W. Norton.

Brown, Francis. 1979. The New Brown–Driver–Briggs–Gesenius Hebrew and English Lexicon. Peabody: Hendrickson.

Fairchild, Mary. 2014. 'What Does the Bible Say About Cremation?' http://christianity.about.com/od/christianfuneral/i/cremationburial.htm (accessed 9 May 2014).

Fox, Michael V. 1999. A Time to Tear Down and a Time to Build Up. Grand Rapids: Eerdmans.

George, Timothy. 2002. 'Cremation Confusion: Is it unscriptural for a Christian to be cremated?' http://www.christianitytoday.com/ct/2002/may21/27.66.html (accessed 9 May 2014).

Harris, Richard L. 1980. She'ol. Theological Wordbook of the Old Testament. Vol 2. Chicago: Moody.

Horn, Siegfried H. 1979 Seventh–day Adventist Bible Dictionary. Hagerstown: Review and Herald.

Kidner, Derek. 1987. The Message of Jeremiah. Leicester: Inter–Varsity.

Knibb, Michale A. 1989. 'Life and Death in the old Testament.' In The Ancient World of Israel. Edited by R. E. Clements. Pp 395–415. Cambridge: Cambridge University Press.

Loader, J. A. 1986. Ecclesiastes. Grand Rapids: Eerdmans.

Motyer, J. Alec. 1980. Burial and Mourning. The Illustrated Bible Dictionary Part 1. Leicester: Inter–Varsity.

Payne, J. Barton. 1994. '2 Chronicles.' In NIV Bible Commentary, Volume 1: Old Testament. Grand Rapids: Zondervan.

Sailhamer, John H. 1992. The Pentateuch as Narrative. Grand Rapids: Zondervan.

Sarna, Nahum M. 1989. Genesis. The JPS Torah Commentary. Philadelphia: The Jewish Publication Society.

Thompson, J. A. 1986. Handbook of Life in Bible Times. Leicester: Inter–Varsity.

Trafton, Joseph L. 1996. Burial. http://www.biblestudytools.com/dictionaries/bakers–evangelical–dictionary/burial.html (accessed 24 April 2014).

Tidball, Derek. 1989. That's Life! Leicester: Inter–Varsity.

Wenham, Gordon J. 1987. Genesis 1–15. WBC 1. Waco, TX: Word Books.

Chapter 5

Comfort All Who Mourn

Michael Kier

Blessed be God, even the Father of our Lord Jesus Christ, the Father of mercies, and the God of all comfort; Who comforteth us in all our tribulation, that we may be able to comfort them which are in any trouble, by the comfort wherewith we ourselves are comforted of God. 2 Corinthians 1:3–4 [1]

In the way of righteousness is life; and in the pathway thereof there is no [eternal] death. Proverbs 12:28

...Let me die the [temporary] death of the righteous, and let my last end be like his. Numbers 23:10b

...the righteous hath hope in his death. Proverbs 14:32b

Blessed are they that mourn: for they shall be comforted. Matthew 5:4

Wherefore comfort one another with these [God's] words [of truth]. 1 Thessalonians 4:18

For whatsoever things were written aforetime were written for our learning, that we through patience and comfort of the scriptures might have hope. Romans 15:4

Keys to understanding this paper:

He [Christ] would reveal Himself in all human afflictions as the Comforter. Signs of the Times, August 15, 1895

Pain cannot exist in the atmosphere of Heaven. The Signs of the Times, January 27, 1888

Let us come to God as little children to learn from Him. When you learn His way you will be comforted by His words, and when you yourselves have been thus comforted, you will then be in a position to speak to others words of comfort. The Wisconsin Recorder, September 15, 1909

Thousands who now reject the message of salvation would accept Christ if they could see the beauty of His character reflected in His followers. The Review and Herald, November 3, 1896

All despair is swept from the soul when Christ is seen in His true character. The Review and Herald, February 3, 1891

INTRODUCTION

It is our privilege and sacred responsibility, as sincere followers of Jesus Christ, to minister to the grieving as Christ's representative. Christ weeps for the mourners who can see nothing more than the surface circumstances of their trouble. Yet the Comforter of the world stands by the side of how many Asian mourners as One still unrecognized, One still not properly introduced.

The intention of this article is to:

Ask the question, How do I locally, and how do we globally, serve together in such a way as to work quickly and most effectively toward preventing another person from dying outside the comfort of salvation in Christ?

Urge you as a sincere reader to determine to continue, begin anew, or take the first step in walking progressively closer to God by receiving every word of divine revelation. In this way you and I invite Christ to live and share His life through us individually and collectively for the purpose of truly bringing comfort those who are otherwise destined for the second death (Rev.21:8).

HUMANLY "IMPOSSIBLE" CALLING

We must never presume to imagine that of ourselves we could genuinely comfort someone whose beloved family member or friend has passed away (John 15:5). It is impossible for any human to thoroughly comfort another who is experiencing the finality of death. To receive and deliver genuine, satisfying and lasting comfort it must originate from the Source of infinite comfort. Fellow mourners must be wisely and tenderly introduced to the God of all comfort who has purposed to comfort all who mourn – through the shared experiences of Christ's disciples who have received His comfort personally (2 Cor 1:3–4).

"The Lord works through human instrumentalities, and has commissioned to his followers the duty of ministering to those who are desponding and distressed. There are hearts all around us that need to be uplifted, that need the bright beams of the Sun of Righteousness. The Lord looks to those whom he has comforted and blessed to enlighten those who are in darkness, and to relieve those who are in sorrow. Those who have received light and peace and joy are not to pass by those who mourn, but are to come close to them in human sympathy, and help them to see a sin–pardoning Savior, a merciful God.

"Christ has borne our griefs and carried our sorrows, and he will give joy and gladness to those who mourn. Will you, my brother and sister who have felt the sorrows of earth, do service for Christ in helping the very ones who need your help? Will you who are strong bear the infirmities of the weak? Our Savior was a man of sorrows and acquainted with grief. He identified his interests with those of the weak and suffering. In looking to Jesus we look to one who comforts all who mourn in Zion. How many more might have been comforted and blessed if human messengers had performed the service which Christ had enjoined upon them to suffering humanity! "Pure religion and undefiled before God and the Father is this, to visit the fatherless and widows in their affliction, and to keep himself unspotted from the world."

"Those who love Jesus will have the mind of Christ, and will comfort all who mourn; those who are poor, tempted, and discouraged they will help to walk in the light of the cross, and not in the shadows and in the darkness. They will point out to them the fact that the blood of Christ speaketh in their behalf "better things than that of Abel." Christians are to minister to all that mourn, to comfort many sorrowful hearts whose memory is filled with pictures of disappointment, of forfeited friendships, and of bitter bereavements, whose history has been one of sorrow and mourning.

"The Lord Jesus has given to his people the special work of comforting all that mourn. Christ is working for this class, and he calls upon human beings to become his instrumentalities in bringing light and hope to those who are mourning in the midst of apparently dark providences. Christ calls upon us to show them a bright side by our sympathy and love, and prevent the troubled soul from charging God with unfaithfulness. Our heavenly Father is never unmindful of those whom sorrow has touched. But many think that God has no care for them, as a result of the negligence of his professed followers; for these fail to act their part as colaborers with Christ in comforting those who mourn." (White 1895:Para 2–7)

CULTURES OF DEATH

"There is a way which seemeth right unto a man, but the end thereof are the ways of death" (Prov 14:12; 16:25, KJV).

The Gospel of Jesus Christ is distinctly separate from all other philosophies and ethical codes including those originating from Asian nations such as India and China.[2] Common Scripture readings for a Seventh–day Adventist funeral seem largely inappropriate for use outside of the Christian context. So how do Christ's followers genuinely cooperate with God's effort comfort all that mourn, including those who have lost a loved one who has never embraced the blessed hope?

THE COMFORT OF TRUTH

During traditional funeral ceremonies people are often moved to ask life's ultimate questions. The Lord of Life invites His sons and daughters to prayerfully seek for appropriately sensitive times and settings to more clearly unfold the truth as it is in Christ that will lead a sinner to salvation from sin and eternal death. God always provides comfort in the truth. Genuine and lasting comfort comes only through the Holy Spirit who ever remains simultaneously the Comforter and the Spirit of truth (John 14:16–17; 15:26; 16:6–7). Thus to be truly comforted, a person must be gently, yet clearly taught how to welcome the truth of God's Word regarding both His justice and His mercy (Prov 1:23; 3:11–12; 4:13; 5:23; Rev 3:19). Apart from genuine comfort by the divine Comforter/"Convincer", the only remaining options will be varying degrees of mere temporary or outright false comfort (Jer 8:11; 23:17; Zech 10:2).

IN LIGHT OF THE SECOND DEATH

Eternal destruction is declared by God to be humanity's greatest fear (Heb 2:14–15). This undercurrent of dread can become a debilitating force moving mankind into a most vulnerable position. Even the sincerest attempts to comfort mourners apart from God's revealed Word will cruelly manipulate most into making little if any difference between the righteous and the wicked in their death. The world is now tempted on an unprecedented scale to comfort mourners with a false assurance that there will be no second death reserved for unrepentant sinners. Our sacred responsibility is to give every soul within the sphere of our influence a compassionate opportunity to understand every Word of God, especially His ultimate victory over all death. As a friend succinctly stated, "If you don't want to die, then you must want salvation from sin."(Roth 2000)

A funeral service conducted in memory of the person who has lived as a whole–hearted follower of Jesus Christ stands in marked contrast to all other religious ceremonies and spiritual traditions. The eternal hope of the genuine Christian makes the atmosphere surrounding the casket bright with the promise of the resurrection of eternal life at Christ's return in the clouds of heaven. However the majority, many who profess religious belief, are shrouded in thick darkness, without God and without true hope in the world though they presume to take refuge in the sayings and traditions of men[3] or doctrines of devils (Is 28:15; Gen 3:3–4; Mat 7:21–23).

PREVENTING CHRISTLESS FUNERALS

Attending a funeral service for someone from a people–group unacquainted with the gospel of Jesus Christ can be an unpleasant awakening. The merit–making ceremonies of spiritualism, conducted in relation to the death of one's soul, can lead us to mourn deeply for all who are dying in a state of eternal separation from Christ. Sensitivity to this preventable horror should break and melt our hearts to press together to proclaim salvation in Christ alone. Of course we must enter into Christ's ways to meaningfully care for mourners in our immediate sphere of influence. At the same time the obvious long–term need is to be able to preemptively care for hurting people well before the heartbreak of the funeral setting.

Individually we can and must make it a personal priority to visit the bedside of the aging, the sick and the suffering ones and gently point them to the only Savior who takes away the sin of the world for "God would have every afflicted soul look to the brightness of Calvary's cross." (White 1895:par 5) Why? Because "All despair is swept from the soul when Christ is seen in His true character." (White 1891:par 10)

"The very first and the most important thing is to melt and subdue the soul by presenting our Lord Jesus Christ as the sin–bearer, the sin–pardoning Savior, making the gospel as clear as possible. "When the Holy Spirit works among us"…" souls who are unready for Christ's appearing are convicted."…"The simplicity of the truth reaches their hearts. It touches all classes." (White 1899:264)

COMFORTING MOURNERS IN THE CONTEXT OF TIMELESS PRINCIPLES

1. Silent Presence. In times of overwhelming grief our presence most often communicates more appropriately than mere language. Job's friends provided more meaningful comfort during seven days and nights of mourning in silence with him than when they later tried to interpret to him the reason and cause for his multiplied concentration of tragedies (Job 2:11–13; 16:1–2). This ancient Eastern example contains potent lessons designed for us living at the very end of time (1 Cor 10:11; Rom 15:4).

2. Blessed Are They That Mourn. Near the beginning of His public ministry, Christ pronounced God's blessing on those who genuinely grieve (Mat 5:4). Every sorrow is allowed for a divine purpose. Sorrow is intended to turn our attention toward the eternal. God reveals our character defects so that we may learn to trust Him to set us free from everything that would prevent us from enjoying eternity with Him. It is God's intention to so refine the sorrowing heart that it becomes His dwelling place. Times of pain, suffering and loss are the very occasions when heaven works to brighten our experience with the precious revealing's of Christ's deeply comforting presence (White 1896:9–12).

3. Sorrow Motivates Wisdom. Grief and tragic loss can provide an intense motivation to open the heart to heaven's wisdom. King Solomon recorded his own observations and personal experience noting that the teachable heart of the wise will be found in the house of mourning, but the largely unimpressionable heart of fools is attracted to the house of mirth (Ecc 7:2–4). The one attending a funeral service and taking to heart the temporary nature of life and the sober realities of death may be especially prepared to respond to the drawing influence of the Spirit of God working through a caring friend's tactful sharing of Bible truth.

4. How to Console Mourners. "Blessed be… the God of all comfort; Who comforteth us in all our tribulation, that we may be able to comfort them which are in any trouble, by the comfort wherewith we ourselves are comforted by God" (2 Cor 1:3–4, KJV). When we can share from our heart how the Lord continues to lift our soul above the daily sorrows and disappointments of life into the realm of His peace, bringing meaning out of our suffering, then our words can become a genuine blessing (White 1896:12).

"Those who are comforted of God, who experience peace and rest in him, will bear rich clusters of fruit in comforting others with the consolation which they themselves have received from the compassionate Savior. The Lord Jesus often draws souls to himself through some human agent to whom he has given a valuable experience in mourning and sorrow. He often reaches hearts by causing those who have suffered to come close to others who are passing through affliction, who can point the mourners to the bow of promise that encircles the throne of God. They can tell those who are in bereavement or in physical suffering that there is One who knows their weakness, and who will be to them hope, comfort, peace, and joy. They can encourage them to trust in God, who desires that the frail human sufferer shall lean hard upon his everlasting arms. Christ would encourage the timid disciples to look up to him. For the purpose of uplifting and encouraging others the Lord has prepared helpers for every emergency. Let every one in the Lord's service be ready to see the needs of others, and to draw from their experience that which will be a blessing to those that mourn. Let them shed forth the bright beams of the Sun of Righteousness" (White 1895:par 1–6).

5. Avoid the "Miserable Comforter" Path. As with any potential soul–winning opportunity, we must guard against carnal motives to restlessly rush in as self–appointed comforters eager to be the influential center of attention (2 Sam 18:19–30). It is possible to sabotage our own best attempts to comfort by pressing ahead without possessing a credible character witness. "God calls for workers. Personal activity is needed. But conversion comes first; seeking for the salvation of others, next" (White 1903:par12). God has given a definite order for us to be effective in finishing the work of comforting all who mourn (ibid. par13). It takes much time with God to be prepared for sacred service.[4]

To speak to the grieving merely from the ability of natural human reasoning can result in more damage than good. If our words are devoid of Christ's selfless love and truth we will be like miserable comforters. "How then comfort ye me in vain, seeing in your answers there remaineth falsehood?" (Job 21:34, KJV). The very people whom we seek to reach will assume a defensive, repelling attitude if they are approached by any power other than the selfless love of God.[5] Without Christ we can do nothing to truly benefit mourners (John 15:5). Since God is love and Christ is God, whatever is done apart from Christ is done without His love (1 Cor 13:1–3; John 15:5; 1 John 4:16). But whatever is done out of pure love, be it ever so little or despised in the sight of others, it will be entirely fruitful for good; for God measures more with how much love our work is done, than by any amount of work we appear to accomplish without His love.[6] Divine love can do nothing but good and it exists in us as a people only as long as God reigns supreme (White 1952:195).[7]

6. Christ's Healing Love. When Christ's parting words are fulfilled, when we love one another as He loved us (John 15:12); when we love the church and the world as He loved both, "then for us His mission is accomplished. We are fitted for heaven; for we have [embraced] heaven in our hearts" (White 1898:641:3). When Christ has all our heart we will then have everything we need to really comfort all who mourn.

7. Each Funeral – Our Opportunity to Be Christ's Channel of Highest Influence. Apart from the truth of God's revealed Word, every funeral is destined to become another platform for the enemy of all righteousness to reinforce his original lie; that God does not mean what He says, that His law can be transgressed without facing the ultimate consequence of one life, the sleep of death, and then the judgment (Gen 3:3–4; Heb 9:27). Yet the sincerely candid and grief–filled heart is better prepared to acknowledge the stark reality – that any degree of evil brings heart–rending and deadly serious consequences. But without the presence of the Spirit of God, no mourning heart will be touched, no grieving sinner will be won to Christ. Yet if we are connected with Christ, no matter how ordinary, or ignorant we may be, God gives us His influence that will tell upon hearts. He designs to make us the channel for the outworking of the highest influence in the universe, in our life – and even in our death.[8]

Below is a fitting illustration from the experience of James White:

"My husband attended the funeral. There were many present who had listened to his [the young deceased] faithful exhortations, and despised them while he was living, and some who had abused him on account of his faith, a short time before. They looked upon the countenance of the dead, which bore a pleasant smile, and turned from the sight with quivering lip and moistened eye. We could but think, though dead, he speaketh. It was the testimony of all present that they had never seen so pleasant and lovely an expression upon the face of the dead. We followed the body to the grave, to rest until the righteous dead awake to immortality" (White 1948:92:1).

The short excerpt below gives an insightful glimpse into how Ellen White herself relied upon God's sustaining presence and the truth of His Word during her nearly overwhelming grief at the death of her husband.

"My physical strength had been prostrated by the blow, yet the power of divine grace sustained me in my great bereavement. When I saw my husband breathe his last, I felt that Jesus was more precious to me than He ever had been in any previous hour of my life" (White 1915:252:1–4).

"At times I felt that I could not have my husband die. But these words seemed to be impressed on my mind: "Be still, and know that I am God." Psalm 46:10. I keenly feel my loss, but dare not give myself up to useless grief. This would not bring back the dead. And I am not so selfish as to wish, if I could, to bring him from his peaceful slumber to engage again in the battles of life. Like a tired warrior, he has lain down to sleep. I will look with pleasure upon his resting place. The best way in which I and my children can honor the memory of him who has fallen, is to take the work where he left it, and in the strength of Jesus carry it forward to completion. We will be thankful for the years of usefulness that were granted to him; and for his sake, and for Christ's sake, we will learn from his death a lesson which we shall never forget. We will let this bereavement make us more kind and gentle, more forbearing, patient, and thoughtful toward the living" (White 1915:253:1–2).

HISTORIC/PROPHETIC PERSPECTIVE

Entire nations stand at the brink of unprecedented grief.[9] Since World War II, the disturbing history of countries such as Japan, Rwanda, Vietnam, and Cambodia, are inadequate to portray the grief foretold in the final unfolding of prophetic events. May the wise in heart look ahead and cherish every funeral service as a fresh opportunity to gain experience in caring for aching hearts as we intentionally prepare together for the predicted time of trouble and mourning just ahead.[10]

Heaven's way is for us to follow the Lamb of God wherever He goes, and He has determined for us to go with Him to comfort all with the endtime truths that will prevent the kind mourning that can never be comforted. To receive this degree of genuine, satisfying and lasting comfort it must originate from the Source of all comfort – the truth of the Word of God. Genuine and lasting consolation can proceed only from Holy Spirit who ever remains the Comforter and "Convincer" of truth at the same time. Thus to truly be comforted, we must learn to daily receive a love of being instructed and corrected by every revealed Word of God (Prov 5:23).

CAREFUL TO COPY PATTERNS OF DIVINE REVELATION

"What thing soever I command you, observe to do it: thou shalt not add thereto, nor diminish from it" (Deut 12:32, KJV).

"The heathen systems of sacrifice were a perversion of the system that God had appointed;..." "...In the instruction given through Moses, God had placed restrictions upon their association with idolaters; but this teaching had been misinterpreted. It was intended to prevent them from conforming to the practices of the heathen. But it was used to build up a wall of separation between Israel and all other nations." (White 1898:28)

"We cannot copy the example of the world at all in anything" (White 1888:859).

Below is an example of a funeral service for one of Israel's spiritual leaders. This history serves to highlight how God is honored by simplicity, even for the burial of the High Priest. Great display and expense were avoided. Adequate time was given for the people to mourn Aarons' death (Num 20:28–29).

"The burial of Aaron, conducted according to the express command of God, was in striking contrast to the customs of the present day. When a man in high position dies, his funeral services are attended with the greatest pomp and ceremony. When Aaron died, one of the most illustrious men that ever lived, there were only two of his nearest friends to witness his death, and to attend his burial. And that lonely grave upon Mount Hor was forever hidden from the sight of Israel. God is not glorified in the great display so often made over the dead, and the great outlay of means in returning their bodies to the dust" (White 1880:par 21–22).

"Concerning the burial of Israel's high priest, the Scriptures give only the simple record, "There Aaron died, and there he was buried." Deuteronomy 10:6. In what striking contrast to the customs of the present day was this burial, conducted according to the express command of God. In modern times the funeral services of a man of high position are often made the occasion of ostentatious and extravagant display" (White 1890:427).

MULTIPLIED FUNERALS: A SIGN OF THE END

As God's Holy Spirit is more fully grieved and withdrawn from the earth by the rejection of heaven–sent light and truth, intensifying disasters by sea, air and land will follow one another in quick succession. All these are God's agencies of mercy to arouse humanity to a sense of eternal danger (White 1917:277). Wisdom is urging us to be united as one in Christ to bear a credible witness before and then during the times of pandemic grief when human hearts will be failing them for the fear of death that sweeps through the earth.

SUMMARY

Comforting all who mourn is one of Christ's highest priorities and so must it be with all who continue to respond to His drawing to become and remain part of the family of God. More specifically, inspiration urges us to address the reality that to fulfill the divine expectations, it will necessitate the seemingly impossible task of our becoming as one with Christ – without compromising a single principle of God's written Word (John 17:21–23; Eph 5:25–27).

When we as a body decide to obey God from the heart to comfort all who mourn, especially in the midst of darkness and crisis, the glory of God will shine forth. It could be again as it was in the days of Jonah when he simply did as God directed. It was precisely then that the people of the doomed city "believed God". God's warnings and corrections always communicate the comfort of hope to each who will turn to trust and obey Him with the whole heart (Jonah 3:4).

FINAL APPEAL

In light of the impending disasters soon to come upon the whole earth, God is calling His church to enter an experience with Him that has not yet been done. "The harmony and the unity of the church are the credentials that must be presented to the world to prove that God has sent His Son into the world to give grace and light and truth" (White 1977:30). God's prophets promise it.[11] "It is self that divides brethren; but self must die. Christ will then be revealed in our words, in our tender regard for one another…" (White 1844).

The Lord will bring to pass the oneness of His remnant people with Himself – internationally, empowered by Christ's righteousness alone. This is God's final method of warning and invitation to convince the world of His loving comfort. Then when Jesus returns He will find faith on the earth! Let us now begin to fully cooperate in giving Heaven's ultimate personal appeal – death to self for glory of God and the saving of the nations. In this final hour of judgment a person cannot yet be considered "reached" and warned until they have had a credible personal introduction to the eternal Comforter.

For all who realize the responsibility, let us pray for the mercy and the power of God's Love to carry His true comfort to all who mourn. For the hour is fast approaching when there will be no time for those who are not warned and separated from the deceptions of false comfort. Their last day to receive divine comfort will have come to an end.

"For whatsoever things were written aforetime were written for our learning, that we through patience and comfort of the scriptures might have hope" (Rom 15:4, KJV).

NOTES

1. *Scripture quotations from The Authorized (King James) Version. Rights in the Authorized Version in the United Kingdom are vested in the Crown. Reproduced by permission of the Crown's patentee, Cambridge University Press.*

2. *"[Ellen White's] writings hold firmly to the doctrine that the gospel, as revealed in the sacred Scriptures, presents the only means of salvation. No recognition whatever is given to any of the philosophies of India or the ethical codes of Burma and China as compared with the gospel of the Son of God. This alone is the hope of a lost world." (White, Ellen G., 1915, "The Funeral Services at Battle Creek." Life Sketches of Ellen G. White, chapter 61, titled Page 472, paragraph 2)*

3. *"Satan has wrought with deceiving power, bringing in a multiplicity of errors that obscure the truth. Error cannot stand alone, and would soon become extinct if it did not fasten itself like a parasite upon the tree of truth. Error draws its life from the truth of God. The traditions of men, like floating germs, attach themselves to the truth of God, and men regard them as a part of the truth. Through false doctrines, Satan gains a foothold, and captivates the minds of men, causing them to hold theories that have no foundation in truth. Men boldly teach for doctrines the commandments of men; and as traditions pass on from age to age, they acquire a power over the human mind." (White, Ellen G., October 22, 1895, "Satan's Malignity Against Christ and His People", The Review and Herald, paragraphs 3–4)*

4. *All who are under the training of God need the quiet hour for communion with their own hearts, with nature, and with God. In them is to be revealed a life that is not in harmony with the world, its customs, or its practices; and they need to have a personal experience in obtaining a knowledge of the will of God. We must individually hear Him speaking to the heart. When every other voice is hushed, and in quietness we wait before Him, the silence of the soul makes more distinct the voice of God. He bids us, "Be still, and know that I am God." Psalm 46:10. This is the effectual preparation for all labor for God. Amidst the hurrying throng, and the strain of life's intense activities, he who is thus refreshed will be surrounded with an atmosphere of light and peace. He will receive a new endowment of both physical and mental strength. His life will breathe out a fragrance, and will reveal a divine power that will reach men's hearts. (White, Ellen G., 1905, "With Nature and with God", The Ministry of Healing, chapter 3, page 3, paragraph 3)*

5. *...the excellence and value of pure love consist in its efficiency to do good, and to do nothing else but good. Whatsoever is done out of pure love, be it ever so little or contemptible in the sight of men, is wholly fruitful; for God measures more with how much love one worketh, than the amount he doeth. (White, Ellen G., May 11, 1886, "The Power of Love", The Review and Herald, paragraph 1)*

6. *Pure love is simple in its operations, and separate from every other principle of action. When combined with earthly motives and selfish interests, it ceases to be pure. God considers more with how much love we work, than the amount we do. Love is a heavenly attribute. The natural heart cannot originate it. This heavenly plant only flourishes where Christ reigns supreme. Where love exists, there is power and truth in the life. Love does good, and nothing but good. Those who have love bear fruit unto holiness, and in the end everlasting life. (White, Ellen G., January 13, 1898, "Because He First Loved Us", The Youth's Instructor, paragraph 9)*

7. *Supreme love for God and unselfish love for one another–this is the best gift that our heavenly Father can bestow. This love is not an impulse, but a divine principle, a permanent power. The unconsecrated heart cannot originate or produce it. Only in the heart*

where Jesus reigns is it found. (White, Ellen G., 1911, "A Faithful Witness", The Acts of the Apostles, chapter 551, paragraph 2)

8. *"The promise of the Spirit is not appreciated as it should be. Its fulfillment is not realized as it might be. It is the absence of the Spirit that makes the gospel ministry so powerless. Learning, talents, eloquence, every natural or acquired endowment, may be possessed; but without the presence of the Spirit of God, no heart will be touched, no sinner be won to Christ. On the other hand, if they are connected with Christ, if the gifts of the Spirit are theirs, the poorest and most ignorant of His disciples will have a power that will tell upon hearts. God makes them the channel for the outworking of the highest influence in the universe." (White, Ellen G., 1900, "Talents" Christ's Object Lessons, chapter 25, page 328, paragraph 1)*

9. *"...there shall be a time of trouble, such as never was since there was a nation even to that same time..." (Daniel 12:1)*

10. *"The end is near and every city is to be turned upside down every way. There will be confusion in every city. Everything that can be shaken is to be shaken and we do not know what will come next. The judgments will be according to the wickedness of the people and the light of truth that they have had." (1902). "O that God's people had a sense of the impending destruction of thousands of cities, now almost given to idolatry." (1903). "The time is near when large cities will be swept away, and all should be warned of these coming judgments." (1910). (White, Ellen G., 1992, "The Cities", Last Day Events, chapter 8, page 111, paragraphs 3–5)*

11. *Hosea 2:19–23; Isaiah 60:1–2; Jeremiah 32:37–41; Ezekiel 11:17–20; Ephesians 4:6, 11–15; Revelation 18:1–4*

REFERENCES

Roth, Larry. August 12, 2000.

White, Ellen G. 1844. Notes of Travel–South Lancaster, Mass. The Review and Herald, January 15.

______. 1880. Death of Aaron. The Signs of the Times, October 14.

______. 1888. Missionary Work. 1888 Materials.

______. 1890. Patriarchs and Prophets.

______. 1891. Sermon at Otsego. The Review and Herald, February 3.

______. 1895. Blessed Are They That Mourn. The Signs of the Times, August 8.

______. 1896. Thoughts From the Mount of Blessing.

______. 1898. The Desire of Ages.

______. 1899. Evangelism.

______. 1903. The Work Before Us. The Review and Herald, September 10.

______. 1915. Life Sketches of Ellen G. White.

______. 1917. Prophets and Kings.

______. 1948. Spiritual Gifts, Volume 2.

______. 1977. Walk In All Humility, Testimonies to Southern Africa, Letter 6b, 1890.

Chapter 6

God's 'Show–and–Tell': The Didactic Power of Ritual in Scripture and Missions

Gerald A. Klingbeil, D.Litt.

INTRODUCTION

Ritual is a powerful communicator. It can speak without words and needs little or no translation. It does not require a college or university degree and is understood in different cultures—and yet, it may be at times confusing, disturbing, or even irrelevant—particularly, if we do not have the right key to unlock its significance. Let me illustrate this last statement.

In the 1980s my father–in–law and his family served in Swaziland in southern Africa. He had recently graduated with a theology degree from Helderberg College and had been born and raised in South Africa. While Apartheid kept races apart, there were increasingly more connections between different ethnic groups in the country. As a white pastor from a foreign country (Swaziland is a small independent landlocked nation, partially surrounded by South Africa), my father–in–law was the compromise candidate for a large local congregation that struggled with some racial tension. The family was warmly welcomed; in fact, my wife who was an adventurous 10–year old at that time, has overwhelmingly positive memories of their time in Swaziland. However, the power of ritual and superstition, even within an Adventist congregation, including long–serving elders and well–established members, came at times to the surface, often associated, as is frequently the case, during transitional life–changing moments (such as birth, rites of passages marking the transition from boyhood to manhood, marriage, and death). My father–in–law still remembers one of his first funerals. Following the service in the church, the family and church members carried the casket with the deceased towards the burial ground. Very periodically, yes nearly rhythmically, my father–in–law noted that the pallbearers stopped and mopped their brows. They seemed exhausted and apparently required a rest. After a number of these surprising stops a seasoned elder marched purposefully forward to the pall–bearers and reprimanded them sharply. As my father–in–law did not understand SiSwati, the native language of Swaziland, he did not understand the words, but clearly "heard" the anger and rebuke. Following this exchange, the remainder of the journey proceeded without any interruptions; apparently, the casket had become significantly lighter. Later, when my father–in–law asked the elder about the incident, the elder, noticeably embarrassed, told him that the young men had enacted a very strong cultural belief, namely that the "soul" had to catch up with the body prior to internment. Obviously, the biblical teaching of conditional immortality and death as a complete sleep, while intellectually accepted by the church members, was superseded (or overridden) by a deep–seated cultural and religious concept inherent in Swazi and many other traditional societies.

This study is divided into three subdivisions: First, I will provide a concise introduction to ritual per se, and more particularly, to how we can interpret this powerful element of everyday and religious life. Second, I will provide a review of God's "show–and–tell" toolbox found in Scripture and suggest a reading strategy that should help us capture the significance of biblical ritual, especially when we consider our distance in time and space to a world that is so different from many key elements of our daily lives. Third, I will review the missiological potential of utilizing ritual in communicating the "Good News" to those who have little or no historical, emotive or intellectual link to Scripture or Christianity per se. Thus my focus is not upon a Buddhist or even Thai context, but rather on ritual per se, which will, hopefully, lead to valid lessons that can be applied to distinct missiological contexts.

THE POWER OF RITUAL

Rituals permeate most aspects of our lives. They enrich our coming–of–age experience; they can be seen in a soccer stadium; they appear most often in moments of transition. Definitions of ritual can be gotten two dozens for a penny (Klingbeil 2007:14–19).[1] They range from very specific to rather broad. Many definitions focus on one particular element of ritual, such as action (Schechner 1987:5) or time or space. Some scholars prefer to emphasize the "ritualization" of life, highlighting the processual nature of ritual (Grimes 1982:55; 1985; 1990). The definition I have adopted in my research is based on the work of Dutch scholar of religious studies, Jan Platvoet. It recognizes the social dimension of ritual—our ritual activities are mostly ritual activities in relationship to others—and also emphasizes the crucial elements of space, time, action, and participants. Furthermore, it underlines the fact that ritual wants to communicate something and thus is not meaningless in itself. Here we go: "[Ritual is] that ordered sequence of stylized social behavior that may be distinguished from ordinary interaction by its alerting qualities which enable it to focus the attention of its audiences—its congregation as well as the wider public—onto itself and cause them to perceive it as a special event, performed at a special place and/or time, for a special occasion and/or with a special message" (Platvoet 1995:41).

Rituals are solidly embedded in specific contexts—be they religious or cultural—and are integrally related to our "operating system" or worldview.[2] In other words, in order to understand a ritual adequately, I first need to understand the worldview and culture of the participants of the ritual—a significant caveat, particularly for missiologists and evangelists serving in unfamiliar environments.[3]

Rituals are not only complex constructs that require careful attention to detail (I will deal with reading strategies in the second part of this study), they are also great means of communicating theology, or, perhaps less academic, the foundational concepts of our lives that drive us to action. Due to the presuppositions of standard historical–critical scholarship in biblical studies and the conviction that ritual activity belonged to a supposedly late strata of biblical texts, also described as the "priestly source," emphasizing law over experience, in the past, few scholars have mined biblical ritual in search of biblical theology.[4] However, it appears as if this trend is reversing. Increasingly, biblical ritual is included in the discussion of biblical theology (McConville 1984; Marx 2003:103–120; Merrill 2004:16–33; Nelson 1993; Gilders 2004; Holman 2001:167–184; Brueggemann 1997:653; and House 1998:126 arguing that Leviticus is "one of the most theologically oriented books in Scripture").

Ritual is also an integral element of the study of liturgy and worship. Liturgical studies have benefitted tremendously from the theoretical advances of ritual theory (Jennings 1987:35–56; Hoffman 1991:22–41; Kelleher 1991:99–122; Kelleher 1993:292–318; Grimes 1992:11–25). In fact, traditional liturgical churches have generally suffered a marked decrease in worship participation, while charismatic church services, often involving multimedia elements and participatory music and worship elements report a tremendous growth. Without sacrificing the essentials of worship, i.e., keeping God at the center and transforming individuals into members of a living community (Dawn 1995:75–80) that can begin to reflect the image of God, the communicative, pedagogical, and community–building dimensions of ritual may just provide the needed impetus as we consider worship paradigms. In contrast to a simple change in methods or techniques, the integration of ritual (and thus ritual theory) in worship services in the 21st century requires careful and conscious reflection.[5]

Finally, shared ritual provides a possible avenue to overcome the increasing isolation of people engaged in digital conversations but often devoid of actual integration within a physical (or real) group or community. Western societies today are mostly characterized by lonely individualism and an "island" mentality. Carefully considered ritual within the context of worship or a church community can overcome this isolation.

RITUAL IN SCRIPTURE

Most readers of Scripture would immediately point to the Old Testament (or Hebrew Bible) when asked about biblical ritual. And indeed, its sacrificial system, together with its sanctuary focus, festivals, and priesthood, does represent one of the major focal points of the Old Testament even though ritual also emerges (in slightly different shape, focusing upon the typological fulfillment) in the New Testament. However, as will be shown below, one should not discard the notion of the pervasiveness of ritual in the New Testament.[6] Beyond the sacrificial system (including the sanctuary/tabernacle/temple construct), there are numerous activities connecting both testaments, such as anointing (or consecration), laying on of hands, fasting, mourning, praying, Sabbath celebration, sharing of food in cultic contexts, etc. that involve ritual elements.

I have argued elsewhere (and repeatedly) that one should not jump to conclusions when observing ritual activity. Gut–feeling interpretations may at times be helpful; ultimately, however, they cannot be the guide for understanding ritual coming from a different cultural or religious background. If we truly want to "understand" we first need to invest time to pay attention to the overall design and the details of the design. In my previous work on biblical ritual, known to us from texts (and, unfortunately, not audiovisual records or personal observation) I have argued that we need to pay attention to nine crucial elements (Klingbeil 2007:127–130, 147–204):

First, we need to pay attention to the required situation and context. What triggers the ritual performance?

Second, we want to understand the overall structure (either textually or literally) of the ritual. What holds the ritual together? What marks it as a complete unit, indicating beginning and end? What is the central focal point of the ritual?

Third, we are interested in form, order, and sequence. Is the ritual action sequential or parallel or a mix of both? What formal characteristics mark the beginning of the ritual, what signals its end? Are there activities that are more important than other, suggesting a hierarchy of ritual activities?

Fourth, we need to understand the geography of the ritual, or, in more technical language, its ritual space. Space, geography, and movement are important elements of any ritual. Location matters, as, for example, a sacrifice that was not offered on the altar of burnt offerings was illegitimate and outside the bounds of Israelite religion. Space helps to focus attention of the audience and may suggest hierarchy (remember, only the high priest was allowed to enter the Holy of Holies during the Day of Atonement ritual in Israel [Lev 16]).[7]

Fifth, we should focus upon ritual time. What marks the beginning of the ritual? How long does the ritual last? Is the ritual part of a larger sequence of events (such as a festival calendar)? Ritual time can be absolute (i.e., on April 1, 2014) or relative (when I realize that I have sinned I need to bring an offering to the temple). Ritual time often involves transition between different states or conditions (Klingbeil 2011:21–34; 2007:168–173; 1997:500–513; cf. Wyatt 2001). As with many things in life, timing is also important in ritual in order to achieve desired outcomes.

Sixth, we need to pay attention to ritual objects (Klingbeil 2007:174–181). A knife or a cup are not always just a knife or a cup. In the appropriate context, they suddenly can become the knife and the cup—to be used exclusively in a particular ritual context, in a specific location, and at an appropriate time. It appears as if objects used in ritual generally cannot be interpreted at face value. Mysteriously, they become transformed and take on different meanings. A rough piece of rock suddenly becomes part of an altar (Exod 20:25; 24:4) or a memorial sign (Gen 28:18; 31:45–54; Josh 4:5). Clothing marks different hierarchy or status (cf. Lev 8) or can become part of a mourning ritual when it is publicly torn (Gen 37:34; Josh 7:6; 2 Sam 1:11). When we consider objects in ritual we need to look beyond the expected.

Seventh, ritual action represents a key element that lies at the core of what ritual is. Action, performed either publicly or privately, communicates progress and sequence. In biblical texts, action is mostly more general than specific. For example, the general sequence of the high priestly actions during the Day of Atonement ritual are generally clear; yet we do not know their specifics (e.g., does the high priest walk slowly, erect, bent?). Furthermore, biblical ritual texts are often also abbreviated, i.e., they include a summary statement without providing the exact description of the involved activities (e.g., Gen 12:7, 8 describes Abraham's altar building activities and the fact that he worshipped at the altar, even though it does not provide the specifics of this ritual).

Eighth, we need to consider ritual participants and their roles. "Who did what when and why?" is a good question to ask when we look at participants. Who is active—who is passive? How are roles determined (by heritage, status, or divine indication)? What kind of authority do the ritual specialists have; what roles do they play? How do ritual participants interact with one another or with other important elements of ritual (as, for example, space) (cf. Klingbeil 2004b:105–134; 2007:189–196)?

Ninth, we should note ritual sounds and language, which—incidentally—represents one of the more difficult categories of biblical ritual due to the textual nature of the data (Hermisson 1965). Does the ritual include nonlinguistic sounds (like moaning, groaning or shouting)? Are music and musical instruments integrated in the ritual? Is the ritual language stylized or free? An interesting example of this category is the role of music (either sung or played on instruments) in mourning rites. In 2 Sam 3:32–34, during the funeral ritual for the slain Abner, King David sings a lament accompanied by communal weeping. Judges 11:40 also refers to a commemoration rite in the context of the yearly event remembering Jephthah's daughter (Klingbeil 2007:196–203 provide more examples).

Right from the outset it must be noted that not every ritual will provide sufficient information regarding all different categories. Even anthropological field research involving observation and interviews may not provide all the necessary information. Textual data is even more limiting. However, the fact that these elements represent core components of ritual per se, provides the observer or researcher with the tools to ask the right questions.

MISSIOLOGY AND RITUAL

Missiologists have long recognized the immense potential of biblical ritual and ritual theory for missiology (Kung 2001; Karecki 1997:598–606 and 1998:309–323; Newson 2002:282–287; Henderson 2006:34–56; Nguyen 2012:455–466; Hibbert 2008:343–355; Zahniser 1991:311–331; Hesselgrave 1999:577–589; Adventist thinking about this topic includes Mwansa 1999:125–131; Maberly 1999:232–240; Christo 2002:1–12; Klingbeil 2006:157–173; Lichtenwalter 201:211–244). While this recognition has not always led to agreement regarding ritual's usefulness in missions,[8] the mere acknowledgment of potential represents an important step forward. Whereas Western societies generally demonstrate a lower density of ritual expressions—especially clear examples belonging into the religious realm—countries located in the "Two–Thirds World" continue to boast a significant heritage of rituals as an integral part of their larger cultural systems. Most people living in these countries will relate more easily to the multimedia dimension of ritual found in the Hebrew Bible and may actually struggle more with relating to the more theoretical theology found in Pauline writings.

Clearly, the conscious integration of ritual into missiological strategies requires careful reflection if one is not to fall into the trap of "paganizing" the Gospel and the particular Adventist message. The reality of this danger can be seen in Roman Catholic theology and practice throughout history or in the early Christian transition from persecuted minority religion to official majority religion in late Antiquity.[9] Missiologists have considered this trap and have suggested a four–step approach to counter this paganizing tendency. These steps are to some extent coinciding with ritual analysis and include (1) a careful phenomenological analysis, considering the practice and significance of a given ritual; (2) ontological reflection, i.e., trying to determine the origins and context of a particular ritual and its meaning within the larger worldview; (3) critical evaluation of the data gathered under (1) and (2); and (4) missiological transformation (Hiebert, Shaw, and Tiénou 1999:20–29; Hiebert 2008; and Grunlan and Mayers 1988). As has been noted by many missiologists, the crucial final step of missiological transformation requires not only good data and a steady "hand", but also constant interaction with key Scriptural principles.

The innovative power of ritual is well documented—even in biblical ritual. In a study on biblical libation rites I have argued that specific subrites can be used in new contexts, thus creating a new puzzle that reflects a new image (Klingbeil 2013). Another good example of ritual innovation involves the (at least partial) transformation of the Passover supper into the communion supper celebration (Klingbeil 2007:144–145, 179–181; 2011:23). The food and drink imagery of the divinely ordained Passover meal gets a new lease on life as Jesus reinterprets it as pointing to Himself. This reinterpretation provides both a link to earlier biblical ritual and a fulfillment of the prophetic typology included in divinely–appointed ritual. While ritual is generally conservative and tradition–building, it has important innovative potential whereby known ritual elements are connected to form a new and distinct whole, communicating new beliefs, structures, and perspectives.

How should missiological practitioners, living in foreign cultures, utilize the communicative power of ritual in their ministry? First, and foremost, very carefully. As highlighted in the example of the funeral ritual in Swaziland in the introductory section of this study, understanding religious ritual involves not only careful observation and detailed analysis but also access to religious specialists or experts of the host country. What does a given ritual mean for local practitioners? Is there a broad spectrum of significance that changes according to participant or practitioner or is the meaning universally clear?[10]

Second, once we understand a particular ritual (as, for example, a funeral rite of a particular country or region) with all its important elements and characteristics, the next step seeks to describe the key principles involved in the ritual. What elements are expressed? What underlying worldview or theology can be isolated? In the example from Swaziland, it becomes clear that the young pallbearers' concept of death involved spirit–movement apart from a body. This concept is widely presupposed and believed in many cultures and its presence in Swaziland should not come as a surprise. If at all possible, it would be helpful to discuss underlying theological or worldview principles with people that can understand and "read" the culture appropriately.

Third, once the underlying principles for a particular rite or ritual complex have been identified, it is now time for creative and Spirit–guided thinking. What ritual activity would express concern for the eternal wellbeing of the deceased, yet at the same time would not compromise biblical principles and theology? As we contemplate options and possibilities we need to remember that rituals do not only function on the rational level. I am sure that my father–in–law preached about the state of the dead in his church—particularly after this first experience with a local ritual expression. He may have even spent time studying the Bible with the young men involved in the funeral march. Yet, most likely their concerns were not primarily intellectual, but rooted deeply in stories and activities that connected to their lives on an existential level. In fact, I would assume that most of them had heard biblical texts stating that the dead "know nothing" (Eccl 9:5) and have no memory (Ps 6:5) and that death is just as a sleep (Job 14:12; John 11:11, 12) that one day will be interrupted when God calls us back to life at resurrection morn' (Dan 12:2; John 5:28, 29). Yet, more often than not worldview trumps intellectual knowledge, requiring a conscious decision to contradict an underlying worldview that is in conflict with a Scripture–based worldview. Carefully considered rituals affirming the biblical worldview and theology are important means of a worldview reset or re–boot (which, in itself, is a long–term process).

Fourth, following the development of ritual activity that is both in line with a biblical worldview and theology and also is able to connect to the ritual universe of the host culture, it is time for a try out. What do people experience and think as they enact a new ritual? This step, equivalent to product testing and market research in a business context, requires open interaction with representatives and members of the host community. It also requires constant tweaking and recognition of concepts and ideas that may (or may not) have been part of the original plan.

Fifth, following the successful testing phase comes a time of teaching and training. Short training sessions, introducing members to the broader issue of underlying worldview and its link to ritual activity, should openly introduce a new ritual activity as part of a missiological drive to connect to people of the larger community. The introduction of new ritual activity may lead to conflict; however, this conflict is often avoided if the larger congregation or community is part and parcel of the earlier steps, involving observation, analysis, deep reflection, creative thinking and innovation, and tentative introduction. At every step of the way, openness to dialogue and additional reflection is required if the process is to succeed.

INSTEAD OF A CONCLUSION

Conclusions often suggest arrival. This is seldom the case in missions and similarly dubious when considering the complex constructs and significance of ritual activity within the larger context of worldview and theology. The power of this often complex activity also represents one of its challenges. The Old Testament sanctuary system, God's "show–and–tell", may provide a helpful window. Exodus 25:8 expresses upfront the all–encompassing importance and purpose of the sanctuary: "And let them make Me a sanctuary, that I may dwell among them" (NKJV) is a key command in the Pentateuch.[11] Divine presence, reflecting the divine presence in Eden, was undoubtedly the underlying rationale of the earthly sanctuary. God wanted to be with humanity. However, since the introduction of sin, divinity cannot coexist with human sinfulness. Sin required a divine solution and the sacrificial system, closely linked to the earthly sanctuary/temple, provided this solution. Considering the yearly religious cycle culminating in the Day of Atonement ritual (Lev 16), every sacrifice offered on the sanctuary's altar represented an illustration and hint to the real "Lamb of God" whose sacrifice would mean the ultimate solution to the sin problem. Yet, the multilayered sanctuary "show–and–tell" did not only point to the true "Lamb of God." Its rituals and festivals also illustrated the larger issues of the cosmic conflict between God and His opponent, involving issues of divine justice (or theodicy), a public investigation and judgment, and, ultimately, the elimination of sin.[12] The complexity of the ritual system with its many layers of symbolism and significance highlights the need for careful analysis—yet, at the same time, it also showcases the potential and power of ritual as a teaching tool or as a communicator. "Rituals are the 'Sistine Chapels' of communication," I wrote some time ago (Klingbeil 2007:241). They represent the pinnacle of potential and artistry—yet are also laden with possible pitfalls and misinterpretation. Both mission practitioners and those thinking about missions need to be mindful of them and utilize them to proclaim the gospel message with a loud cry and in a way that is understandable to millions of people who otherwise may not be able to "hear." The task is huge; the challenges are many; yet He, who gave to us the sacrificial system and the temple economy is surely able to inspire us to utilize this powerful tool in a way that will honor Him and also speak to those who have not yet heard.

NOTES

1. *Beard, See also the collection of 24 different definitions suggested between 1909 and 1990 in Platvoet (1995:42–45).*

2. *See Grenz (2000:37–51) for convincing arguments that highlight the close connection between worldview, culture, and theological thinking.*

3. *An unfamiliar environment is not only cipher for foreign missions but can also include large or subtle cultural differences within a particular country, involving educational, social, or economical differences. For example, a member of an Amazonas tribe living in the jungle of Peru, will have significantly different experiences and rituals than a MBA living in Miraflores in Lima or a campesino living on an isolated farm in the Altiplano.*

4. *I have made a strong case for this in the past (Klingbeil 2004a:495–515; cf. Klingbeil 2007:227–230).*

5. *A good example is the practice of coming forward and leaving one's "burden" during the pastoral prayer time.*

6. *Concerning the early Christian's attitude toward synagogue prayer see Horbury (1998:296–317). For a discussion of terminology, biblical references, theology, and the often diverging history of interpretation of the communion meal throughout the Christian era see Bieritz (2001a:163–166; 2001b:173–176), Roloff 2001:166–168, and Schnurr*

(2001:168–173). McGowan (1999:1–32; 218–249) has provided a fascinating study of the bread–and–water tradition in the NT and the early Christian communities. His introductory section on the importance of food in ritual is very helpful. Cf. also Gruenwald (2003:231–266).

7. *I have published repeatedly on the important category of ritual space. See, for example, Klingbeil (1995:59–82; 2002:283–309; 2007:159–168). Cf. also Wightman (2007), Ragavan (2013), Hundley (2011), Bergmann (2007:353–379), and Beard (2005:235–260).*

8. *See, for example, the critical remarks in Hesselgrave (1999:577–589).*

9. *Note the discussion in Wonderly (1967:241–248) and Holler (1995:108–127). Note also the helpful discussion in Dally (2003:171–181). A more general discussion involving the relationship between the Bible and missions can be found in Goheen (2010:208–235).*

10. *In some religious systems the point of a ritual may not be significance but rather the performance of the ritual per se and the involved participants. See here the helpful considerations found in Brown (2003:3–18).*

11. *The following is based on more detailed research published in Klingbeil (2012:66–85).*

12. *There are a number of relevant studies in the DARCOM series, published by the Biblical Research Institute at the General Conference dealing with these macro–issues involving the sanctuary. See also the work of my colleague Roy E. Gane (2005) in a volume that is very cognizant of ritual theory as well.*

REFERENCE LIST

Beard, Luna. 2005. From Barefootedness to Sure–Footedness: Contrasts Involving Sacred Space and Movement in the Bible. Journal for Semitics 14:235–260.

Bergmann, Sigurd. 2007. Theology in Its Spatial Turn: Space, Place and Built Environments Challenging and Changing the Images of God. Religion Compass 1:353–379.

Bieritz, Karl–Heinrich. 2001a. Eucharist: Overview. In The Encyclopedia of Christianity, ed. Erwin Fahlbusch et al. Transl. Geoffrey W. Bromiley, vol. 2:163–166. Grand Rapids, MI: Eerdmans / Leiden: Brill.

Bieritz, Karl–Heinrich. 2001b. Eucharist: Contemporary Practice. In The Encyclopedia of Christianity, ed. Erwin Fahlbusch et al. Transl. Geoffrey W. Bromiley, vol. 2:173–176. Grand Rapids, MI: Eerdmans / Leiden: Brill.

Brown, Gavin. 2003. Theorizing Ritual as Performance: Explorations of Ritual Indeterminacy. Journal of Ritual Studies 17:3–18.

Brueggemann, Walter. 1997. Theology of the Old Testament. Testimony, Dispute, Advocacy. Minneapolis, MN: Fortress.

Christo, Gordon. 2002. Staying Within the Boundaries: Contextualization of Adventism for India. Journal of the Adventist Theological Society 13:1–14.

Dally, Ortwin. 2003. Alte Rituale in neuem Gewand? Zu Fortleben und Umdeutung heidnischer Rituale in der Spätantike. In Rituale in der Vorgeschichte, Antike und Gegenwart: Studien zur Vorderasiatischen, Prähistorischen und Klassischen Archäologie, Ägyptologie, Alten Geschichte, Theologie und Religionswissenschaft, ed. Carola Metzner–Nebelsick. Internationale Archäologie 4, 171–181. Rahden, Germany: Verlag Marie Leidorf.

Dawn, Marva J. 1995. Reaching Out without Dumbing Down: A Theology of Worship for the Turn–of–the–Century Culture. Grand Rapids, MI: Eerdmans.

Gane, Roy E. 2005. Cult and Character. Purification Offerings, Day of Atonement, and Theodicy. Winona Lake, IN: Eisenbrauns.

Gilders, William K. 2004. Blood Ritual in the Hebrew Bible: Meaning and Power. Baltimore, MD: Johns Hopkins University Press.

Goheen, Michael W. 2010. Bible and Mission: Missiology and Biblical Scholarship in Dialogue. In Christian Mission: Old Testament Foundations and New Testament Developments, ed. Stanley E. Porter and Cynthia Long Westfall. McMaster New Testament Studies Series 9, 208–235. Eugene, OR: Pickwick.

Grenz, Stanley J. 1990. Culture and Spirit: The Role of Cultural Context in Theological Reflection. Asbury Theological Journal 55, no. 2: 37–51.

Grimes, Ronald L. 1982. Beginnings in Ritual Studies. Lanham, MD: University Press of America.

Grimes, Ronald L. 1985. Research in Ritual Studies: A Programmatic Essay and Bibliography. ATLA Bibliography Series 14. Metuchen, NJ: American Theological Library Association / London: Scarecrow.

Grimes, Ronald L. 1990. Ritual Criticism: Case Studies in Its Practice, Essays on Its Theory. Columbia, SC: University of South Carolina Press.

Grimes, Ronald L. 1992. Liturgical Renewal and Ritual Criticism. In The Awakening Church. 25 Years of Liturgical Renewal, ed. Lawrence J. Madden, 11–25. Collegeville: Liturgical.

Gruenwald, Ithamar. 2003. Rituals and Ritual Theory in Ancient Israel. Brill Reference Library of Judaism 10. Leiden: Brill.

Grunlan, Stephen A. and Mayers, Marvin K., eds. 1988. Cultural Anthropology: A Christian Perspective. 2nd ed. Grand Rapids, MI: Zondervan.

Henderson, Ian H. 2006. Mission and Ritual: Revisiting Harnack's Mission and Expansion of Christianity. In The Changing Face of Judaism, Christianity, and Other Greco–Roman Religions in Antiquity, ed. Ian H. Henderson, Gerbern S. Oegema, and Sara Parks Rickers. Studien zu den jüdischen Schriften aus hellenistisch–römischer Zeit 2, 34–56. Gütersloh: Gütersloher Verlag.

Hermisson, H. J. 1965. Sprache und Ritus im alttestamentlichen Kult. Wissenschaftliche Monographien zum Alten und Neuen Testament 19. Neukirchen–Vluyn: Neukirchener Verlag.

Hesselgrave, David S. 1999. Third Millennium Missiology and the Use of Egyptian Gold. Journal of the Evangelical Theological Society 42:577–589.

Hibbert, Richard Yates. 2008. Defilement and Cleansing: A Possible Approach to Christian Encounter with Muslims. Missiology 36, no. 2:343–355.

Hiebert, Paul G. 2008. Transforming Worldviews: An Anthropological Understanding of How People Change. Grand Rapids, MI: Baker Academic.

Hiebert, Paul G., Shaw, R. Daniel, and Tiénou, Tite. 1999. Understanding Folk Religion. A Christian Response to Popular Beliefs and Practices. Grand Rapids, MI: Baker.

Hoffman, Lawrence A. 1991. Reconstructing Ritual as Identity and Culture. In The Making of Jewish and Christian Worship, ed. Paul F. Bradshaw and Lawrence A. Hoffman, 22–41. Notre Dame–London: University of Notre Dame Press.

Holler, Stephen. 1995. The Origins of Marian Devotion in Latin American Cultures in the United States. Marian Studies 46:108–127.

Holman, Jan. 2001. An Approach from Biblical Theology of the Passover. A Critical Appraisal of Its Old Testament Aspects. In Christian Feast and Festival. The Dynamics of Western Liturgy and Culture, ed. Paul Post et al. Liturgia Condenda 12, 167–184. Leuven: Peeters.

Horbury, William. 1998. Early Christians on Synagogue Prayer and Imprecation. In Tolerance and Intolerance in Early Judaism and Christianity, ed. Graham N. Stanton and Guy G. Stroumsa, 296–317. Cambridge: Cambridge University Press.

House, Paul R. 1998. Old Testament Theology. Downers Grove, IL: InterVarsity.

Hundley, Michael B. 2011. Keeping Heaven on Earth: Safeguarding the Divine Presence in the Priestly Tabernacle. Forschungen zum Alten Testament II.50. Tübingen: Mohr Siebeck.

Jennings, Jr., Theodore W. 1987. Ritual Studies and Liturgical Theology: An Invitation to Dialogue. Journal of Ritual Studies 1, no. 1:35–56.

Karecki, Madge. 1997. Religious Ritual as a Key to Wholeness in Mission. Missionalia 25:598–606.

Karecki, Madge. 1998. Mission, Ritual, World–View. Missionalia 26:309–323.

Kelleher, Margaret M. 1991. A Communion Rite: A Study of Roman Catholic Liturgical Performance. Journal of Ritual Studies 5, no. 2:99–122.

Kelleher, Margaret M. 1993. Hermeneutics in the Study of Liturgical Performance. Worship 67:292–318.

Klingbeil, Gerald A. 1995. Ritual Space in the Ordination Ritual of Leviticus 8. Journal of Northwest Semitic Languages 21:59–82.

Klingbeil, Gerald A. 1997. Ritual Time in Leviticus 8 with Special Reference to the Seven–Day Period in the Old Testament. Zeitschrift für die alttestamentliche Wissenschaft 109:500–513.

Klingbeil, Gerald A. 2002. 'Up, Down, in, Out, Through and Back'. Space and Movement in Old Testament Narrative, Ritual and Legal Texts and Their Application for the Study of Mark 1:1–3:12. Estudios Bíblicos 60:283–309.

Klingbeil, Gerald A. 2004a. Altars, Ritual and Theology—Preliminary Thoughts on the Importance of Cult and Ritual for a Theology of the Hebrew Scriptures. Vetus Testamentum 54, no. 4: 495–515.

Klingbeil, Gerald A. 2004b. 'Who Did What When and Why?' The Dynamics of Ritual Participants in Leviticus 8 and Emar 369. In Inicios, fundamentos y paradigmas: Estudios teológicos y exegéticos en el Pentateuco, ed. Gerald A. Klingbeil. River Plate Adventist University Monograph Series in Biblical and Theological Studies 1, 105–134. Libertador San Martín, Argentina: Editorial Universidad Adventista del Plata.

Klingbeil, Gerald A. 2006. 'Empty Forms or Vital Teacher'? The Role of Ritual in Spiritual Growth and Nurturing. Journal of Asia Adventist Seminary 9:157–173.

Klingbeil, Gerald A. 2007. Bridging the Gap: Ritual and Ritual Texts in the Bible. Bulletin for Biblical Research Supplements 1. Winona Lake, IN: Eisenbrauns.

Klingbeil, Gerald A. 2011. 'Of Clocks and Calendars': The Cohesive Function of Time in Biblical Ritual. Biblische Zeitschrift 55:21–34.

Klingbeil, Gerald A. 2012. El santuario, el ritual y la teología: En busca del centro de la teología adventista. Theologika 27, no. 1:66–85.

Klingbeil, Gerald A. 2013. 'Between Innovative and Traditionalizing Forces': A Closer Look at Libations in the Biblical World. Paper read at International Meeting of the Society of Biblical Literature, in Ritual and Innovation consultation, St. Andrews, Scotland.

Kung, Matias H. 2001. The Ritual Dimensions of the Tabernacle Worship and Their Missiological Implications. Ph.D. diss., Trinity Evangelical Divinity School.

Lichtenwalter, Larry L. 2010. Worldview Transformation and Mission: Narrative, Theology, and Ritual in John's Apocalypse. Journal of the Adventist Theological Society 21, no. 1–2:211–244.

Maberly, Clifton. 1999. Buddhism and Adventism: A Myanmar Initiative. In Adventist Mission in the 21st Century, ed. Jon L. Dybdahl, 232–240. Hagerstown, MD: Review and Herald.

Marx, Alfred. 2003. The Theology of the Sacrifice According to Leviticus 1–7. In The Book of Leviticus. Composition and Reception, ed. Rolf Rendtorff and Robert A. Kugler. Vetus Testamentum Supplements 93, 103–120. Leiden: Brill.

McConville, J. Gordon. 1984. Law and Theology in Deuteronomy. Journal for the Study of the Old Testament Supplement 33. Sheffield: JSOT Press.

McGowan, Andrew. 1999. Ascetic Eucharists. Food and Drink in Early Christian Ritual Meals. Oxford Early Christian Studies. Oxford: Clarendon.

Merrill, Michael S. 2004. Masks, Metaphor and Transformation: The Communication of Belief in Ritual Performance. Journal of Ritual Studies 18:16–33.

Mwansa, Pardon. 1999. Healings and Miraculous Signs in World Mission. In Adventist Mission in the 21st Century, ed. Jon L. Dybdahl, 125–131. Hagerstown, MD: Review and Herald.

Nelson, Richard D. 1993. Raising Up a Faithful Priest: Community and Priesthood in Biblical Theology. Louisville, KY: Westminster John Knox Press.

Newson, David. 2002. Christian Ritual and the Meaningful Language of Loss. Currents in Theology and Mission 29:282–287.

Nguyen, Vanthanh. Dismantling Cultural Boundaries: Missiological Implications of Acts 10:1–11:18. Missiology 40, no. 4:455–466.

Platvoet, Jan. 1995. Ritual in Plural and Pluralist Societies. In Pluralism and

Identity. Studies in Ritual Behaviour, ed. Jan Platvoet and Karel van der Toorn. Studies in the History of Religions 67, 25–51. Leiden: Brill.

Ragavan, Deena, ed., 2013. Heaven on Earth: Temples, Ritual, and Cosmic Symbolism in the Ancient World. Oriental Institute Seminars 9. Chicago, IL: The University of Chicago/Oriental Institute.

Roloff, Jürgen. 2001. Eucharist: NT Texts. In The Encyclopedia of Christianity, ed. Erwin Fahlbusch et al. Transl. Geoffrey W. Bromiley, vol. 2:166–168. Grand Rapids, MI: Eerdmans / Leiden: Brill.

Schechner, Richard. 1987. The Future of Ritual. Journal of Ritual Studies 1, no. 1: 5–33.

Schnurr, Günther. 2001. Eucharist: Development in the Church and Theology. In The Encyclopedia of Christianity, ed. Erwin Fahbusch et al. Transl. Geoffrey W. Bromiley, vol. 2:168–173. Grand Rapids, MI: Eerdmans / Leiden: Brill.

Wightman, G. J. 2007. Sacred Spaces: Religious Architecture in the Ancient World. Ancient Near Eastern Studies Supplement 22. Leuven: Peeters.

Wonderly, William L. 1967. The Indigenous Background of Religion in Latin America. Practical Anthropology 14:241–248.

Wyatt, Nicolas. 2001. Space and Time in the Religious Life of the Near East. The Biblical Seminar 85. Sheffield: Sheffield Academic Press.

Zahniser, A. H. Mathias. 1991. Ritual Process and Christian Discipling: Contextualizing a Buddhist Rite of Passage. Missiology 19, no. 1:311–331.

Section II

Issues in Ministering to Mourners

Chapter 7

SDA Christian Funeral Practices that Breathe Life in the Thai Buddhist Context

Christopher Sorensen

INTRODUCTION

I am a missionary from the United States currently living and working in Khon Kaen, Thailand. I was raised in an American SDA family and baptized in 1985. When I was 14 years old, I caught the "mission bug" on a short term mission trip, and after receiving a BA in Theology from Southern Adventist University in 2001, my wife and I joined Adventist Frontier Missions with the purpose to reach the Northern Khmer people for Christ. With the help of a local Thai pastor, we have assisted in planting a SDA church in Surin, Thailand, and now we have joined a larger missionary team in Khon Kaen, Thailand with the purpose of helping the SDA churches to create evangelistic tools and develop a "complete Christian culture." Part of that goal involves developing contextually relevant and meaningful ceremonies for life's great events, not the least of which are funerals.

The ministry topic that I am going to address is entitled "SDA Christian Funerals that Breathe Life in the Thai Buddhist Context." I intend for this project to be a brief survey of Christian funeral principles and practices that are meaningful and effective both in ministering to grieving Christians and in planting evangelistic seeds in the hearts and minds of Thai Buddhists. In Thailand and other Buddhist countries in South–East Asia where, according to Whitsett, funerals are arguably the most important religious ceremony[1], in order to be relevant and effective in our work among Thai Buddhists, the SDA church needs to learn to conduct Biblically sound contextualized funerals well (Whitsett 2013:6).

The problem that I will be addressing is: What can be done in the Thai SDA church to make Christian funerals more meaningful and inspirational to both SDAs and their Buddhist friends and relatives?

The first research question which relates to my theoretical foundation and will be answered in the first section is: "What are the principles that should guide our Thai SDA funeral practices?" The second research question which relates to the Thai ministry context is, "What are some good funeral practices that are currently being done in SDA Thai churches and in other protestant denominations in Thailand?" Or more specifically, what funeral practices can we discover that are based on solid Biblical principles while at the same time contextualized and meaningful both to Christians and nonbelievers?

My primary methodology to answer the questions above was to conduct personal interviews with pastors and church leaders in Thailand. I tried to consult some scholarly articles and SEANET publications that are relevant to the topic.[2] And of course, I sought to identify guiding principles from the Scriptures, the Spirit of Prophecy, and official SDA church publications.

I will conclude the project with a summary of the main principles and tips that will make our Thai SDA funerals the most powerful, meaningful, fruitful, and cost–effective forms of ministry and outreach that we can possibly do, keeping in mind that there is still grace available as we grow in our competence in conducting funerals.

PURPOSE AND GUIDING PRINCIPLES FOR THAI SDA FUNERALS

Jane Barlow, a protestant missionary to Thailand for more than 20 years, has pointed out that "much of what is done at funerals is a response to fear—fear of what will happen to the deceased, but also, what is often articulated more, fear of what the deceased's *pii*[3] will come back and do to the living. So when death occurs, rituals and ceremonies are performed with two main goals based on these fears: (1) to improve the merit status of the deceased and so enable the winyan (spirit) to go to heaven, and (2) to protect the household and community from the return of the pii of the deceased" (Barlow 2011:99).

While much of what takes place at Buddhist funerals may be based on fear, none should deny that there are other motives (good motives) at work too: i.e. enduring gratitude for the beneficial actions which the dead performed while still living, and loving concern for the deceased's future well–being, etc.. But do these good motives mean that the Christian should adopt those practices? Not necessarily. For while Christian "ministry to the bereaved calls for respect of traditions and culture in dealing with death," yet it must "always" do so "in the context of Christian principles and the biblical understanding of death" (SDA Minister's Handbook, 2009, emphasis mine).

The fact is, Biblical teachings and principles necessarily preclude the Christian from adopting many Buddhist funeral practices either in whole or in part. For example, the Biblical teaching that salvation and eternal life in heaven is by grace through faith in Christ Jesus prevents the Christian from trying to make merit for the dead (Eph. 2:8–10 cf. Jn. 3:16; 17:3). And the Biblical teaching which states that the dead "know nothing" and "never again will they have a part in anything that happens under the sun" (Eccl. 9:5, 6, NIV) makes it completely fruitless for the Christian to ask the dead for forgiveness and unnecessary to perform many of the folk Buddhist practices that are intended to "confuse the pii and prevent it from returning" to their house to bother the living family members (Barlow 2011:100).

Understanding this, Pastor Samart Wongnaphaphaisan, the SDA pastor of the Hua Hin SDA church at the time of writing, says that in light of Jesus' complete salvation already received by faith during the lifetime of the believer, funerals are really unnecessary as far as the well–being of the dead are concerned. Nevertheless, he reasons that Christians living among Buddhists should still conduct funerals.

Why? He gives three reasons which are the first three of Thirteen Suggested Principles for SDA Christian Funerals:

1. God's Glory:

God should be glorified (1 Cor. 10:31) through our good works (Matt.5:16) or righteous acts which must necessarily be in harmony with His commandments (Isa. 60:21 cf. Ps. 119:172).

2. Not Offending Fellow Believers:

Many people, believers included, would be greatly offended, and perhaps even stumble in their faith by the apparent lack of sympathy and care which they expect to receive through our participation in a funeral ceremony.

3. Not Offending Unbelievers:

If even Christians would be offended by not conducting a funeral service, how much more offense would a Buddhist feel by the Christian community's lack of care? (Wongnaphaphaisan 2014).

4. Orderliness:

"Everything (including our funerals, if they are to really bring glory to God) should be done in a fitting and orderly way" (1 Cor. 14:40, NIV, commentary added). This calls for serious study, planning and clear communication with family, church members and the community.

5. The Golden Rule:

"Do unto others as you would have them do unto you" (Matt. 7:12). This principle calls for Christians to imagine ourselves in the place of the grieving, and to try to do for them what we would want done for us were we in their situation.

6. Christ–like Love:

"Love each other as I have loved you" (John 15:12, NIV). This command of Jesus makes more concrete the selfless service that we are to offer to the mourners.

7. Empathy:

"Mourn with those who mourn" (Rom 12:15, NIV). Jesus demonstrated this principle of empathizing with the mourners as White explains: "When [Jesus] met a funeral, He did not pass by indifferently. Sadness came over His face as He looked upon death, and He wept with the mourners" (White 1982:57.3).[4]

8. Encouraging Words:

"Encourage each other with these words" (1 Thess 4:18, NLT). Paul presents the principle of encouraging the mourners by speaking words of the 2nd coming of Jesus, the resurrection and reunion that we will have with those who died in Christ. Pastor Chanchai Kiatyanyong, currently the President of the Thailand Adventist Mission, concurs that encouraging the living is one of the primary purposes of Christian funerals (Kiatyanyong 2014).

9. Sharing burdens:

"Carry each other's burdens, and in this way you will fulfill the law of Christ" (Gal 6:2, NIV). Whether they are financial, emotional, or one of the many logistical burdens, Paul argues that when we help our mourning brethren to bear their burdens, we are thereby fulfilling Christ's law to love each other. Pr. C. Kiatyanyong also points out that when Christians offer assistance and show love in this way, even though they are not blood relatives, this makes a powerful positive impression on Buddhist friends and relatives (Kiatyangyong 2014).

10. Timeliness and Tact:

Pr. C. Kiatyanyong also says that funerals are a great opportunity to preach about the hope we have in the present and future life (Kiatyanyong 2014). Therefore, we should "Preach the Word," being "prepared in season and out of season; correct, rebuke and encourage–with great patience and careful instruction" (2 Tim 4:2, NIV). This principle of preparedness for patient and careful Christian witness applies to the entire Christian life. It includes "in season" and "out of season" moments—the planned and foreseen opportunities, as well as those that are unexpected. Though funerals are often "out of season" events, they are nevertheless great opportunities for witnessing–"golden moments" such as White urges to take advantage of with promptness (1915, pp. 133, 134).[5] To that, Peter adds that when giving our ready answer, we should do so with "gentleness and respect" (1 Pet. 3:15). This calls for courage, clarity, and tact.

11. Showing Honor to Others:

"Give to everyone what you owe them: If you owe taxes, pay taxes; if revenue, then revenue; if respect, then respect; if honor, then honor" (Rom 13:7, NIV). Even in Christian funerals we must seek appropriate ways to honor our fellow believers, friends, relatives, and even the deceased. One way the Thailand Adventist Mission has recommended that Christians show respect to the dead, instead of waiing the dead and lighting incense, is by "standing silently in front of their picture for a brief minute" (Seventh–day Adventists and Thai Ways 2009:13).

12. Living Honorably In the Eyes of God and Man:

Whitsett points out that just as Christ lived "in favor with God and man" (Luke 2:52), his "followers" today should strive to live with conduct that is first of all, approved by God, then also "honorable among the Gentiles" (1 Pet 2:12, NKJV) – including the South–East Asian Buddhist communities. This, he says, must include the way in which Christians "bury their dead" (Whitsett 2013).

13. Frugality:

Ellen G. White writes that "In modern times the funeral services of a man of high position are often made the occasion of ostentatious and extravagant display. . . God is not honored in the great display so often made over the dead, and the extravagant expense incurred in returning their bodies to the dust." But there must be a delicate balance between the principle of "Frugality" and that of "Showing Honor." (White 1890:427). And careful explanation and teaching during the funeral service can make the wisdom of this principle plain. Pr. S. Wongnaphaphaisan says that from his experience, when he has conducted funerals that were not extravagant, but clearly explained and smoothly executed, the response from Buddhist relatives is often positive, such as, "Wow! The Christians conduct funerals in the right way!" (Wongnaphiphaisan 2014). They appreciate how Christian funerals are not a huge financial burden.

EIGHT CHRISTIAN FUNERAL TIPS AND CONTEXTUALIZED PRACTICES

Having laid the foundation of Thirteen Guiding Principles for SDA Christian Funerals, let us now explore some good Christian funeral tips and contextualized practices that are being done or are recommended by some pastors and missionaries both inside and outside the SDA church of Thailand. Eight Thai Christian Funeral Tips:

1. Formulate a General Contextualized Plan for Christian Funerals:

Greg Whitsett recommends Paul Hiebert's four–step Critical Contextualization Model as a guide for church leaders and their congregations in formulating a funeral plan that is as familiar and meaningful to the local community as possible while at the same time completely faithful to Biblical teachings and Christian values (see Hiebert, as cited in Whitsett, 2013).[6]

And if certain funeral practices need to be completely replaced, we would do well to remember the counsel of Dale Goodson, one of the trainers of AFM church planting missionaries, who said, "When cultural practices conflict with biblical teaching, I am convinced it would be better to apply biblical principles directly to the concerns that gave birth to the offending practices rather than to simply find a non–offending replacement. While it is true that we don't want our behavior to stand in defiance of God's will or clear biblical teaching, we also need to remember that God is honestly concerned with our welfare. Applying what He teaches within scripture should improve things, not just change them. These improvements need to fill the gap left by the rejected practices, as well as relevantly address all the other cultural elements they were associated with or depending on for success. . . Effective replacement requires good integration" (Goodson, n.d.).[7]

2. Assist Church Members in Personalizing Their Own Plan Before Their Death:

All members, especially older ones, should give due consideration to their funerals, recognizing that their funeral is their last chance to influence their relatives and friends for Christ. As such, the pastor or an elder should feel it a duty to tactfully educate the new church members about the practices and options available for a Christian funeral. This could be presented privately or in the format of a seminar which would very likely be largely attended with great interest. For nearly all Buddhists who've ever considered Christianity have at some point asked, "What will happen to me when I die?" Sadly, few have ever received clear and comprehensive answers. And if Christians themselves are in the dark about what constitutes a Christian funeral, they won't likely talk much about it with their Buddhist relatives, and will be even less likely to request one.

However, if a church member does expressly request that their relatives conduct a 100% Christian funeral appealing to their children's responsibility to pay back the parent's good favor, then by their own belief system, they would likely feel bound to fulfill their parents' wishes. The Office of the National Culture Commission in Thailand (ONCC) has written a book entitled The Tradition of Conducting Low–Budget Funerals. Under the heading "Fulfilling the Wishes of the Dead" ["การปฏิบัติตามเจตนาของผู้ตาย"] they recommend that in "fulfilling the purposes of the dead, whether in regard [to donating body organs] or to any other virtuous intention of the dead—children, grandchildren, heirs, and other people close to the dead should pursue the opportunity to act according to those purposes because this is one way of paying back the dead for their good favor" (ONCC 1995:13).

3. Be Present:

Barlow laments that in Thailand many Buddhists and Christians tend to avoid the "subject of imminent death. . . Sadly, this often means that the dying, when near their time of death, are not able to talk about their fears or wishes as far as death is concerned because others leave them alone. . ." (Barlow 2011:103). The sad result that I've seen on several occasions is that the dying member feels abandoned and the unbelieving family members are negatively impressed. Then after the death, when Christians finally show up, if no solid plans have been laid for the care of the dead believer, there can be varied levels of contention and pushing between the Christians and the Buddhist relatives over the right to conduct their respective ceremonies for the dead. How much easier it would be for the Buddhist relatives to allow for a Christian funeral if they have seen the Christian pastor and friends often present ministering in loving and practical ways before, during, and immediately after the death! For even when a church member has expressly requested a Christian funeral, if the pastor or fellow Christians are slow to arrive after the death, the relatives and the community will quickly default to the Buddhist ceremony that they know so well and would prefer anyway.

4. Have a Detailed Funeral Task Check–List:

This list details tasks that could or should be done when a member dies as well as who is responsible to do them. Such a list could include details such as the following:

Who is responsible for notifying church members and family members of the church member's decease and the location and times of services?

Who is responsible for embalming the body? (hospital/other)

Who is responsible for washing and dressing the deceased?

Who is responsible for renting a wooden and/or refrigerated casket?

Who is responsible for preparing flowers, decorations, and a picture of the deceased?

If needed, who is responsible for renting the tents, tables, table cloths, chairs, dishes, outdoor lights and wiring, sound system, dishes, drinking water, ice, etc.?

Who is responsible for making and serving food for the guests in attendance?

Who is the pastor/elder responsible for the ministry of presence—organizing church members for practical ministries (i.e. child care, house cleaning, etc.), as well as ministering to the emotional and spiritual needs of the family members?

Who is the pastor/elder responsible for the ministry of programming (i.e. coordinating programming with the family, organizing sermon topics, music, researching and recording the life history of the deceased, etc.) for the morning and evening programs and explaining how the family and community can participate?

Who is responsible for inviting the honored guests and community leaders to attend the final burial/cremation service and explaining their role?

Who is responsible for preparing the burial plot/crematorium reservation?

Who is responsible for preparing the bulletins and other gifts to give to all the guests who attend the program/s?

Who is responsible notifying the proper government offices, bank, and funeral insurance groups, etc. of the death of the deceased? Who is the legal executor of the will of the deceased?

Who is responsible for paying all the outstanding bills and debts of the deceased?

Who is responsible for collecting and distributing monetary gifts for all the funeral expenses?

The value of a check–list such as the one above becomes obvious when one considers how difficult it often is for families to think of all the details of a complex funeral service while they themselves are grieving. And the more organized and helpful the church appears in the eyes of the Buddhist community, the higher will be everyone's view of Christianity and our God.

5. Invite and Involve as Many People as Possible:

Prometta shares a personal story about how people reacted when they saw a Christian funeral procession that had only 8 people participating. He heard people say, "Oh, look at that! No way am I ever going to be one of them! I wouldn't dare tell anyone I was part of a group like that! Too embarrassing. Pitiful!" At that time, he determined that if he could help it, something like that would never happen again. Nowadays, he tells his church members to invite everyone–the more, the better. He even tells them to use moderate pressure, such as, "If you don't come to this funeral, I won't come to yours." It works! And he finds that those funerals that have lots of people make others curious to join, even monks (Prometta 2000).

6. Aim to create a positive experience for the Buddhists in attendance:

Pastor Ricardo Palacios, AFM missionary to Khon Kaen, Thailand shares some interesting advice when he says, "Perhaps, when given only a short amount of time to share at a funeral, it would be better to focus on creating a positive experience for the Buddhists than to try to heavily indoctrinate them with a long sermon. If they experience a taste of joy in the worship of Jesus, the love within the body of Christ, and the hope of His coming and resurrection, these, more than a hard push to explain the state of the dead, would perhaps make the relatives more likely to come back to church later" (Palacios 2014).

7. Teach and Explain Everything Clearly:

Prometta said, "If there is something you do but have no answer to those who ask you why you are doing it, then you shouldn't do it. . . In order to communicate effectively, it is imperative that every time we have a Christian Isaan [north east Thailand] funeral we explain what is happening". For example, if people ask why it is that Christians don't put a coin in the mouth of the deceased, a good answer would be: "No money is able to buy heaven for the dead" (Prometta 2000).[8] Nearly all the pastors that I interviewed said something similar. For without explanation, much of the Christian service appears meaningless or worse. But, for example, if we explain the fullness of Christ's salvation and His ability and promise to return and resurrect His people, this will help the Buddhists to understand the logical reason why we don't try to make merit for the dead. And Pastor Samart Wongnaphaphaisan emphasized that it is only when such explanations have been given that the Buddhists can conclude, "Oh, you have done [this funeral] well, and correct!" (Wongnaphaphaisan 2014).

8. Follow–up with Relatives in the weeks and months after the funeral:

"Ministering to those who are grieving only begins with the funeral, and should continue for many months afterward." This is part of comprehensive Christian care: being present, patiently listening, and encouraging the grieving ones to stay active (SDA Minister's Handbook 2009:203–4). But more than just promoting emotional healing, we must also try to water the gospel seeds that were planted during the funeral so that in the end, there might be a real spiritual harvest.

AN EXAMPLE OF A CONTEXTUALIZED NORTHEASTERN THAI FUNERAL

One concise, yet fairly comprehensive description of a contextualized Christian funeral that I've read was written by Barlow who says that in her rural church, church members there try to help the grieving family by making food, donating rice or money, etc. But she is careful to explain that "they do this not to make merit but to show practical love and care." While they go against the rural Buddhist norm by serving no alcohol, they retain many cultural forms like how they decorate the coffin with lots of "flowers, fairy lights, and a large photo of the deceased." Another similarity to a Buddhist funeral is their use of a loud speaker system "to play loud music day and night." They hold daily "Christian services," both morning and evening at the times that the monks would normally come and chant. And they continue this for several days following the burial or cremation. That is because they seek to take full advantage of this opportunity to evangelize! (Barlow 2011)

Perhaps the most impressive part of their funeral ministry is how "church members stay with the family through the night, as they do at a Buddhist funeral, singing, talking, and laughing together, not to keep the evil spirits away, but to show love."

Then "on the day of the burial" (or cremation) they have a "special service. . . at the house." There are preferably "many church leaders" present. Then they have a large procession transporting the coffin to the graveyard. It is led by "a large wooden cross followed by church leaders in robes. This is to indicate that the cross is the way to heaven, and the respected leaders are there to give honor to the deceased." They have a band that plays music to which people dance while following along behind the coffin—again to "show respect," and to "celebrate the resurrection in Christ." Before the actual burial, they read "a short history of the deceased's life" and apparently distribute it among the attendees. Their purpose here is again to show honor. While the service's main elements still appear very "Western," with prayers and Bible verses or a short evangelistic sermon, yet it is contextualized in the end when "the hosts throw coins and sweets into the crowd—not to make merit, but as a fun way to thank people for coming, and to break any emotional tension." Barlow concludes her description by explaining that her church has "actively looked for the traditional symbols they can incorporate without being syncretistic (e.g., the food, the community event going over days, the decorations, the loud music, and the procession)." And as to its effectiveness, she points out that "in places where this is happening, Buddhists notice and barriers are broken down" (Barlow 2011:108). Barlow also quotes Prometta, who said that after such a contextualized Christian funeral, he heard someone comment, "If this is what happens when Christians die, I want to die! Dying this way is great. Heaven must be more fun than this. Those who die in God are really happy" (Prometta 2011).

CONCLUSION

In this brief paper, I have attempted to answer the question, "What can be done in the Thai SDA church to make Christian funerals more meaningful and inspirational to both SDAs and their Buddhist friends and relatives?" There is much more that could be said. But in summary, I would reaffirm that we should keep in mind Thirteen Guiding Principles for SDA Christian Funerals: 1) God's Glory, 2) Not Offending Fellow Believers, 3) Not Offending Unbelievers, 4) Orderliness, 5) The Golden Rule, 6) Christ–like Love, 7) Empathy, 8) Encouraging Words, 9) Sharing Burdens, 10) Timeliness and Tact, 11) Showing Honor to Others, 12) Living Honorably in the Eyes of God and Man, and 13) Frugality. With these guiding principles in mind, we should be able to organize a meaningful and effective funeral service by: 1) formulating a general contextualized funeral plan, 2) assisting church members in personalizing their own plan before their death, 3) being present to minister before and immediately after the death, 4) having a detailed check–list of funeral tasks, 5) inviting and involving as many people as possible, 6) aiming to create a positive experience for Buddhist attendees, 7) teaching and explaining everything clearly, and 8) following–up with relatives after the funeral is over. When we have prayerfully done our best to accomplish the above tasks, I believe SDA funerals in Thailand will truly breathe life among our fellow church members and Buddhist friends! Such funerals will be the most powerful, meaningful, fruitful and cost–effective forms of ministry and outreach that we do.

However, if the above principles and tips seem too complex and hard to remember, I would encourage church leaders to at least remember (1) the principle of "Christ–like love" and (2) the ministry of "being present." For even if we fall short of all the other ideals and our programs are not as organized as we would have wished—if the above two points have been accomplished, all is not wasted. Remember that "love covers all offenses" (Prov. 10:12 ESV). And in a special sense, our grieving members and honest hearted Buddhist friends will forgive and soon forget many of our clumsy "offenses,"–our imperfectly executed plans– if it is only apparent that we truly love them from the heart.

NOTES

1. *Whitsett, director of the Global Missions Center for East Asian Religions (CEAR), references a field study conducted by Adventist Frontier Missions where he and his colleagues discovered that "the most important rite of passage in Tai–Kadai culture is the funeral." Tai–Kadai is a tonal language family group that includes the Lao and Thai speaking peoples (Tai–Kadai_languages, n.d.).*

2. *SEANET refers to a "group of evangelical mission theologians and practitioners" who have "been holding annual assemblies that brought together various key leaders (church leaders, mission leaders, missiologists, missionaries, and pastors) to reflect, discuss, and plan programs and projects that will help in the evangelization of Buddhist peoples and nations" (Lim & Spaulding, 2003).*

3. *Barlow translates "pii"as "malevolent spirit".*

4. *The small handbook entitled Seventh–day Adventists and Thai Ways (2009) p, 13 counsels that "Christians, while not joining in the sprinkling of water over the corpse, can still show love to the host family by simply attending the funeral and displaying solemn behavior that expresses sorrow (emphasis mine).*

5. *I do not know of any other time in the life of a Thai Buddhist when they are more open to hearing the Christian message of hope than at a funeral. Their interest is higher, their attention span is longer. They are, due to the circumstance, a captive audience until the body is buried/cremated. Compared to conventional evangelistic outreach, the funeral is usually much better attended by non–believers, and there is little to no evangelism budget required.*

6. *Paul Hiebert's Critical Contextualization Model is as follows: 1) Christian leaders must recognize the need to deal biblically with all areas of life in the local community. 2) Christian leaders must guide the local church in respectfully and uncritically gathering and analyzing the customs associated with the matter being studied. 3) The pastor or missionary will next guide the local church in a Bible study related to the matter at hand in order for them to clearly un-*

derstand and accept the biblical teachings and principles that apply to the cultural situation. 4) The congregation evaluates critically their own past customs in the light of their new biblical understandings and makes a decision regarding their use. (1985:186–187)

7. *As an example, Goodson points out that a missionary who tries to organize a Christian soccer camp as a substitute for an initiation–to–manhood ceremony that has some demonic elements could completely miss many of the legitimate needs the initiation ceremony was trying to address: ie. learning to submit to authority, accept discipline when one is in the wrong, seek counsel from elders, protect one's family, bear one's share of community responsibilities, etc.. The competent pastor/missionary will be careful not to "throw out the baby with the bath water." And he/she will seek to create substitutes that are not only Biblically "non–offensive," but also completely relevant and functional, meeting the needs and addressing the original concerns even better than does the local cultural practice.*

8. *Even knowledgeable Buddhists will admit that this is true. In the Thai book entitled, Death and Merit–Making Ceremonies for the Dead (1998), the author concedes that putting a coin in the mouth has "no purpose and is against Buddhist teaching" [*เป็นไปโดยไร้เหตุผล และผิดหลักธรรมใน พุทธศาสนา*] (p, 8).*

REFERENCES

Barlow, J. 2011. Suffering, Death, and Funerals in Thailand. In Suffering: Christian Reflections on Buddhist Dukkha., ed. Paul H. DeNeui, 93–114. Pasedena, CA: William Carey Library.

Theeranantho (Ed.) 1998. Death and Merit–Making Ceremonies for the Dead. Bangkok: Duang Kaeo Publishing House. [การตายและพิธีการทำบุญศพ (พ.ศ. 2541) ธีรานันโท (บรรณาธิการ) กรุงเทพฯ: สำนักพิมพ์ ดวงแก้ว (หน้า 8)].

Goodson, D. (n.d.) An Introduction to Culture, Worldview, and Discipleship. [unpublished manuscript] Berrien Springs, MI: Adventist Frontier Missions.

Kiatyanyong, C. March 21, 2014. Telephone interview.

Lim, D., & Spaulding, S. 2003. Sharing Jesus in the Buddhist World. Pasedena, CA: William Carey Library.

Palacios, E.R. March 13, 2014. Personal communication.

Prometta, T. 2000. Allowing Jesus to be Reborn at Funerals. In Proceedings of Isaan Congress II, translated by Paul De Neui. Khon Kaen, Thailand. http://thaicov.org.

SDA Minister's Handbook. 2009. The General Conference of Seventh–day Adventists Ministerial Association.

Thailand Adventist Mission. 2009. Seventh–day Adventists and Thai Ways.

Tai Kadai Languages (n.d.) Retreived March 24, 2014, from Wikipedia: http://en.wikipedia. org/wiki/Tai–Kadai_languages.

The Office of the National Culture Commission (ONCC). 1995. The Tradition of Conducting Economical Funerals. [ประเพณีการจัดงานศพแนวประหยัด (พ.ศ. 2538) จัดพิมพ์โดย สำนักงานคณะกรรมการวัฒนธรรมแห่งชาติ กระทรวงศึกษาธิการ (หน้า 13)].

White, E. G. 1982. The Upward Look. Hagerstown, MD: Review and Herald Publishing Association.

__________. 1890. Patriarchs and Prophets. Hagerstown, MD: Review and Herald Publishing Association.

__________. 1915. Gospel Workers. Hagerstown, MD: Review and Herald Publishing Association.

Whitsett, Gregory P. 2013. Living in Favor with God and Man: Honorable Christian Living in a Theravada Buddhist Context. Presented at SDATS: Shame and Honor Conference, Sept 19–21, 2013.

Wongnaphaphaisan, S. March 21, 2014. Telephone interview.

Chapter 8

Christian Funeral: Opportunity to Share the Good News with Buddhists

Surachet Insom

Every true disciple is born into the kingdom of God as a missionary. (DA 195.2) Christians understand their role as peculiar citizens in this world. We realize that newborn life is the beginning of becoming Christ's representative. We are to have the same mind as Paul says, "For to me, to live is Christ and to die is gain" (Phil. 1:21, NIV). With this conviction in mind, we seek opportunity to share the good news at all times as Paul urges us to "preach the word; be ready in season and out of season. . ." (2 Tim. 4:2 ESV).

Often relatives of deceased church members approach me as minister and ask me to use the occasion of a funeral to share the good news of Christian salvation. Their wish is that the funeral of their love one can be a time for sharing of what they believe and their hope after death. They often say, "This is the only chance for our relatives, friends and guests of honor to hear about Jesus."

This approach has given me ideas on how to share the hope of resurrection (not only with Christians but Buddhists also). The message of hope is not only for believers but is also for others to hear about Jesus, some for the first time. After my first attempt many church members told me that non–Christians benefited from the message. They were pleased that even at the death of their loved one we could still share hope in Jesus. Aa Christian funeral provides an opportunity for their friends to learn why they believe in Jesus.

CHALLENGES IN THAILAND

There is freedom in Thailand to proclaim the Good News. There are a few times when our Thai friends will join and worship with us in churches or homes without resistance. One of these times is at a funeral service, because most Thais feel obligated to participate in an end of life service.

A funeral service is a great opportunity for Christians to share our hope in Christ's resurrection. However we need to realize that Thais are not interested in embracing Christianity. There are several reasons why Buddhists including Thai Buddhists are reluctant to attend Christian religious meetings and accept the gospel.

REASONS WHY THE LOWLAND THAI ARE RELUCTANT TO ACCEPT THE GOSPEL:

1. Thai's assume that Christians are trying to convert people into Christianity. Thailand is a Buddhist nation, so in their mind to be Thai is to be Buddhist.

2. People would rather so other things that are familiar rather than to attend a religious meeting that is strange to them.

3. Thai Buddhists have little knowledge of Christian teachings, beliefs and services, and they are not familiar with 'Christian language.'

4. The beliefs of Buddhism, Hinduism, Brahmanism, and Animism have been woven into Thai society and have become an inseparable part of their culture, worldview and practice; a part of everyday living.

5. Strong family ties and ancestor worship have become the duty of each family member. In refusing to take part in family worship activities that person removes himself from the family circle.

6. Christian beliefs about life and death are in stark contrast to Buddhist beliefs. Buddhists feel obligated to care for their dead relatives by providing all that is necessary for the after-life (money, food, clothing, etc). Christians do not share this belief

THE RARE OPPORTUNITY

Although Buddhists seldom attend Christian programs there are a few that are acceptable. These include weddings, Christmas programs and funerals which are familiar to Buddhist practice. It is our opportunity to share the love of Christ with them at these times.

THOUGHTS ON SHARING THE GOOD NEWS WITH BUDDHISTS

Traditional Thai Beliefs	***SDA Beliefs***
Thai Proverb: Gone forever, asleep forever, no resurrection, death is inescapable.	Death is a sleep. Christ will raise the righteous dead to eternal life at His return.
Fear of sin and hell. Belief in reincarnation into any of several life forms—human, animal, ghost, demon, angel, or a god.	Assurance that every person is offered eternal life now as a gift from Jesus Christ. No reincarnation.
No assurance after death. The goal is to accumulate merit in hope of a better life in the next reincarnation.	Through Jesus's resurrection, there is escape from death and into eternal life.

Traditional Thai Beliefs	*SDA Beliefs*
Funeral atmosphere of hopelessness. Music at funerals are mournful.	Funeral atmosphere includes comfort and hope of reunion with loved one. Songs rejoice in the hope of a resurrection.
Uncertainty of salvation. Salvation is determined by the accumulated merit earned by the deceased and rituals performed by others.	Confidence in Christ's provisions for salvation and God's judgment.
Funerals are expensive but based on the resources of the family.	Funerals are simpler and less costly.
The family continues to make merit on behalf of the dead as long as they are alive.	The family continues to abide in Christ to ensure a happy reunion of the righteous at the 2nd coming.
Fear of sin and punishment in hell which will result in be reborn into the lower life forms.	Assurance of God's perfect plan, no fear of eternal hell or rebirth into a low life form.w

SUGGESTED SERMON TOPICS FOR BUDDHISTS

Thai Buddhists believe in the reality of evil spirits, so the theme of a controversy between good and evil, God and Satan is meaningful to them. I introduce this theme at the beginning of funeral sermons. This leads people to realize the nature and genesis of life and death. I can then develop the theme to include where life and death originated and how God has and is now dealing with the problem of sin. Buddhists believe in evolution. The story of creation and the fall of man can open their minds to the Christian concept of how evil entered our world.

Since Buddhism is atheistic by nature, it contrasts with man's desire to have deity protection. Somehow most Thai Buddhists imported Hindu gods to secure their desire for divine protection. We see these gods around the country. The most popular gods are Shiva, Narayan, Vishnu, Ganesh and Brahma. Polytheism has changed Thai Buddhists to accept other divine beings. We can use Paul's method used in Athens to introduce the Creator God who has power to give life after death.

SOME THEMES THAT WILL CAPTURE THE BUDDHIST MIND:

– The origin of life, sin and death.

– How God deals with human life.

– Biblical teaching of evil spirits and the end of all evil.

– The consequence of sin and the effects of Satan's work in human life, family and society.

– Christian belief in life and death.

– The hope of resurrection and a new life with loved ones.

– The reality of eternal life in contrast to reincarnation.

– Jesus, the originator of life and conqueror over sin and death.

– The hope of Christ's Second Coming and the New Earth.

– Death has been conquered by Christ's death on the cross.

– Heavenly life on earth. Life of hope, love and everlasting life. Christians are practicing eternal life on earth.

There is no limit to applying Christian teachings to reach Buddhists even at the death of a believer. We must make sure we share valuable eternal beliefs at valuable times.

REFERENCE LIST

Aarayan. Buddha History, Bangkok: Amnoy Sarn Publishing, 1984.

Dictionary of Buddhism, Bangkok: Mahachulalongkorn Rajavidhayalai, 1985.

Inspiration Dharma: Buddhist Funeral. http://www.asoke.info/09Communication/DharmaPublicize/Sanasoke/sa285/136.htm

Marja–Leena, Heikkila–Horn. Buddhist with Open Eyes, Bangkok: FahApai Co., Ltd. 1997.

Mettraiya, The World Great Prophet of the Future. Somchai Suwanpodok, Medsai Printing, 2550.

Pin, Mudhukan. The Presentation of Buddhist Teaching, Bangkok: Klang Vidhaya Publishing, 1976.

Satian, Pantarangsri. New Discover Buddhist History, Bangkok: Kaona Press, 1963.

White, Ellen G. The Desire of Ages. Review and Herald Publishing, 1898.

CHAPTER 9

FUNERAL HOMILY: A FRESH LOOK AT SERMONS IN THAI CHRISTIAN FUNERALS

Soontorn Thanteeraphan

MINISTRY TO THE BEREAVED

This section will discuss the sermon that is being use in the funeral in a Thai context. There will be three major points that contribute to an approach toward present funeral homilies. First, I will analyze the role of the sermon in a funeral service. Next, I will analyze the typical funeral sermon being preached by most pastors in Thailand. And lastly I will analyze the message heard by those who attend the funeral.

The Seventh–day Adventist Minister's Handbook says that ministry to the bereaved calls "for respect of traditions and culture in dealing with death, but always in a context of Christian principles and the biblical understanding of death" (General Conference of Seventh–day Adventists Ministerial Association 2009:195). The Seventh–day Adventist Church sets its foundation upon biblical understanding and principles toward death. The Minister's Handbook says "The funeral sermon should be both realistic about death and hopeful for the resurrection, recognizing the contribution of the deceased and the loss to the family, to the community, and to God" (2009:198). The expectation of funeral sermons is to include these three key aspects: 1) sound biblical foundation, 2) recognition of the contributions of the deceased, 3) bring hope and comfort to those who attend, especially family, relatives and close friends of the dead.

WORD OF HOPE

In a Buddhist funeral, the ceremony concentrates on only one objective: bringing blessing to relatives and attendees.[1] Monks have the duty to bring words of blessing. They chant in the Bali or Sanskrit language. The words of blessing focus on the reality of life in both a physical and spiritual sense. The chant contains the reminder that life is suffering and people should set goals to achieve nirvana. The highlight of the funeral is the chant. For Buddhists, the chant is considered a blessing to receive. Each night of the funeral service there is chanting which demonstrates how important the chant is to the Buddhist.

Adventism in Thailand is leaning toward the conservative approach in operating churches. The churches in Thailand follow the advice of the Union Office, Division, and General Conference closely. While Buddhist funerals contain only chanting, Adventist funerals have other elements in the service based on common practice in America and Europe. The Ministerial Association of the Seventh–day Adventist Church directs that funeral services should contain songs of comfort to bring hope; eulogy and obituary in honor of the dead; and testimonials by the attendees sharing what they remember about the person (2009: 198).[2] These are preliminary items before the sermon is preached.

By the time the sermon is delivered the funeral guests do not necessarily feel a special blessing. The primary source of comfort in funeral should be derived from the word of God. Several experts on homiletics, such as Morris, Fanwar, and Robison, are convinced that only the word of God can bring change, hope, and comfort (Morris 2012:11, Fanwar 2006:14, Robinson 2001:21).

FUNERAL SERMON

Pastors should be aware that Thai culture is heavily influence by pluralism.[3] Merriam–Webster's Online Dictionary defines pluralism as "situations where different social classes, religions, races are living in the same society while they still continue with their own faith." Thailand is the land of pluralists. Thai Buddhists may send their children to a Christian School yet remain Buddhist. A common peasant may accept all religious services yet still remain faithful to Buddhism.

As guests attend an Adventist funeral, they expect to listen to words of hope found in the Bible. Instead of focusing on exposition of the word of God, pastors frequently aim to convert the funeral guests. They use an evangelistic sermon to prove that the SDA belief about death is correct. The sermon follows the classic evangelistic approach. Pastors begin with condolences to the grieving family, and then shift to either a second coming sermon, which is based on 1 Thessalonians 4:13–18, or the doctrine on the state of the dead. Some also go through the "Great Controversy" plan of salvation, and then the pastor will conclude with another condolence to the family. While the 15–20 minute sermon of this style might cheer up the family members and may serve to convert those of different faiths. The question is, does this resonate in the heart of the Thai Buddhist?

In every occasion in life from the happiest (baby dedication) to the saddest (bereavement of a loved one), the only way to sooth needs, feelings, and emotions is in sharing the Word of God. Without the Bible, speech is just human opinion and will not be able to fill the needs of life (Morris 2012:11). Robinson (2001:19) strongly emphasizes that preaching the word of God alone can redeem and nothing can replace it. In this section, I will look at the elements that I have found to be vital to the sermon in a Buddhist context to effectively reach their hearts. I have purposely omitted the section on basic biblical exegesis, as Adventist pastors are experts in the Bible doctrine.

THREE ELEMENTS

There are three elements pastors need to give special attention to as they prepare their sermon: 1) mystical power, 2) life of demonstration, and 3) an invitation to the listeners.

1 – MYSTICAL POWER

The phrase "mystical power" is referring to the power of the Holy Spirit moving in the hearer's heart when the Word of God is being preached. Song (1979:62–63) gives an example of the Zen Buddhist concept of satori or "key to unlocking the mystery of life."[4] Thai Buddhists have a similar concept to satori. Funeral attendees know that the truth the monks chant unlocks the mystery of life: birth, old age, illness, and death. Christian sermons should address satori as well in the following ways.

Mystical power in this article refers to two dimensions. The first dimension refers to the mystery of the word of God. When the preacher properly exegetes and prepares the sermon, it contains power that can convict the hearts of the people. The Holy Spirit is the power that softens people's hearts and allows truth to change their lives.

The second dimension is the mystery of the providence of God. God allows people present at Christian funerals to hear Biblical truth and find satori from hearing the word of God spoken in the sermon. God will impress their hearts. They should leave with a satori that is found in the word of God. At one of the funerals I conducted, a lady asked, "Does the Bible really teach what you shared?" The Holy Spirit convicted her of truth.

2 – LIFE DEMONSTRATION

Dr. Ubolwan Mejuton (2006:10) used the term life exegesis to refer to the real life examples used in the sermons. Real life examples create a bridge and uplift the heart of pluralistic listeners. Yap Kim Hao (1990:64–65) elaborates on a real life example that "Theology as praxis is directed toward action. It is the involvement with actual life.

This involvement is in concrete human history. It is a real response to the actual situation of the people with all their needs and their hopes and expectations." In other words, Yap is saying that pluralistic listeners are much more interested in real life stories rather than made up stories.

With this thought in mind I would recommend 2 things: use illustrations from the life of the deceased in the sermon and integrate points from the obituary in the sermon rather than having a separate reading of the obituary.[5] The sermon maybe inductive, deductive or another style, but when using an illustration, the preacher must use a life real life story to illustrate the point. This may mean that the preacher will have to find a great deal of information in advance from the family, but it is very worthwhile if it serves to lead someone to Christ.

3 – INVITATION TO THE LISTENERS

I believe that no sermon is complete if the listener isn't invited to make a decision. When the phrase "making decisions" occurs, the thought of conversion and public evangelism come to mind.[6] I use the term "making decisions" because it is the common term for people to understand. However, I really mean the invitation for the listeners to follow the life example of the deceased. (See Sample Sermon in Appendix.)

CONCLUSION

This article seeks to provide a fresh look at funeral sermons from a Thai context and to give direction to those who are asked to officiate at Christian funerals. The paper fulfilled the above goal by discussing the role of the sermon, giving an analyses of types of sermons, and exploring the feeling of the people after listening to the sermon. It also explores the elements that could help funeral sermons become more meaningful through mystical power, life illustrations and a personal invitation. I don't claim to be an authority on preaching at funerals, rather I seek to provide direction and offer a new perspective. I hope that those who read this may continue to develop better tools.

APPENDIX: SAMPLE SERMON[7]

On behalf of Bangkok Adventist Hospital Church; we would like to send our condolences to Ms. A's family. She is a person who sacrificed herself for God's institutions and His Church. On behalf of the church, we would like to thank Ms. A's family for continuing to support the hospital and His church. May God watch over your family and continue to bless you. Let us pray.

(Prayer) "May God's blessing dwell upon this memorial service and may we experience your presence as I bring your Holy Word to encourage and create hope in your soon return. In the name of Jesus, I pray."

In Psalm 127, the Psalmist expressed the things that God expects from each member of a family. The scripture reads "If the Lord does not build the house, then those who build it work in vain. If the Lord does not guard the city, the watchman stands guard in vain. It is vain for you to rise early, come home late, and work so hard for your food. Yes, he can provide for those whom he loves even when they sleep. Yes, sons are a gift from the LORD, the fruit of the womb is a reward. Sons born during one's youth are like arrows in a warrior's hand. How blessed is the man who fills his quiver with them! They will not be put to shame when they confront enemies at the city gate." (paraphrase)

King Solomon said that if God is not the one who gives; whether it be the house that we have, a city that is being watched or those who toil for work, everything is in vain. When we invest in something we expect something in return. If we plant mangoes, we hope to eat its fruits. When we work, we desire our salary. When we teach nursing students, we hope to have good nurses who serve as nurses. But Solomon suggests that if the Lord does not permit whatever we hope for it is in vain. It is in vain if we rise early to work. Sometimes, we are too stressed and we can't sleep. But God promises that he will provide sleep for those whom he loves.

Ms. A understood this promise very well. On January 8, 1949, about one year before she graduated with her nursing degree as part of the first class of nursing at the college, she and her two classmates

Ms. B and Ms. C decided to accept Jesus as their personal savior and were baptized. Ever since then she dedicated her life to support the School of Nursing at Bangkok Adventist Hospital, and God's church. Ms. A realized that God graciously provided her with the opportunity to study at this institution, and to be able to work at both the hospital and the school of nursing. She always realized that God directed her life and was watching over her. She knew that the result of her work for Him would not be in vain.

Solomon says children are gifts from God, and he compares children to arrows in a quiver. He said that the more we have, the better it is. At the time that Solomon lived arrows were not made by machine that makes them uniform and perfect like those you can buy today. Good arrows were made by hand. The arrow maker would first search for good wood. He would cut and shape the wood to be the right size and weight. The head of the arrow was made from bones or rocks which the maker had to cut and sharpen until it was the right size and shape and would fit the arrow shaft. The maker would have to find rope and tightly lash the arrowhead and shaft together.

Making one good arrow took a long time. It required patience, perseverance, and skill. The diligent person always made good quality arrows and kept them. When a difficult situation occurred, those arrows would protect the owner from danger. Solomon is comparing good arrow to well–trained children; children who benefit society and are not a burden to their parents; children who bring joy to their parents not sadness.

In the Thai Language, the word "students" has been used only recently. Thai would always use the word "Lukesit" or children whom I teach. Ms. A had a lot of children. She had her birth children and the children who she taught. Like the arrow maker she spent time fashioning the wood to become the right size. She also used a lot of energy in sharpening the stone into the arrowhead. She used her many abilities in equipping and training young people in the classroom, and she was a good example for the young people to follow. The children she taught are her legacy.

Today, we have seen the word of God fulfilled in Ms. A's life. She chose to serve the Lord, and her labor was not I vain, but full of happiness. She chose to dedicate her time in making arrows to support God's institution and his church.

Once again on behalf of Bangkok Adventist Hospital Church we would like to send our condolences to Ms. A's family. It is our greatest hope that God will impress each one of us here today to follow in the footsteps of Ms. A in dedicating our lives to serving the Lord.

NOTES

1. *This ceremony is concentrated on the evening session due to the similarity to Adventist's memorial service. However, during the day, the relatives may do different activity to earn merits for the dead. The evening service is different than the cremation ceremony; which is opened for further study.*

2. *The current Minister's Handbook is the 2012 edition. I only have access to the 2009 edition.*

3. *This information is from my personal experience as a Thai pastor who has pastored and planted churches in Thailand.*

4. *[Merriam–Webster defines Satori as: sudden enlightenment and a state of consciousness attained by intuitive illumination representing the spiritual goal of Zen Buddhism.]*

5. *Funeral services for both Adventists and Buddhist contain a bulletin where an obituary is always printed.*

6. *Making a decision is similar yet very different from an evangelistic approach. It is similar because both call for taking a stand for something. However, there is one important difference in that it is assumed that the listeners come to an evangelistic–focused event for the purpose of conversion. However, at a funeral the call should be related to demonstrating respect toward the God whom the deceased believed, and hopefully lead the listeners to ask to know more about Him at a future time.*

7. *This sermon is translated from Thai to English. I have purposely omitted the name of the deceased.*

REFERENCE LIST

Fanwar, W.M. 2006. The Gourmet Pulpit: Preaching with Panache and Power (1st ed.). Nakhorn Ratchasima, Thailand: Somchai Press.

General Conference of the Seventh–day Adventists Ministerial Association. 2009. Seventh–day Adventist Minister's Handbook. Maryland, USA: Ministerial Association.

Kim, Y.B. 2005 (May). Asian Meet Jesus the Asian. Quest 1: 17–40.

Koyama, K. 1999. Water Buffalo Theology (rev. ed.). Maryknoll, NY: Orbis Books.

Mejuton, Ubolwan. 2006. Life Exegesis. In Communicating Christ in Buddhist World, ed. Paul DeNeui and David Lim, 2–24. Pasadena, CA: William Carey Library.

Merriam–Webster Online Dictionary. http://www.merriam–webster.com/dictionary/pluralism (accessed 02 April 2014).

Morris, Derek. 2012. Powerful Biblical Preaching: Practical Pointers from Master Preacher (rev. ed.). USA: Trilogy Scripture Resources.

Paksangkhanet, Thechathut. 2013. Funeral Chant. http://www.mbuslc.ac.th/web/การสวดอภิธรรมในงานศพ–โดย–พระดร (accessed 02 April 2014).

Robinson, H.W. 2001. Biblical Preaching (2nd ed.). Grand Rapids, MI: Baker Academic.

Song, C.S. 1979. Third–eye Theology (rev. ed.). Maryknoll, NY: Orbis Books.

________1988. Theology from the Womb of Asia. Maryknoll, NY: Orbis books.

Thanteeraphan, S. 2008. Life Exegesis: The way to share Christ with Central Thai. Research paper for THST 585 Principles of Biblical Hermeneutics, Griggs University, Mission College, Muak Lek, Thailand.

Yap, K.H. 1990. Doing Theology in a Pluralistic World. Singapore: Methodist Bk. Room. Methodist Center.

Chapter 10

How to Honor the Dead and Minister to the Living in Laos

Khamsay Phetchareun

INTRODUCTION

When death occurs it causes the most painful experience in the family of the deceased. It makes the family members feel numb, confused, lost, and vulnerable. It is a very sensitive time for the bereaved family. Ministering to the bereaved family is the most delicate task of a minister of the gospel.

This paper does not attempt to deal with Lao Buddhist funerals, but rather focuses on funerals according to the rites of the Lao and Hmong Adventists. It takes special interest in how the Adventist pastor is to respond to the bereaved family who is either Adventist or non–Adventist. Finally, attempts will be made to suggest what Adventists should do in relation to some practices associated with the funeral services without offending the bereaved family.

BEFORE DEATH OCCURS

When a pastor arrives at a particular location, where there is no Adventist cemetery, it is mandatory that he asks around for local cemetery elders or committee members. Then, he should try to pay a visit to those leaders and also village or district leaders. He should let them know that he is a religious leader and is willing to work towards the betterment of the community. He should get involved in community projects and become known to the community as a person of integrity and high moral standards. Once he has attained such a reputation it will be easier for him to ask permission to use the local cemetery for burial or cremation of his deceased church members. In the past, there was a case in which the local village elders refused to allow a deceased Adventist to be buried in their local cemetery unless the family allowed Buddhist monks to officiate over the funeral service. Fortunately, the village was not too far from Vientiane so the Vientiane Church asked for the body to be taken to the church for an Adventist funeral and cremation in Vientiane. But what if the body is in a rural area and the local cemetery elders refuse to allow the deceased Adventist to be buried in their cemetery? This will certainly become a real problem for the pastor and the bereaved family. Our God will also lose face in this situation. His name will be tarnished and His cause will suffer. That is why it is very important for the pastor to develop a good relationship with the local cemetery elders and village or district leaders.

WHEN DEATH OCCURS

When death occurs, the pastor should try to be with the family immediately. Often the family will be in shock and feel confused. They will not be in the right state of mind to make logical decisions, so the pastor needs to be with the family immediately. There is nothing more important than being physically present with the bereaved family. In my opinion, even when death occurs during the divine service and the pastor is in the middle of his sermon, the pastor should arrange for an elder to preach on his behalf and should immediately go to the deceased family. By doing this he will win the hearts and minds of his church members as he demonstrates his care.

Once he arrives at the house of the deceased he should consult with the family as to what kind of coffin they would like to use and help them decide where to keep the coffin – whether at the church or at the home. Most of the time these decisions will depend very much on the family's financial status. This is the most sensitive and delicate point of time because the family's emotional strength is at its lowest. Often, it is the closest friend of the family who will be the best person to come in and organize everything on behalf of the family, acting as a master of ceremony (MC) or a host. All decisions made, however, should be in consultation with the family.

The next important thing to do is to organize the memorial services. According to our Lao Adventist tradition, there are three memorial services per day: morning, lunch time, and evening time. Again, as the religious leader, it is the pastor's responsibility to organize the memorial services. Depending on where the funeral is being held, he may be the one who conducts all of the services. However, if there are other pastors or elders around, he can ask for their help in leading out in the memorial services.

According to the Lao culture the body can be kept at home or, most preferably, at a Buddhist temple. Most Buddhist temples in Laos and Thailand have at least one chapel available for funeral services and also offer crematory services. In some temples there are several funeral chapels. However, in some cases the body can be kept at home. During this time extended family members, relatives and friends (sometimes even former enemies) will come to pay respects to the deceased. In the traditional Lao and Thai culture, the one who pays respects to the deceased is given a couple sticks of incense to place in a sand–filled vase in front of the coffin while at the same time addressing the deceased by recalling good times or stating how they remember the deceased. Other nice words or a prayer for the deceased to ascend to paradise are spoken. Former enemies use this time to beg for forgiveness from the deceased. Extended family and friends contribute monetary gifts for the merit making ceremonies.

In our Adventist tradition, however, we do not give incense to guests who come to pay respects to the deceased. The gifts and contributions brought by the guests are used for the funeral expenses. In Lao Buddhist, Hmong Animist, and Adventist traditions, most close friends and relatives will stay with the deceased family until the burial or cremation is finished. During this time food is provided for the guests. In the Lao culture, eating is mostly optional. Guests may or may not eat at the home of the deceased. Some guests, especially pregnant women and children, do not like to participate. However, in the Hmong culture, eating together is much more significant to the family of the deceased. The family expects guests to eat and will feel offended if they don't. Traditionally, the Hmong will cook three meals a day, often pork, chicken, and beef, to offer the spirit of the deceased. The guests then eat what is left from the offerings (Lee 2009:23–27). This practice, however, can become a financial burden to the surviving family. Often, in the case of a prolonged illness of the deceased prior to death, the family has already spent most or all of their money and there is nothing left to take care of the funeral and related expenses.

PRACTICES IN REGARDS TO VIEWING THE DEAD

The Lao and the Hmong differ in the practice of the viewing of the dead. While the Lao do not normally ask to see the face of the deceased when they pay their respects, the Hmong do (Leepalao 2013:23). In Hmong culture it is expected. Often, close relatives will also touch the face of the deceased and cry. This practice can pose a health hazard, especially if the deceased died from a contagious disease. The Bible speaks against touching the dead body, saying the person who touches the dead will be unclean and requires proper purification (Numbers 19:11–13). Even during Bible times, the Lord was concerned about the health consequences of those who touched corpses.

In contrast, the Lao will only open the coffin at the cremation site just before cremating the body. Coconut water is used to wash the face of the deceased, often performed by the male next of kin. Close surviving family members are allowed to view the face of the deceased for the last time. Normally the only ones to touch the body of the deceased are those who help with the initial preparation and placement of the body in the coffin.

SOME THEOLOGICAL ISSUES

Although this paper does not focus on what to do when attending a Lao Buddhist or a Hmong Animist funeral, some of these cultural practices have unknowingly been brought into Lao or Hmong Adventist funeral rites. Some of them may not be harmful to one's faith, while others may pose some risk. Thus it is a desire of the author to discuss some of the cultural practices related to Lao and Hmong Adventist funeral rites. This paper, however, does not presume to be the final authority on what can or cannot be done. Rather the goal is to give a balanced explanation of both sides with the hope that later proper Lao and Hmong Adventist funeral rites can be formulated and used in the Lao field. In this section, several issues such as burial and cremation, performance of traditional songs, eating at the home of the deceased, talking to the "deceased," giving or contributing to the "deceased," and crying for the deceased will be discussed.

TO BURY OR TO CREMATE?

When death occurs, the first thing that comes to mind is whether to bury or cremate the body. Some cultures practice burial and others cremation. Even among Christians, some prefer burial over cremation. Yet, some Christians totally object to cremation. The Bible, however, while it seems to favor burial, does not explicitly condemn cremation. Those who are against cremation refer to most of the burnings in the Bible which are associated with punishment from God (Lev 21:9; Amos 2:1; Mat 5:19). Yet, there are also occasions when cremation was used not as a punishment. In the case of King Saul and his sons, is seems that cremation was used to preserve the dignity of the deceased (2 Chr 16:13–14; 1 Sam 31:12–13). However, the real issue "is not whether one is buried or cremated but the meaning given to these acts" (George 2014:66). Unfortunately, in an attempt to show the even more honor and dignity to the deceased, some have unnecessarily added more practices, such as elaborate caskets and other elements. In modern days, burial certainly costs much more than cremation. Thus, before death, some people often instruct their loved ones to cremate them and scatter their ashes in the river. These people trust that God does not need to have their raw materials, namely bones, to raise them to life again. To be fair, one must be aware that the Bible also mentions other ways of disposing the dead such as placing the body in a cave (Gen 23:19) or in a sepulcher (Mat 27:61). Therefore, it seems that it is not so much how fast (in cremation) or how slow (in burial) one returns to dust, but rather it is about what is acceptable to the surviving family (Gen 3:19).

TO SING OR NOT TO SING?

Singing is part of Christian worship programs, including weddings and funeral services. The Hmong people of Laos have a special song called "End of Life Song" that they sing at funerals. It is believed that singing the song guides the soul of the deceased back to the ancestors where it belongs. Besides this song, there are other songs designed to give blessings to the surviving family. These songs are sung at Hmong funerals (Thao 2008).

Just because singing is a part of pagan funerals does not mean that Christians should refrain from singing at Christian funerals. In fact, the same should apply to cremation. Just because some pagans cremate their dead should not mean that Christians should refrain from cremation. In Christian funerals singing plays a very important role in comforting and providing hope to the surviving family members and others who are present. Indeed, the Buddhists find it very interesting that Christians sing at funerals. They see that instead of crying uncontrollably, Christians instead can sing. For this reason, singing at Christian funerals provides a wonderful opportunity for non–Christians to be interested in the spiritual message that is preached during the funeral.

TO EAT OR NOT TO EAT?

Eating at the home of the deceased is also a topic for discussion. It is not so much the Lao, but the Hmong tradition that is in question. The Hmong believe that the surviving family members have to provide three meals a day for the deceased (Lee 2009:26). After the deceased is 'served', the rest of the food is given to the guests who come to be with the family during the days of morning. Some feel that because the food was meant for the soul of the deceased, it is not permissible for Christians to eat at Hmong funerals. Refusing to eat, however, risks greatly offending the host. Hmong will see this refusal to eat as a denial of their hospitality as well as a sign of disrespect toward the deceased, and will shame the surviving family in front of their other guests. This kind of action will certainly be very harmful to the relationship between the Christian and bereaved family as well as the Hmong community at large.

As for the Lao funeral, the house of mourning will always have people, family and friends. Food will be cooked and served three times a day and as needed. The Lao, however, are not as sensitive as the Hmong when it comes to eating or not eating. However, pregnant women and children are typically not allowed to eat at the home of the deceased. Nor are they supposed to look at or participate in the funeral procession because of a belief that the spirit of the deceased may enter them and bring bad luck.

In the Bible, the Apostle Paul addressed the issue of food offered to idols quite extensively in 1 Corinthians chapters 8 and 10. If one reads the advice carefully one will know that Paul's main concern is about causing another spiritually weak member to stumble (1 Cor 8:8–9, 13). The most serious advice against eating in the temple of idols is this, "You cannot drink the cup of the Lord and the cup of demons. You cannot partake of the table of the Lord and the table of demons" (1 Cor 10:21, ESV). Still at this point Paul's main concern is still for the spiritually weak member, for he said, "Let no one seek his own good, but the good of his neighbor" (1 Cor 10:24, ESV). Therefore, when it comes to eating foods prepared at Hmong funerals, Paul would use the same advice. The concern is not so much for the one who eats, but for the one who will stumble. So, if you decide to go to a Hmong non–Christian funeral, it would be better to eat the food. However, if you don't want to eat the food, it is advisable not to attend the funeral in the first place.

TALK TO THE DEAD?

After death occurs, in both Lao and Hmong tradition, the body of the deceased is kept in a coffin inside the house or church so family and friends can pay their last respects. Often the visitors talk to the coffin, addressing the deceased lying inside. They mention the good times and the bad times, or give blessings and beg for forgiveness from the dead. Is this permissible in Christian faith? What does the Bible have to say on this topic?

In various Bible passages we see that the Lord commanded His people not to practice divination, tell fortunes, interpret omens, sorcery, or inquire of the dead (Deu 18:10–12; Lev 19:31; 20:6, 27). The command is for God's people to avoid seeking advice from the dead, as it is actually not the dead but Satan's agent that replies. This is like having an "extra–marital" affair with Satan while having God as your "husband." However, talking to the deceased at the funeral or the tomb is different. People of all cultures and religions, including Christianity, do it all the time. They think of, talk about, and talk to the deceased (in the coffin or tomb). This action is more about keeping a memory alive rather than consulting the dead for advice as King Saul did (1 Sam 28:7–20).

TO GIVE OR NOT TO GIVE?

When there is a death, the surviving family has a lot of financial expenses. They need all the support they can get, both emotionally and financially. Often, Christians are reluctant to give money to their Buddhist friends as their Buddhist friends would normally say, "Thank you for helping Gin Tarn (give alms to the dead) with us." It is not known if the money will be part of the offering given to the dead through a ritual in which Buddhist monks chant blessings thereby sending it to the spirit world for the deceased to use. While this may happen, the majority of the money donated is used to cover funeral expenses as well as to pay for feeding the guests. Depending on how close a friendship the Christian has with the bereaved family, some Christians may be able to say, "This money is to help pay for the food and other funeral expenses, not for the Gin Tarn." Looking from another angle, one never can be sure that one's monetary gifts and donations, regardless of the cause, will always be spent wisely. There is always the risk that the recipient may use the money for alcohol, drugs, prostitution, or other illegal or spiritually immoral activity.

As for Christian funerals in Laos, whether of Lao or Hmong tradition, money is the most acceptable gift to give to the bereaved family. As mentioned above, the bereaved family has a lot of expenses such as purchasing food for the guests as well as other funeral–related expenses. Giving a flower wreath is also another popular gift that close friends like to give. These flower wreaths stand with the casket, the number of which is often associated with the reputation of the deceased. Christians should be careful to ensure that what is written on the wreath reflects Christian beliefs and teaching regarding the hope of resurrection at the Second Coming of the Lord. Wreaths given by Buddhist friends may have messages such as, "May the soul of Mr/Mrs… ascend to Paradise". However, as Adventists, we do not believe that the deceased has a soul that is capable of ascending to Paradise or anywhere else. Instead of the typical Buddhist saying, a Christian message could be something like, "May Mr/Mrs… sleep peacefully awaiting the return of the Lord. See you on that morning of resurrection". Such messages may give opportunities for us to share our faith and hope of resurrection as non–Christians read them and begin to ask questions about their meaning.

TO CRY OR NOT TO CRY?

The Bible advises against immoderate grief and uncontrollable weeping at funerals "as others do who have no hope" (1 Thes 4:13, ESV). It is acceptable to cry during funeral, but excessive crying may represent weak faith. Jesus also cried three times while He was on earth (see Luke 19:41; John 11:33–35; Heb 5:7). One was at the funeral of Lazarus (John 11:33–35). However, unlike the crying of the Jews, Jesus' weeping was controlled and silent. The Greek word used in Jesus' case was δακρύω (dakruō) which means "to shed tears" or "cry silently." On the contrary, elsewhere when there is weeping in association with funerals, the Bible uses the word κλαίω (klaiō) which means "weep aloud," as in the case of Mary and the Jews who were with her. According to the ancient Jewish funeral custom, it is believed that professional mourners were also hired to weep at Lazarus' funeral as well as in the cases of the widow's son at Nain (Luke 7:11–15) and Jairus' daughter (Luke 8:41–42, 50–56) (Edersheim 1993:693). Nowadays, professional mourners are available for hire, as people judge how popular the deceased is based on how many people attend the funeral (New 2013).

Note that Jesus did not rebuke people about their excess weeping or klaiō. We, as Christians, who have stronger faith, should never act in any way that suggests our disapproval of other people or Christians who cry excessively at funerals. We can discourage Christians from hiring professional mourners to add colors to their funerals, but we also should not judge those who choose to hire them either.

OTHER TRADITIONS TO BE ADDRESSED IN THE FUTURE

There are other practices and superstitions related to Lao Buddhist and Hmong Animist funerals. The Lao set the coffin in such a way as to prevent it from laying in the same direction that the rest of the family members lay when they sleep. Traditionally, when they take the coffin from the house, they will not take it out through the door. Instead, they break a hole in the wall of the house and take it out through the hole.

The Hmong funeral is more complex and often requires three to seven days to perform it properly. There are many practices assigned to different people to carry out and great care is taken to be sure they are done in an orderly manner. The whole process is overseen by the funeral director or master of ceremonies. Due to the limitations of this paper these additional practices will not be discussed here. However, they warrant further study and consideration in order to formulate a comprehensive funeral guide for the Adventist Church in Laos.

CONCLUSION

All of us who are ministers must remember that all funeral services are designed to assist the remaining family members and relatives of the deceased. The deceased knows nothing – whether the funeral is conducted following Buddhist, Muslim, Hindu, animist, or Christian rites. The salvation of the deceased depends on their faith before they died, not on what religious or traditional rites are followed.

As Adventists in Laos, we are challenged with the background of two major religions: Buddhism and animism. It is important that ministers understand the religious backgrounds of their people so that he has a clear explanation of what rites are allowable and which are not. Because people's minds are very sensitive during the time of grief, the pastor must do everything with extreme care. Yet he must also keep in mind that the funeral rites do not determine the fate of the deceased. With this in mind, he should be willing to accept any practice that is not forbidden by God for the sake of the surviving family members, even if he personally doesn't feel comfortable with it.

There are still many issues that remain to be discussed. Perhaps they can be addressed in future articles.

REFERENCES

Edersheim, Alfred. 1993. The Life and Times of Jesus the Messiah. Peabody, MA: Hendrickson Publishers.

George, Timothy. 2002. Cremation Confusion. Christianity Today 46, no. 6 (21 May): 66. [electronic form: accessed May 2, 2014].

Lee, Kirk. 2009. Rituals, Roles, and Responsibilities Included in a Hmong Funeral: A Guidebook for Teachers to Better Understand the Process their Hmong Students Experience in a Time of Family Loss. Master Thesis., California State University.

Leepalao, Tougue. 2013. Hmong Funeral Procedures, trans. Xai Lor, Txongpao Lee, and Kou Yang. St Paul, MN: Western and Southern Life.

New, Catherine. 2014. 'Rent A Mourner' Helps You Look More Popular at your Funeral. The Huffington Post, March 27. http://www.huffingtonpost.com/2013/03/27 /rent–a–mourner_n_2964280.html (accessed May 7, 2014).

Thao, Shong Ger. 2008. Religious and Cultural Expert Testimony. Paper presented at the United Nations Special Rapporteur Consultation on Grave Desecration of Hmong Graves in Thailand. 10 December.

Chapter 11

A Missiological Reflection on Chinese Qingming Festival

Samuel Wang

INTRODUCTION

Perhaps one of the biggest stumbling stones in the path of the Chinese embracing the Christian faith is related to the way the dead are treated by Christians, both during the funeral and afterwards. Chinese not only place great importance on the ceremonies of funerals, but also have various ways and customs to pay tribute to the dead. Historically, these differences in practice can be seen in the Chinese Rites Controversy, a dispute among Roman Catholic missionaries to China during the 17th and 18th centuries over ritual practices of honoring family ancestors and the Catholic response to these practices.[1]

Even today every April 5, Chinese around the world observe the Qingming Festival as an important day of showing reverence to their deceased elders and parents. Each year at this time new and mature Chinese Christians are conflicted as to how and to what degree they should participate in the ceremonies on this day. They indeed want to show proper respect to their dead parents and ancestors, but they also desire to stand firm for their faith in Jesus Christ. It can be a challenge for Christians to find the right balance while not offending their non–Christian family members.

Agreement or disagreement over customs of honoring the dead is a pivotal factor in the final decision making of Chinese when deciding whether to convert to Christianity. Following these customs is viewed as a sign of family loyalty and of true filial piety, a value which is highly regarded in Chinese society. Because this issue looms so large in the minds of would–be Christian converts, the matter demands missiological reflection for developing practical guidelines for Christians on Qingming Day or in other ancestral honoring ceremonies.

IMPORTANCE OF THE QINGMING FESTIVAL TO CHINESE FAMILIES

Qingming (April 5) is one of the more important festivals in a yearly cycle that is intimately connected with folk religions and especially with the cult of the ancestors. Its origin can be traced back to 636 BC, but Qingming was officially made a public holiday for honoring ancestors in AD 732. The name of the festival, Qingming, means 'pure and bright', which refers to the struggle between yang (the force of light) and yin. It coincides with the beginning of warm weather and the start of the agricultural season in North China. It is known for Chinese ancestral veneration and the tending of family graves. During Qingming, families typically visit the graves of ancestors, sweep the tombs, pray before the ancestors, leave offerings of food, and burn ghost money (fake paper currency) in honor of the departed, symbolically renewing the bond between the living and dead relatives.

Qingming is not only observed in Taiwan, Hong Kong, and Mainland China (where it was reinstated as a public holiday in 2008) but also in Vietnam, Japan and Korea. Despite the holiday having no official status in countries further abroad the Chinese communities in Southeast Asian nations, such as Singapore and Malaysia, also take this festival seriously and observe its traditions faithfully. The holiday is very much a family celebration and family obligation. This festival is seen as a time of reflection to honor and give thanks to their forefathers.

CHINESE WORLDVIEW OF THE DEAD

We do well to take a missiological look at this festival of the Chinese as a way of discovering the Chinese worldview and their values. By so doing, good mission opportunities may be discovered.

From the customs of Qingming festival one can see that in the Chinese worldview the dead exist in a separate world with full knowledge of this world. One of the symbolic points of connection between the living and the dead is the graveyard. The Chinese tend to believe the dead are not only conscious, but also powerful and can provide protection or bestow blessings upon their families.

Ancestor worship is a tradition established over time based upon this worldview and is widely practiced even among those who may not share the same belief that the dead are still living. For instance, Confucius himself did not necessarily believe that when a man died, he still existed in some form and in some place. Nevertheless, he supported the long–established custom of honouring parents, as can be seen from the following two passages from Confucius Analects, which typically reflect the national sentiment and psychology regarding how to treat the deceased parents.

Meng Yi asked what filial piety was. The Master said, "It is not being disobedient." Soon after, as Fan Chi was driving him, the Master told him, saying, "Mengsun asked me what filial piety was, and I answered him, – 'not being disobedient.'" Fan Chi said, "What did you mean?" The Master replied, "That parents, when alive, be served according to propriety; that, when dead, they should be buried according to propriety; and that they should be sacrificed to according to propriety." (Legge 1983:5)

The philosopher Zeng said, "Let there be a careful attention to perform the funeral rites to parents, and let them be followed when long gone with the ceremonies of sacrifice – then the virtue of the people will resume its proper excellence." (Legge 1983:11)

The Chinese consider showing respect to one's parents and ancestors as an active way of practicing filial piety and building one's morality. As the saying goes, "When drinking water, think of its source." or "When you drink the water, think of those who dug the well." Chinese believe that one's body—from a single hair to a piece of skin—are derived from one's parents. Thus one must not, even in the very least, injure or wound one's own body. This is the beginning of filial piety. Therefore, paying tribute to the departed elders, parents and ancestors is a way to be thankful and to show gratitude to those who were responsible for bringing us into this world and to those who have rendered help and support for our growth. Families come to the grave site to present offerings of food and burn ghost money to symbolically provide for the departed ancestors, to show the continuation of the clan and to repay the ancestors for their grace unto the living. Practical morality is thus trained and molded from the family circle. This is a typical way of the pragmatic Chinese develop good principles such as gratitude and thankfulness from real life experience. They are not interested merely in abstract ideas or dogma.

Paying tribute to the departed ancestors is believed to be an essential channel by which to receive blessings and protection from them. Families come to the grave site not only to give thanks but also to pray for protection. It should be noted that people normally understand their ancestors are lower than the supreme God of Heaven. In the incense they offer, it is customary to offer incense to the God of Heaven first before burning incense to ancestors. Interestingly, the incense offered to Heaven can be used as an offering to ancestors, but not vice versa. Ancestors serve somewhat as intercessors between the person making the offering and God. It is thought that one is not virtuous enough to approach heaven directly for blessings. Therefore, family members come to ask their ancestors to pray for blessings on their behalf. However false this way of practice might be, one detects a sense of humility and dependence on something besides oneself.

EDUCATIONAL FUNCTION OF THE QINGMING FESTIVAL

"It is better to go to the house of mourning, than to go to the house of feasting: for that is the end of all men; and the living will lay it to his heart" (Eccles 7:2, KJV). In a practical way, Qingming creates a teaching moment for parents or other elders in the family to teach the younger generations, not only about the family history, but also positive values of thankfulness, gratitude, humility, and unremitting self–renewal. It is also a valuable opportunity to pause the business of life and contemplate the heavy subject of death, which would otherwise hardly be on the minds of younger generations.

WELLNESS ADDRESSED BY THE QINGMING FESTIVAL

Once in a while, human beings need an emotional exit from life's insistence on personal composure and external façade of confidence. Qingming provides such an exit for the Chinese to express their emotions and feelings for their deceased beloved. Many use this opportunity to express their emotions, their secret thoughts, their desires, and other family matters before the family grave. In a way, their burdens are thus relieved, their spirit somewhat renewed, even though the communication and dialogue they seek is not bidirectional. Releasing the stress and inner emotions is a need of all humanity, not just the Chinese.

Despite the opportunity for emotional release on this holiday, Qingming is not considered a sorrowful day. The name of this holiday suggests that this is a time for people to go outside and enjoy the greenery of springtime, the word tà qīng, or "踏青", means "treading on the greenery". After a long winter, April is a good time to go out and enjoy nature. Proper consideration is also given for health reasons. The day reflects the holistic thinking of the Chinese.

MISSIOLOGICAL IMPLICATIONS OF THE HOLIDAY FOR CHINESE ADVENTISTS

How should Chinese Adventists use the Qingming festival to reach their fellow Chinese for Christ? What practical guidelines can we derive from these missiological reflections?

First of all, Adventists should present themselves as keepers, not destroyers of meaningful traditions. The Qingming festival is a good time for Chinese Adventists to make known that they are still Chinese though they have accepted Jesus Christ as their personal Savior. Within the family circle, Qingming is a rare time to meet with family members and relatives to strengthen family ties and enhance relationships. Do not discard the festival simply because some Chinese place food in the graveyard and pray to the dead. Try to improve this opportunity for Christ.

Secondly, look for ways to adopt some of the traditional practices in each family. When changes in the customary in the observance of the festival are considered, do not make a big issue out of it. The goal is to preserve harmony and relationship within the family. For most Chinese ancestor worship comes more from respect than religious worship. Historically ancestor worship was strongly religious, but over time religious overtones have lessened greatly. This is especially so in mainland China where the "Cultural Revolution" turned the country to atheism.

Customs may vary, but the essence is similar. Adventists should be open enough to show sincere respect and heartfelt thankfulness for their ancestors, but care must be taken not to over–step the boundary of our faith in Christ. Adventists can join their family members in some activities on this occasion such as weeding the grass in the graveyard. In churches it is a good time to remember pioneers of the church as a means to pass on the torch and to educate the newer members about those who have made contributions to the cause of the Gospel and one's local church.

Thirdly, Chinese Adventists should reflect on the biblical teachings about life and death when opportunities arise. It is customary for families to show their gratefulness to their ancestors or others, and to burn incense to Heaven, the real source of all blessings. Adventists can carefully share truth about Jesus as the fountain of life and source of everlasting blessings. The Adventist understanding of death as soul sleep, the hope of resurrection of the righteous to eternal life, and the ultimate destruction of death itself can be a great comfort can be a great comfort and encouragement for many Chinese.

In addition, Qingming is a good time to organize outings into nature to meditate on God's wonderful plan of redemption through creation. Adventists can be share with their family members that we can pray directly to Jesus and unload our burdens before Him. And that He will not only hear our prayers but answer them as well, giving us peace and rest.

CONCLUSION

When ministering to the Chinese, be like the Chinese. At Qingming Festival, Chinese Adventists can suse this opportunity to show respect to their deceased parents and elders, to be humble and grateful, to be serious and enlightened about life and death through the biblical truth. Although some customs need to be adjusted, they still can participate in other activities of this festival and use it for winning souls for Christ. Chinese Christians should keep in mind that we should celebrate Qingming without participating in those parts of the festival that are in conflict with biblical teachings. We still need to exercise great caution and discernment.

"The water that bears the boat is the same that can swallow it up."

NOTES

1. *The Chinese rite controversy was started mainly between the Jesuits, Dominicans and Franciscans, but many more were involved, including the Holy See and the Chinese emperor Kangxi (1654–1722). It was finally put to rest in 1939 when Pope Pius XII issued a decree on December 8, 1939, authorizing Christians to observe the ancestral rites and participate in Confucius–honoring ceremonies. The controversy involved three major points: 1) whether the ancestor veneration ritual was civil or religious in nature; 2) whether the ceremonies performed in honor of Confucius by Chinese scholars at the time were secular or religious; 3) disagreement by the missionaries over the best Chinese word to express the Christian concept of God.*

REFERENCE LIST

Legge, James. (1983). Confucius Analects in Chinese Classics, Vol I. Taipei: Southern Materials Center.

Chapter 12

Mission Blockade: Ancestor Worship

Daniel M. Hung

EDITORS' NOTE: This paper was originally published over 30 years ago (January 1983) in the Evangelical Missions Quarterly or EMQ. The article is a case study by the author based on his personal experience when his mother had a death–bed conversion and the subsequent funeral. This article is included in this volume because it describes the Taiwanese ancestor and funeral beliefs and customs and the very real challenge of knowing how to navigate the strong emotions and social dynamics of a religiously pluralistic family at the time of a death. Clearly, not participating in the funeral is not an option. In addition, this article is included as it serves as a second perspective on Chinese funerals (the other one being by Samuel Wang). This author is not a Seventh–day Adventist and therefore this article contains statements about the condition of death that does not reflect Seventh–day Adventist understanding of biblical teachings about unconscious soul–sleep (See Eccl. 9:5, etc.) and the righteous dead awaiting Christ's second coming to receive their eternal reward (1 Thess. 4:16–17). Despite different biblical understandings, the editors trust the reader will by our decision to include this article.

Many people have written on ancestor worship as outsiders, but I am writing as a convert from it. I became a Christian at age 20, but I still live among my own people, the Chinese; more specifically, the Taiwanese, 98 percent of whom continue to worship with great zeal idols and ancestors as gods. Ancestor worship is the greatest obstacle to the Christian mission among the Chinese. As a giant rock blocking the flow of water in a river, it prevents the great majority of the Chinese from coming to Christ.

What is the nature of ancestor worship? The Chinese believe in polytheism. They believe human beings instantly become gods when they die and thus are able to bless or curse their living families. To offer burning incense to the deceased signifies this point.

The deceased, on the other hand, need to "eat" food sacrifices offered by the living families; otherwise, they would become hungry, miserable, unfortunate ghosts. To the Chinese, it is a great sin and an unforgivable breach of filial piety to fail to offer incense and food sacrifices periodically to the deceased ancestors because ancestor worship is the traditionally authorized way to honor and remember them. That's why a Chinese couple must have at least one son to ensure ancestor worship, since daughters become outsiders when they get married. If their first children are girls, the couple will continue to bear children until they have a son.

A few years ago a couple in Taiwan who had begotten 13 girls in a row got a baby boy as their 14th child at long last. They were so happy that they gave a big feast to their relatives, friends and neighbors. According to the traditional Chinese virtues, to have no sons is a great sin against ancestors. This has resulted in population explosion. No wonder Taiwan is the second most densely populated place in the world. I have six brothers. When I accepted Christ as my Savior and stopped taking part in ancestor worship, my mother said, "Fortunately, I have six other sons to offer food sacrifices to me after I die."

Of course, some people have died without any sons to offer sacrifices to them. In this case their daughters, nephews, nieces or relatives worship them. But there are a few "homeless" wandering hobo ghosts around. They died without any relatives to offer sacrifices to them. In Lunar July people in Taiwan offer special food sacrifices to such hobo ghosts by the main door of their houses, by the roadside, and even at one end of a bridge for the convenience of the "homeless" ghosts, lest they should bring misfortune to them.

Failure to worship ancestors is not only considered as a great sin and rebellion against ancestors, but is also believed to result in disasters and misfortune for the living. There are many such stories circulated everywhere in Taiwan.

It is also believed that the deceased need houses to live in and money to spend. Therefore, the living burn for them paper houses, or palaces with paper maids, paper household facilities, including paper TV and stereo sets, paper cars, etc. Special paper money is burned at the end of periodic rituals of food sacrifices. Most Mainlanders, who came to Taiwan from Mainland China after World War II, worship ancestors in a simplified way. They offer only incense and fruit.

How can Christians convince ancestor worshippers that the deceased do not need to "eat" food sacrifices? Well, you may say, it is easy to do that since it is obvious that the food sacrificed to ancestors never disappears. After the sacrificial rituals, the living eat it. But the ancestor worshippers insist that the ancestors do "eat" food in a spiritual and sentimental sense. You may argue that this is absurd, primitive and unscientific, but you get nowhere.

At the death anniversaries of our ancestors, my illiterate mother, who has a good memory, would place cooked food on the table with 13 wine cups and 13 pairs of chopsticks, for she remembers only 13 of the deceased in our family, including my father. She would offer incense and then orally invite the spirits of the ancestors to come and enjoy the delicious food. Often I said to her, "Mom, how about those many other ancestors you don't remember and don't invite to the feast? Won't they starve and be angry with us? Furthermore, they can eat only one meal in many days. Won't they suffer very much from hunger? Since food eaten by spirits or ghosts doesn't disappear a bit, they don't need to wait for your food sacrifices. They can go to restaurants at any time on any day and enjoy all kinds of foods free of charge." She would frown at me and say, "Shut up! I don't want to argue with an educated barbarian like you." Later, I realized that I could never win ancestor worshippers to Christ by arguing in terms of logic, reason or science. I must learn to contextualize the biblical truths for them. But how?

Being anxious to convert the Chinese to Catholicism, the Catholics in Taiwan compromised with ancestor worship. On Chinese New Year's Day in 1971 the late Cardinal Yu Ping staged a public Catholic ancestor worship with incense, food sacrifices without meat, and prayers offered to heaven and Chinese ancestors in general. It was attended by over a thousand people, mostly Catholics and some government officials and, alas, even a few prominent Protestants. The Cardinal declared that ancestor worship is not idolatry, but in accordance with God's will, the fifth commandment. Understandably, TV, radio and newspapers made a big fuss over it because Catholicism seemed to uphold Chinese culture. Since then the Catholics have been repeating the public ancestor worship at every Chinese New Year, sometimes inside a Catholic church building.

In spite of the fact that the Catholic Church compromises with ancestor worship in Taiwan, the membership of the Catholic Church has actually declined. The Catholic Church lost 10 percent of its members from 1970 to 1980: from 303,800 members down to 276,700.

I don't know how much my attempt to contextualize the gospel for my dying mother contributed to her sudden conversion to Christianity and immediate baptism in her hospital ward. The Holy Spirit performed a miraculous regenerating work in her heart. She was terminally ill with heart diseases, urema and general edema, barely surviving on kidney dialysis, and half–asleep and half–awake most of the time. Suddenly, she opened her eyes wide and shouted several times she wanted to believe in Jesus and go to heaven. My wife Lily said to her, "If you believe in Jesus as the Savior and have your sins forgiven, and go to heaven, Jesus will provide a beautiful heavenly place for you to live in. You don't need to worry that you have no paper house to live in." I assured her that the Lord Jesus would provide her and other Christians in heaven with feasts every day and that they would never starve. (Matt. 8:11; Rev. 21:1–5.) I believe this kind of positive presentation of biblical truths is more effective than negative denunciation of ancestor worship in our evangelistic work.

In short, we cannot ask people to give up ancestor worship without giving them proper substitutes. In the Christian mission it is wise to present God the Father as our heavenly Father, the Creator of human beings, who created man's first ancestors, Adam and Eve. Most Chinese revere Heaven as the Greatest and Highest Being. Indeed, God the Father is the Ancestor, the only Source and Root, in terms of man's origin. Chinese culture emphasizes that one should not forget one's origin, but honor and remember it.

Though it is true that conviction of sin must precede conversion, it doesn't follow that Christians must preach against sin at the very beginning on every occasion. Most Chinese equate sin with crime, and claim they have no sin and don't need Christ as the Savior. Therefore, sin would be meaningless to them without reference to God as the heavenly Father and the source of man and every blessing.

Furthermore, we have to present feasible and acceptable biblical ways of remembering ancestors: "Sweeping the ancestors' graves" on the ancestors' death anniversaries ensures the graves look attractive; holding memorial family meetings; hanging up ancestors' pictures in the living room; keeping the family genealogy with short statements of ancestors' deeds; emphasizing the Bible's teaching's about filial piety and its importance (the fifth commandment; Deut. 21:18–21; 32:7); and above all, remembering man's Creator (Eccl. 12:1).

For the sake of contextualizing the gospel, I maintain that Christians should not unwisely denounce anything Chinese or Oriental simply because it is a Chinese or Oriental tradition. In other words, Christians should not go to extremes. Christians should preserve and honor anything cultural or traditional so long as it is not against biblical principles or the Ten Commandments.

Christians should honor and respect the dead or ancestors in biblical ways, or Chinese ways, without violating the Ten Commandments.

But they must not take part in idol worship or idolatrous ancestor worship rites. They must not offer incense to the dead, since incense signifies deity. They must not burn paper money, or offer sacrifices, or burn paper palaces for the ancestors. They must not pray to them. I oppose lighting candles for the dead because they are associated with incense.

Bowing before the picture of a dead person is a delicate question. At Chinese funerals and ancestor worship rites non–Christians do bow to the picture, pray to it, offer incense and sacrifices to it, and burn paper money before it. The picture is often regarded as an idol. In such circumstances I would not bow to the picture, lest non–Christians should think that I agree that the deceased is divine. I do think it is all right to offer flowers to the deceased.

If there are no candles, incense, or sacrifices placed before the picture of the dead, bowing before the picture is another matter since it is a part of the Chinese culture and tradition to bow to a person to show respect. It is not against biblical principles to bow to the picture to pay one's respects, if the circumstance is not idolatrous. In Chinese or Oriental society people customarily greet each other by bowing when they meet. It is neither idolatrous nor against the Ten Commandments.

Strangely enough, I still cannot bring myself emotionally to bow to the picture of the dead, even though I hold to the above position intellectually. Maybe it is because bowing has been much associated with idolatry. As a matter of fact, the great majority of Christians in Taiwan do bow to pictures at the weekly Monday morning meeting, and many of them bow to the pictures of the dead under idolatrous circumstances.

When I tried to contextualize the gospel with regard to ancestor worship and my illiterate mother, I used some very old Chinese sayings or proverbs that illustrate biblical truth and with which she was familiar. For example, "It is better to give a bean to living parents than to offer a pig's head after their death." This Chinese proverb clearly states that the deceased cannot eat food sacrifices. Another Chinese saying that "Heaven begets and nourishes," illustrates that Heaven (or

God) is greater than one's parents or ancestors; therefore, Heaven is to be revered and worshipped above all others.

As my mother realized that she was in critical condition and might die at any time, like most dying persons, she seemed to be afraid to take her dangerous journey into the unknown spirit world. So my wife and I assured her that if she believed in Jesus the Savior, he would be with her all the time and would guide her safely to heaven; she did not need to be afraid to leave this world.

In order to show to my unbelieving brothers, their wives and relatives that we Christians do respect and remember the deceased and our ancestors, my Christian brother and I tried to contextualize a Christian memorial service for our mother at our church. I had my mother's large picture framed with flowers and put in front of the pulpit among flower crosses and baskets of flowers. On the church walls were hung large pieces of white cloth with Chinese words, such as "Enjoy heavenly blessings," "Receive glory at resurrection," and "Forever enjoy Jesus the Savior's mercy and love." This was done exactly according to the Chinese setting of the Taipei City Funeral Home, the only public funeral home in Taipei.

I invited members of the Hung clan to attend the memorial service so that they might see for the first time in their lives what we Christians do for the deceased. They attended a church service and heard the gospel fully for the first time in their lives. They heard the tape recording of my mother's conversion and baptism in her hospital ward. They also took home the memorial service program in which was printed my mother's picture, hymns, and a statement of my mother's conversion, and the simple gospel of Christ.

We had expected 40 non–Christians of the Hung clan to come to the memorial service, but only 13 of them showed up. My sister–in–law, wife of my elder brother, who is most superstitious and anti–Christian, prevented people from attending the service. When her collegeage daughter told her she wanted to come to the memorial service, my sister–in–law threatened to break her legs if she attended. So the daughter did not dare to come.

In order to contextualize the gospel, it is very important to invite as many non–Christian relatives and friends to Christian funerals or memorial services. Usually, they will not come to church to attend Sunday services or evangelistic rallies, but some of them are willing to attend Christian memorial or funeral services out of their respect for the deceased.

Lily and I had to absent ourselves from Easter service to attend my mother's funeral, for the sake of family solidarity, of keeping the door of future evangelism open, and avoiding unnecessary antagonism against Christianity. The coffin of my mother remained in my youngest brother's apartment for 36 days. My elder brother, who wanted to show that he was most filial to mother, slept by the coffin for 36 nights. Some of my younger brothers also did occasionally. Pre–funeral Taoist and Buddhist rites and mini–feasts started as soon as my mother passed away. Since five of my six brothers are not Christians, they disregarded the fact that mother was baptized as a Christian. They were determined to have traditional Taoist and Buddhist funeral rites for her.

My mother's Taoist and Buddist funeral was one of the most elaborate, complicated, and expensive in Taiwan. The whole cost was roughly $16,000; coffin, $950; paper palace, $960; grave, $6,600; flower–decorated huge hearse like that of the late President Chiang Kaishek, $790; fees for Taoist priests and Buddhist monks, $790; plus sumptuous meals, sleeping quarters, and funeral feast for about 320 people, $3,000; other expenses, about $2,700, such as those of pre–funeral rites and mini–feasts.

There were three Western brass bands and two Chinese music bands in the funeral procession. About 70 flower–decorated jeeps, pick–ups and cars preceded the hearse, which was followed by two buses filled with mourners. We seven brothers and most of our wives and some others sat by the coffin in the hearse.

Lily, my two children and my Christian brother refused to offer incense, bow to the coffin or picture of my mother, prostrate before the coffin or pray to it, or before the picture. In short, we refused to take part in any idolatrous funeral rites. Naturally, we Christians were in the spotlight at the funeral service. There was whispering gossip about us, but nobody rebuked us or persecuted us on the spot. We pinned a small black cross on our sackclothes to show that we are Christians. Many of our relatives knew that we had had a Christian memorial service for my mother. Nevertheless, behind our backs bitter and venomous criticism of us persisted. My sister–in–law declared that my wife, my Christian brother and I were "dead" because we had failed to do our filial duties—we refused to take part in Taoist and Buddhist funeral rites and ancestral cult.

One of the reasons why most Taiwanese are against Christianity is the fact that Christians don't mourn for the deceased the way non–Christians do. So the unbelievers conclude that Christians are "unfilial" and disrespectful to the deceased. In Taiwan, women must say or speak something when they wail at mourning, especially at the funeral procession in the street, to show their filial piety. They shout aloud, "Oh, how can I live on without you?" "How I wish you could live three or five more years!" "How much I shall miss you!" "I'll never be able to see you again."

Often such speech–wailing and mourning are only hypocritical performance for onlookers. The mourners covet other people's praise. The louder and longer they speech–wail, the more people will praise them as very filial. Thus they gain great "face"–glory and honor. It is only a show.

The surviving family can hire professional mourners for the funeral procession. The Taiwanese regard as most unfortunate those who die without people to mourn for them with speech–wailing. Only the Christians fit into this category. So, "Die without people mourning" has become a stinging nickname for Christians in Taiwan.

Christians here do weep and cry at the death and funeral of a family member, but without wailing speeches. I suggest we should encourage Christians to wail or cry aloud, possibly with such words as, "Lord, be with us and comfort us." "Lord, sustain us in times of sadness." "Lord, guide so–and–so to heaven safely and into thy bosom." "Rest so–and–so in heavenly peace," etc.

"Saving face" is very important in Oriental society. In private most ancestor worshippers admit that the deceased cannot eat food sacrifices and that the traditional Taiwanese funeral customs are wasteful, impractical and cumbersome. But they don't dare to not worship ancestors or follow traditional customs, because they are afraid of losing face. They are afraid of other people's criticism that they are "unfilial." They are afraid of verbal persecutions, especially those of their living elders.

How can we overcome this problem of "face?" There is no pat answer. We may present the biblical truths in love and give them opportunities to see Christian ways of remembering and respecting ancestors, so that they may see the contrast. There must be other ways to solve the problem. May the Lord grant us wisdom to find them.

When we realize that the monthly income of the average breadwinner in Taipei is $300 to $350, the funeral cost of $16,000 is horrifying and wasteful. But the Chinese will go into deep debt to have costly funeral services to save face. In my mother's case, since I have many brothers in business, many people gave consolation money gifts toward the expenses of mother's funeral. My elder brother, who has many business friends, received more than $3,000. All the money gifts amounted to more than $5,000, including gifts from relatives, neighbors, and church members. I have written this to show how urgently and desperately we need to preach the gospel of Jesus to the 18 million non–Christians in Taiwan.

Copyright © 1983 Evangelism and Missions Information Service (EMIS). All rights reserved. Not to be reproduced or copied in any form without written permission from EMIS.

CHAPTER 13

A HINDU–CHRISTIAN FUNERAL: INTERFAITH DIALOGUE OR CAPITULATION?

Ramesh Chand

EDITORS' NOTE: Ramesh Chand wrote this very helpful article about attending his Hindu father's funeral while he was a post–graduate student at Fuller Theological Student. This personal story depicts the very real battle that wages within Christians who have close family members or friends that are Hindu, Buddhist, or Taoist and how they struggle to find the right balance between honoring their loved one and remaining loyal to God. This paper is not included as an authority for the reader on what to do if the reader is in a similar situation but to encourage Bible study, dialogue, and prayerful reflection on the principles of handling pluralistic situations such as non–Christian funeral rituals where full participation will likely meet up against conscientious objections. This article first appeared as a two–part article in the fall 2012 and spring 2013 issues of Fuller Theological Seminary's journal, Evangelical Interfaith Dialogue, and is reprinted here with permission and a few minor changes to make it suitable as a single article as well as to clarify the author's meaning.

Introduction

This article is a short narrative of my interaction with my Hindu parents. In this article, I will give a few examples of my attempts at interfaith dialogue which was initiated due to the death of my father. Subsequently, I will mention a few hermeneutical principles which I followed in the interactions with my parents. I hope and pray that this article inspires interfaith dialogue on a personal and professional level.

At the outset, I want to mention that this article does not portray the doctrinal standard of a particular church or theological institution. I followed my own hermeneutical principles, although I wish the church and theological institutions would address this need. In a very personal way, this article highlights the fact that bringing people of other faiths to the saving knowledge of Jesus is but the first step in the walk with the Lord. First generation Christians must be encouraged to interact with their family members and society regardless of other faiths. They must be given Christ–like spiritual formation and biblical hermeneutical principles to guide them in their interfaith interactions. The inability of the evangelical church and theological institutions to formulate theology with contextual needs has given rise to many post–colonial and liberal contextual theologies.

My Background

I was born into a Hindu family in India. My father worked in a Hindu temple. Both of my parents were sick when I was born. When I was about 4 years old, my parents' health worsened to the point where it was no longer safe for my sister and me to remain at home. We were sent to a boarding school (Children's Home). It would be 16 years before I lived with my parents again. At the Children's Home, which was run by the Reformed Presbyterian Church, I was educated and I learnt about Jesus.

When I was 16 years old, I received Jesus Christ as my saviour. My parents did not approve of my decision because they thought that this meant I would cut myself off from the family and rebel against my family obligations. However, my desire was to share Jesus Christ with my parents. I wanted to honour my father and mother as God commanded in the Bible. On one of the visiting days at Children's Home, I gave a Bible to my parents and promised to take care of them. Since then, Jesus became another god for my parents in addition to their many others as is customary for Hindus. Years later, when I went home, I saw the Bible placed next to Krishna's idol.

After finishing school, I enrolled in a seminary. In 2000, during my theological studies, I got a call from my mother asking me to return home because my father had a stroke and was paralysed. I discontinued my study immediately, went to stay with my parents and took care of my father. Since I had first left home 16 years prior, this was the first time I had lived with my parents for an indefinite time period. I knew that my faith in the Lord Jesus Christ would be challenged during my stay with my parents who were strong Hindu believers; I wanted to stand firm in my faith and yet love and honour my parents. There were many occasions that challenged my loyalty to Jesus, and during these occasions I found that I developed an interfaith methodology. The following are a few short examples of interfaith dialogue as I experienced them.

My Father's Death

In 2004, while I was in my first year of postgraduate study, my mother called to tell me my father was seriously ill. He had suffered another stroke that caused multi–organ failure. His condition was complicated by his diabetes. By the time I reached home the doctors had given up on my father's health. My father, realizing that he was going to die, started the preparations for his death. According to a promise to his gods and goddess, he shaved his head and beard and offered his hair to them. (This was significant because these served as a mark of his office as a Hindu priest.) In his last days, he talked constantly about his religion and my faith in Jesus Christ. He wanted to change, but due to communal and social pressure, he did not dare to take that stand. His last words were that he was proud of me and that sending me to a Christian institution was a good decision. His death led to one of the most challenging parts of my interfaith dialogue.

As the only son in my family, the funeral responsibilities for my father were placed solely on my shoulders. I could not ask anyone else to perform the funeral procedures. According to Hindu belief, if I abandoned my responsibilities and did not lead the cremation, the soul of my father would not rest in peace. Moreover, according to social custom, I would be expelled from the community and my family.

Having an intimate knowledge of the requirements of the funeral and cremation, I dreaded what I would have to do. Many times I wished that I could just leave and forsake my family responsibilities. I could call it a sacrifice for the Lord. After all, should I not leave my father and mother to follow Jesus? I considered leaving but my mother wept inconsolably and asked me to fulfil the funeral duties so that the soul of her husband could rest in peace.

During this difficult time, I called friends and teachers for their guidance on my participation in the cremation procedure. Most of the views suggested finding an alternative to actual participation in the cremation ceremonies because it would be very difficult not to compromise my faith in that situation. However, there were a few Christian friends who told me that the fulfilment of the cremation was also part of honouring my parents, although they had no ideas as to how I would lead the Hindu cremation ceremony without compromising my faith. However, they assured me of their constant prayer support. In this most difficult time in my life, I cried to the Lord and prayed like Namaan, "I will honor my parents even in death, and while I do so if by mistakes I stumble, the Lord please pardon your servant."

[EDITORS' NOTE: Naaman was a Syrian military leader who was healed of leprosy and asked Elisha for God's pardon when he needed to accompany his master to worship and bow before Rimmon. Elisha told him "Go in peace" 2 Kings 5:17–19.]

The Cremation

(Only the main rituals are mentioned. Events are mentioned chronologically.)

I was asked to shave my head and beard and wear a white robe as a sign of mourning and respect. This is usually done with religious mantras or slogans. However, I shaved my hair and requested it be done without any religious mantras.

Rituals:

- Immediately after death, the body is laid on the floor. An oil lamp is lit and placed near the body. This is kept burning continuously for the first three days.

- The body is bathed with water and dressed in new clothes. A few drops of holy Ganga water and a small of piece of gold are put into the mouth so that the soul may attain liberation.

- The body is then placed on a stretcher and adorned with flowers until the whole body is completely covered.

- Some members of society then carry the stretcher on their shoulders to the cremation ground chanting, "Ram naam satya hai," (The name of Rama is the true name).

My response:

The cremation site was three kilometres away, located on the banks of the Yamuna River. I had to lead the funeral procession on foot, holding fire in a black earthen pot, which was kindled at home with a special ritual of purification. While I led the procession I chanted my own prayer, "Yesu naam satya hai" (Jesus is the True name).

Post–Cremation

Post–cremation mourning rituals are difficult and exhausting. They end on the 13th day after death. We were bound by the many rules and regulations of ritual purity. For the next 13 days, I had to offer rice balls and vessels of milk to the departed soul by leaving the food under a tree. My mother kept a photo of my father in a room with a clay lamp in front of the picture for the next 10 days. During this time I was asked to refrain from combing my hair or wearing shoes. I had to wear a dhoti (a single piece of white cloth wrapped around the body). We were not allowed to cook any food at home, and everything we ate was unsalted and boiled. We slept on the floor. It was believed that if these, along with many other rituals were not performed correctly the departed soul would become a ghost and haunt both family members and society. My mother and the elders of the society kept watch over my actions. Since they knew I was a Christian and did not say any mantras while doing the cremation ritual, the society thought that the departed soul would haunt me.

On the third day after the funeral, I returned to the cremation site to collect the remains and put them in an urn. These remains were later immersed in the Yamuna River with the rite of immersion. During this rite, one of my Hindu friends came with me to recite the mantras and drink the holy water from the river.

After the immersion rites were completed on the 3rd day, I had to feed all those who went with me to the cremation. The food was cooked in front of my house with firewood as fuel. Later a bowl full of ash was collected from the fireplace and spread on the small portion of the floor in the veranda, covered with a basket, and left overnight with a burning lamp on it. Participation in this ritual was a difficult decision as this practice helps determine the stage of the departed soul. The belief is that the departed soul's imprint will be on the ash. The next morning, people came and saw the form of a snake in the ash. The pundit told us that the departed soul had taken the form of a snake and the soul was with Lord Shiva. If we were to organise a havan (sacred purifying ritual which is made to the fire god, Agni) on the 13th day, the soul would take the form of a human being and might return to our family.

It is believed that on the 12th day after the death, the soul passes on to the next life. Therefore on the 13th day, I had to feed the community after a havan which marked the ending of the mourning period. I knew that this havan involved reciting mantras and idol worship, so I went to the priest and told him about my faith in Jesus Christ and the fact that I could not participate in the havan. I suggested that as a mark of respect, I would be present during the havan but would not recite mantras, or bow and worship the idols. The priest agreed on the condition that I would have to start the havan by participating in singing the aarti (devotional song). I led the aarti by omitting the word "Om" (considered to be absolute reality, a mantra or mystical sound of the universes origination), the believed energy force while singing and offered the song to Jesus. Here is the translation of two verses of the aarti from Aum Jai Jagdish (devotional hymn).

Oh, Lord of the whole universe,
Thou art Mother and Father.
At Thy feet I seek eternal truth,
Lord, at Thy feet I seek eternal truth.
There's none other than Thee, Lord.
There's none other than Thee, Lord,
Guardian of all our hopes.
Oh, Lord of the whole universe,
Thou art godly perfection,
Omnipotent Master of all,
Lord, omnipotent Master of all.
My destiny is in Thy hand.
My destiny is in Thy hand.
Supreme Soul of all creation,
Oh, Lord of the whole universe.

The havan lasted for two hours after which I became the head of my family.

Since then, God has used this experience in various marvelous ways. My mother, who is still a Hindu believer, now prays with me when I go home. Family members and people from my society who saw a Christian boy honoring his Hindu parents began asking, "Why?" I then had the privilege of sharing God's love with the community.

Hermeneutical Principles

The hermeneutical principles I followed for the interfaith dialogue with my parents were not suggested by any church or theological institute but were developed in a difficult situation through the guidance of the Holy Spirit. I read the Bible and the Reformed Confessions of my Reformed Presbyterian Church; I ensured that my conscience was guided by the Holy Spirit; I followed the socio–cultural values. These formed the hermeneutical guidelines upon which I based my principles for interfaith dialogue.

Principle #1: The Bible is the main source of authority for all my actions. When I started reading the Bible, I found biblical ways to interact with my Hindu parents. This applied especially to the time of my father's death as I knew that the responsibility of his cremation would lie with me. In my readings I did not find specific events or commands which addressed my contextual need. However, I found the following biblical truths which helped me stay true to God in the situation:

- I based my interfaith engagement on God's assurance of His Lordship and commandment to serve Him alone. This theme resonates throughout Scripture. Commitment to Jesus Christ as the ultimate authority was the basis for this interfaith dialogue.

- I analyzed my relationship with my parents in light of the biblical command to honour our father and mother.

I participated in this dialogue believing and expecting that the Holy Spirit could and would use this situation to glorify God. Therefore I submitted my actions as a witness of God's mercy and grace.

Principle #2: Gain Lessons from the role and experience of the church in dealing with similar issues. The Reformed Confessions and the Reformed Church in India stress both loving and worshipping God alone and honouring parents. In my inquiries about similar situations, I found that most people either compromised biblical truths and lived in guilt or turned their backs on social obligations considering it a sacrifice for the Lord. However, years later, I read 'An Asian Catechism' by Dr. Mohan Chacko, an Indian theologian and a senior pastor of Reformed Presbyterian Church of India, which seemed to address the issue. He writes,

> *Q 127. How shall we honour our family members or ancestors?*
>
> *We honor our family members or ancestors by recognising the work of God's grace in their lives, seeking to imitate their good example, listening to their counsel, and by showing respect to them in culturally appropriate ways. But we must refrain from worshipping them or their spirits through offerings or ceremonies.*

Principle #3: Allow your conscience to be guided by the Holy Spirit. However, the work of the Holy Spirit in personal experiences should not be disengaged from Scripture. I believe that the Spirit does not guide us in ways that are independent of Scripture. The Holy Spirit ministers by guiding our conscience.

Principle #4: Recognize the important role of social values. In the Hindu community where my parents lived, there were certain things that were emphasized. Honoring parents and heeding the advice of elders, caring for parents in times of sickness, proper funeral rites and support of the bereaved family, encouraging peace and religious harmony, and participation in the betterment of society. These social values were tested by the Bible. The most difficult situation was to disengage Hindu beliefs from socio–cultural values. Therefore, I performed the rituals without saying the mantras or bowing in front of the gods and goddesses. Thus the rituals became a socio–cultural practice.

In conclusion, I confess that the method I used may seem like capitulation under the weight of social and religious tradition and runs the risk of syncretism. However, it is my firm belief that interfaith dialogue demands faith in an unchangeable God in changeable circumstances. It demands vulnerability and is impossible without God's grace.

Chapter 14

Appeal for Contextualizing Malagasy Funerals

Jacques Ratsimbason

INTRODUCTION

About 50 percent of Malagasy people follow traditional religions; about 45 percent of the population is Christian and 5 percent Muslim. Traditional religion retains a strong hold on those who are Christians. The task of this paper is to develop an understanding of traditional beliefs and practices in the light of the Bible, and to suggest a strategy for contextualization in the Malagasy funerals.

The following points list some reasons for this paper. First of all, many Malagasy Christians have a syncretistic faith that retains traditional beliefs and practices, which must be confronted by the gospel. This requires techniques for meeting them in their doctrinal arguments. Second, this paper helps the church to present a clearer message to people in Madagascar and to remove syncretistic beliefs and values among Adventist church members. In addition, it provides insight into Malagasy history and cultural background, equipping me with deeper understanding as I work as a teacher of this people group. It also can serve to educate church members to become more uplifted in their spiritual life, and it provides strategies for pastors to equip their members for ministry.

A study of Malagasy animistic beliefs and values is developed using Paul G. Hiebert's model of critical contextualization. Hiebert outlines four principles for success in contextualization: (1) understand what the people believe about the problem, (2) create a bridge between Scripture and the problem, (3) let people evaluate their customs in light of Scripture, and (4) practice a contextualized ethic.

THE PEOPLE OF MADAGASCAR

The indigenous people of Madagascar are known as Malagasy. The Malagasy came to the island from Africa and Asia. In fact, the people of Madagascar are primarily of Malaysian and Indonesian ethnic background later mixed with East African and Arabs. The African influence in the Malagasy population stems mainly from the eighteenth and nineteenth centuries, in which period many slaves from Mozambique and South Africa were transported to Madagascar, thus bringing an African feature to the Malagasy culture. The Arab origin can also be seen in the Arabic elements present in the Malagasy language, such as in the names of months and days of the week. Indeed, the Asian, African, and Arab backgrounds in Malagasy culture are evident. However, interestingly, Malagasy people developed their own religious system, in which their beliefs are manifested through symbols found in their own myths, proverbs, music and songs.

BELIEFS ABOUT DEATH

Malagasy people believe that when a person dies, he rises to an invisible and sacred life. He then gets a higher status because he is nearer to God than to living people. Consequently ancestors are believed to be able to guide living people's lives. Malagasy people take great care of and cherish their ancestors. In Malagasy traditional religion three significant ceremonies accompany death—funeral, exhumation, and sacrifice. Malagasy people see the authority of ancestors through taboos and sacrifice. To infringe on a fady (taboo) is equivalent to being guilty towards ones ancestors.

Beliefs about death reveal some interesting implications for Christian mission. The Malagasy concept of fihavanana expresses a core human value and a very deep Christian value. First, the idea of fihavanana can be used to open Malagasy people to the divine plan of salvation. In the Malagasy Bible, the words "peace" and "reconciliation" are translated by fihavanana (Rom 5:1; 2 Cor 5:18; Eph 2:14; Col 1:21). Second, Malagasy people use the word fihavanana to express a relational ideal. For them, human life is a network of fihavanana, which consists of relationship with God, ancestors, spirits, the living, and even with nature. In a similar way, Christianity is a relationship not a religion. It is a relationship with Jesus Christ, the God who came down to dwell with men (John 1:1–3, 14; Gal 2:20), but also a relationship with other people as expressed by Jesus in His teaching concerning duty and responsibility to one's neighbor.

The Malagasy people believe that ancestral spirits are closer to the living than God. Similarly, they regard ancestors as intermediaries between the Supreme God and the living. They also believe in the division between the soul and the body and embrace the concept of reincarnation.

MALAGASY FUNERAL RITES

When a member of the family dies, there are ceremonies to perform. First relatives wash the body. Then the wake (fiandrasampaty) begins, which lasts day and night until the burial, to keep witches and spirits away. Everybody is expected to cry as a sign of compassion for and sympathy with those who have this "heavy burden to carry" (fiarahamitondra izay mavesatra).

Usually, the deceased is wrapped with a lambamena (red cloth). This hand–woven textile is a sign of authority. Wrapping the deceased or the coffin in the lambamena demonstrates respect for the dead and is necessary for their life in the afterworld.

When the corpse is moved out of the house, it must be carried out feet first. Some tribes such as the Tanala, the Betsimisaraka, and the Antaisaka have a special door on the eastern wall, which is used only when carrying corpses out of the house. Those bearing the corpse to the grave must also avoid going straight forward (mivantana). Instead, must zigzag because to walk straight forward would mean that 'death' would follow that same route back to the living.

When they arrive at the grave (tomb), an additional ritual is performed. A sacrifice is offered to introduce the newly deceased to those already dead, so that he will be received by them. While returning home, the family must be very careful not to look back, because doing so would encourage the spirit of the deceased to accompany them on their way to the village. In addition, as I recall after my brother's death, a fire is placed at the doorstep of the family's home. Before entering the house, each household member who was present at the funeral must step over the fire in order to prevent the spirit of the dead from entering the house.

After the burial, the family goes to a 'living river' where they can be cleansed from the impurity of death.

Beyond these common funeral rites, several tribes have periodic ceremonies that reconnect the living with the dead. In the Mahafaly and Antandroy groups, the coffin is violently shaken in all directions by some men while the women beat their hands. The sacrifice of zebus (cow) accompanies the ceremony, the number depending on the wealth of the deceased. The tomb will be decorated with horns and zebus sacrificed.

It is necessary to note that for the Betsileo, a week after the burial a chief of the family returns to the tomb, asking the dead to remain quiet and not to return to the village and worry the people there.

Throughout Madagascar, tribes have elaborate and expensive rites for reconnecting with the dead.

THE CHALLENGE

After understanding the Malagasy traditional values and worldview, the task of the evangelist is "to open their eyes and turn them from darkness to light, and from the power of Satan to God, so that they may receive forgiveness of sins and a place among those who are sanctified by faith in me" (Acts 26:18, NIV). Present cultural values must be shaped and molded by biblical thought and content. The evangelist must encourage the Malagasy people to:

1. Reorder their view of reality around God and His desires for human life.

2. Point out the idea of one mediator between God and humankind—Jesus.

3. Teach concerning the sending of the Holy Spirit so they do not need intermediaries like ancestors.

4. Instruct the Malagasy about the Hebrew concepts of humanity (no division between soul and body), and the source of spirits and powers (fallen angels).

5. Teach that each person is a unique creation and discuss the power and implications of a creator God to refute the idea of the reincarnation.

The question is: "How do we go about changing traditional worldviews or values?" The evangelist must teach new believers the core of the gospel—the essentials to which all other parts are linked, and through which the Scriptures as a whole must be interpreted. In fact, people must understand the one, true, and living God as Person, Creator, and Lord. All things were created and brought into existence by His will (Rev 4:11; Eph 3:9; Gen 1:1). As the Maker is master of what He has made, God is sovereign over the whole of His creation. All forms of idolatry are an offence to God. In that case, His creation should give Him glory, honor, and praise.

God is always in control of all things and is constantly at work in accomplishing His plan. Moreover, humans are God's creatures and God guides their affairs (Ps 115:3; Hab 1:1–11; Isa 10:5–6). Thus He cannot be manipulated or controlled.

Humankind has fallen short of God's standard, and yet God has a deep desire to be known and understood. God demonstrates His love for humanity by establishing a relationship with His creation through His Son Jesus Christ, His messenger and the incarnation of His nature (John 1:14). Through Jesus' death on the cross and His resurrection there is forgiveness of sin and reconciliation with God for those who repent. God has come to humanity in Jesus Christ. Therefore, God is not distant.

The power of God is seen in His creation and His power that sustains the universe. He is the provider of humanity's needs (1 Cor 8:6). His love and mercy are revealed in Christ and His victory over Satan, the spirit world, sin, and death.

Evangelists also need to point out the idea of one mediator between God and humankind. He forbids us to use any spirits as mediators. Furthermore, the concept of the protection of the Holy Spirit for believers should be emphasized. New converts must realize that the greatest spiritual power in the universe is available to them through the indwelling Holy Spirit (Acts 1:8; 1 Cor 12:13).

New believers must know the source of spirits and powers. Satan and his hosts are dreadfully real and are the powers of darkness.

In the Bible there are numerous references to fallen angels (Gen 6:1–4; Ps 82; Isa 24:21–23; Dan 10:13, 20), demons (Deut 32:17; Ps 106:37), and evils spirits (Judg 9:23; 1 Sam 16:14, 23; 18:1; 19:9; 1 Kings 22:19–23). Biblical teachings about the state of the dead and the concept of reincarnation will be developed.

The conversion of the Thessalonians is a "model" not only to "all the believers in Macedonia and Achaia" (1 Thess 1:7, NIV) but also to Malagasy people coming to Christ out of an animistic background. These early Christians made a definite break with their animistic traditions. They "turned to God from idols to serve the living and true God, and to wait for his Son from heaven" (1 Thess 1:9, 10, NIV). Such a definite break from traditional power sources is characteristic of change as animists come to Christ.

THE CHRISTIAN LEADER'S TASK

The main task of leaders is to educate members in order to be transformed from their old worldview into a biblically shaped worldview. Christian leaders should give answers to questions raised by traditional folk religions, answers rooted in a biblical worldview. Below are some themes new members have to deal with.

THE COMMUNITY–CENTERED LIFE

The clan life is the most important entity in Malagasy society because an individual has meaning only in the context of community.

When faced by the collectivism of the Malagasy, the Christian leader's task is to redefine Christian community so that the new member has a new identity created in the image of God. The new convert is now in Christ who is Teacher, Lord and Savior. Therefore he has a new status as a son or daughter of God.

In addition, the new converts now belong to a new family, a new community—the church. It is a new 'community of the Spirit'—a gathering in which God is at work (Phil 1:1–11).

Members are called to learn to live together in harmony, and dedicate themselves to one another's wellbeing (Acts 2:42).

THE WORSHIP OF ANCESTORS

Malagasy people regard the dead with awe and reverence, and give the afterlife as much importance as the present. Therefore, the dead play a role in the life of the living. To deal with this problem, Christian leaders first need provide a biblical perspective of death. Malagasy Christians must be taught that when someone dies, the whole person dies and there is no part that exists in some other form of being (Ps 146:4; Eccl 9:5; 12:7). And the ultimate hope of Christians is the resurrection by Jesus (1 Thess 4:13–18).

Second, leaders must explain the difference between respect for ancestors and worship of ancestors. In the Malagasy context, it is crucial that this difference be well understood. To do so, the community and the leaders should strive for a debate and work at a discussion on how to respect the ancestors without worshiping them. Note some suggestions to deal with this problem. First of all, since Christians do not believe that the dead have power to bless or harm, there will be no prayers for the salvation of the dead. Second, Christians can and must celebrate the heritage and memory of ancestors. Third, they also can praise God for the influence of those who have lived godly lives, giving thanks for the faithful who have departed (Heb 11; 12:1, 2). Christians must honor their parents and praise them, even they are dead. But there definitely should not be prayers to the dead (Lev 19:31, 32). At the time of the funeral the cult also is essential in Malagasy process for celebrating death and grieving.

THE POWER OF SPIRITS

Animistic beliefs suggest that people possess immortal souls. At death, the soul is free to wander near the grave, travel the earth, or enter the world of the spirits. In the Malagasy culture, the soul—the fanahy, the ambiroa, the lolo, and the angatra—are present in the daily lives of the living. The exacting rituals of burial and cleansing among the Malagasy also give evidence of this belief.

Again, the Bible provides an answer to this concept. Indeed, the Bible defines the term "soul" as the human body—the organism, the mind, and the spirit. The word translated "soul" in Gen 2:7 refers to the organism as a whole, not to some part of it. The soul is not something that can be separated from the person. It is the person in its entirety. Thus, at death, the existence of these three entities, which form a whole, comes to an end (Ezek 19:20).

The evangelist also needs to provide clear teaching on fallen angels and their power to deceive. The witch of Endor described in 1 Sam 28:3–25 is a good example. The Philistines were gathered to battle King Saul's army and the frightened king knew he could not win but hoped he could find help. There had been a time when God guided him, but now he had sinned against God so he could not expect a blessing from that source. In desperation, Saul turned to the witch at Endor to contact the dead Samuel for advice. Because Samuel was dead and could not actually respond to the witch, evil spirits (fallen angels) impersonated him giving the witch the information she needed to convince Saul she had really seen and spoken to Samuel. She told Saul his army would indeed lose the battle the next day and he and his army would be killed. The battle occurred a few days later and Saul and three of his sons were killed (including David's close friend, Jonathan). Evil spirits, the fallen angels, are working with Satan to continue the lie. Satan told Eve in the garden: "You will not surely die" (Gen 3:4, NKJV). Mediums claim they receive information from those who have died, but God's Word assures us that the "dead know not any thing" (Eccles 9:5, KJV). Spirits desire to deceive Christians (2 Cor 11:14) to the point of receiving worship from them (1 Cor 10:20) and therefore must be firmly resisted (Eph 6:12–18; Jas 4:7; 1 P 5:8).

To deal with the concept of reincarnation, the Bible informs us that the body (the physical organism) is a constitutive aspect of human existence: "Then the LORD God formed a man from the dust of the ground and breathed into his nostrils the breath of life, and the man became a living being" (Gen 2:7, NIV). Moreover, the Scripture is clear that "it is appointed for men to die once, but after this the judgment" (Heb 9:27, NKJV). There is, therefore, no scriptural allowance for anyone to be reborn into another earthly existence.

To conclude, the new believer must have a new view of death. It is normal if they feel frightened by death because it is an enemy (1 Cor 15:26). However, it is a conquered enemy, its power over us is broken by Christ's victory, and it will ultimately come to an end (1 Cor 15:26, 54–55; Rev 20:14).

CONTEXTUALIZATION

Because missions must begin with the wishes of God yet function within a social context, strategy is "the practical working out of the will of God within a cultural context." (Gailyn Van Rheenen) Thus, strategy involves contextualization.

First of all, the gospel should be perceptible by every humankind. Second, the biblical truth can be transmitted with its original intent in any culture. Third, the essence of contextualization is Jesus Christ.

Therefore, leaders should ask: How does God desire that we minister within a cultural context? Ideally, as they seek God's will for the culture, church leaders should work with community leaders to develop creative, God–centered, biblically critiqued strategies with well–defined goals.

Although leaders must present Christianity in a culturally relevant way, they are to maintain biblical integrity in their teachings. In order to successfully contextualize Scripture, leaders must work among the people. Hiebert outlines four principles for success in contextualization: (1) understand what the people believe about the problem, (2) create a bridge between Scripture and the problem, (3) let people evaluate their customs in the light of Scripture, and (4) practice a contextual ethic (Hiebert 1987:109).

It could be argued that the whole Bible itself is an example of divine contextualization. Charles Kraft presents four principles for seeing the place of contextualization in the Bible. First of all, the Bible reveals the truth and demonstrates how truth is transmitted. Second, God communicates with humanity according to His acquaintance of people. Third, God gives to humanity a chance to participate in God's plan. Fourth, God's revelation is in accordance with a specific situation (Kraft 1979).

POWER, TRUTH, AND ALLEGIANCE ENCOUNTERS

The Seventh–day Adventist themes of the Great Controversy clearly explain the conflict between good and evil, the warfare between God and Satan, how fallen angels appear as spirits and demons in the world, and the struggle between the people of God and the principalities and powers must be clearly taught. In biblical warfare the cross is the ultimate and final victory (1 Cor 1:16–25). On the cross

Jesus bore the sins of the world and triumphed over all the powers the evil (Heb 2:14). We must teach that Jesus Christ, at the cross, defeated Satan' s kingdom. Satan is a fallen foe. Christ was victorious over him when He came from the grave. God's people have nothing to fear "because greater is he that is in you, than he that is in the world" (1 John 4:4, KJV). Teaching about the two sources of power and a warning about the consequences of returning to the old power sources must be clearly taught to Malagasy people. To be fully understood and to be persuasive, the gospel must be expressed within the cultural and historical contexts of the Malagasy people. They need to experience three types of encounter: a power encounter, allegiance encounter, and a truth encounter.

A truth encounter is concerned with understanding and challenging the worldview of the person. Teaching is the vehicle of this encounter as the mind and the will are exercised and challenged. Faulty understandings are confronted with biblical truth. This teaching is not just concerned with the transfer of information, but instead is designed to challenge the animistic beliefs and values. Some important areas of teaching should include: the Kingdom of God and the dominion of Satan; the place and role of God; motivations for seeking deity; the role of sin and salvation; the nature of human/Divine relationship. Therefore, the sovereignty and the nature of God must be understood by people. God, as the Creator is expected to be worshiped. People must realize that the power of Satan is broken by Jesus as the manifestation of God's love.

A power encounter is concerned with freedom from the enem's captivity. Satan uses many things to keep people from commitment to God and truth. Jesus destroyed the works of Satan and gave people freedom from sickness, disease, and demonic possession allowing people to consider the truth and to make a commitment to God. In a power encounter, people receive the needed emotional freedom to move forward with God. The vehicle of this encounter is spiritual warfare and prayer. In this sense, the transformed life of a Christian is a type of power encounter in that it plays the same role of attracting and leading people to trust in God. To get to the point, a power encounter confronts culture at the point of allegiance and calls people to come under the sovereignty of God. The eternal and universal truth must confront every culture (and individual). It leads to conversion because people accept Him as God of gods and Lord of lords.

An allegiance encounter is concerned with a relationship with Jesus Christ and the rescuing of people from wrong commitments. This encounter aims to help people commit to Jesus Christ and a growing relationship with God, His people, and His mission. The primary vehicle of this encounter is witness as people are challenged to respond to the new understanding and freedom that they have obtained. One example of an allegiance encounter would be the decision to trust in God's power for healing and protection instead of in animistic practitioners. By the type of encounter, people must have a relationship with eternal God in Jesus Christ, and declare their allegiance to the God of universe.

SPIRITUAL FORMATION OF CHURCH MEMBERS

The spiritual formation for new church members coming out of animism is not in how much knowledge someone has, but how his or her life has been changed. Thus, this test cannot be measured over a week or a month, but over a lifetime of immersion in the Body of Christ and faith lived out in the world. Therefore, the focus of spiritual formation in the emerging church is developing the whole person in the context of community. Giving people more life experiences to encounter God, along with appropriate knowledge, helps them incorporate their faith in ways that transform lives.

The following represent some of the principal activities of spiritual formation. First, it should encourage people to evaluate their customs in the light of the Scripture. The analysis could lead to one of the following results: 1) The particular cultural element is accepted, because it is compatible with scriptural principles; 2) The particular cultural element is modified to make it compatible with Christian principles; 3) The particular cultural element is rejected, because it contradicts the principles of Scripture (Guidelines 2003).

Second, spiritual formation should be organized to encourae and expose our members to missions. The point is that people should be encouraged to act upon what they have learned. This, of course, should be ultimate subject of all teachings. The hearer should be encouraged to tell others in his group or culture what they need to do in order to obey the gospel (2 Tim 2:2) and live faithfully before the Lord (Rev 2:10). From my experience, I found that the message is more efficient when the indigenous share and communicate among themselves their own experience.

Third, spiritual formation includes prayer, reading the Word, periodic (a lifestyle of) fasting, the constant exercise of faith, confession of sins, and worship. Such an emphasis gives new members guidance, support, and holds them accountable.

To conclude this section, we have seen that contextualization is a needed of part of any strategy for evangelism in Madagascar. Adventism must also teach a biblical worldview of mission, teach how to reflect on biblical theology, and include formal spiritual formation training for pastors, church leaders, and church members.

CONCLUSIONS

The purpose of this paper is to develop a strategy to contextualize Malagasy funerals. This paper attempts to meet this need as well as challenges leaders of the Seventh–day Adventist Church in Madagascar to deal with newcomer Christians who still maintain their traditional beliefs.

This paper includes traditional values, beliefs, and their expressions in Malagasy society, traditional beliefs concerning morality, the stages of life and the rites of passage in Malagasy culture. This description contains an analysis, which taught us that the lives and beliefs of Malagasy people constantly revolve around ancestors, spirit powers, and taboos.

A method for contextualization in the Malagasy context with suggested strategies was developed in the last part of this paper. The strategies discussed include: teaching of missional theology at the

Adventist University Zurcher, organization of spiritual formation for Church leaders and church members in order to prepare the ground for contextualization.

It is within the context of these cultural analysis about Malagasy funerals, critical contextualization in the Malagasy context, and under the present understandings of Church mission, that I offer the following suggestions and recommendations in the hope that they can be of help both the Church in general and its workers in particular. The following recommendations are divided into three categories: vision for the future, contextualization, and appropriate training.

The vision must be one that has to do with desiring and executing the Great commission (Matt 28:18–20) because "this gospel of the kingdom will be preached in all the world as a witness to all the nations, and then the end will come" (Matt 24:14, NKJV). Ellen G. White reminds us that we should "let every workers in the Master's vineyard, study, plan, devise methods, to reach the people where they are (White 1946:122–123).

In order to understand the holistic nature of God's message and His gospel we need constantly to contextualize the ministry and mission of the Church. Contextualization means, quite simply, communicating the gospel in understandable terms appropriate to the audience. If we are to target other cultures and religious groups, we need a "contextualized" approach which uses their languages and engages with their concepts.

Appropriate and relevant training should be given in three modes. The first training refers to classroom instruction within the Adventist University Zurcher. The second is nonformal training intended for church leaders—Union staff, Conferences staff, and pastors in the field. The third is informal training, recommended for members.

REFERENCES

Guidelines brought to the General Conference of Seventh–day Adventists Administrative Committee for approval in June and July, 2003

Hiebert, Paul G. 1987. Critical Contextualization. International Bulletin of Missionary Research, July.

Kraft, Charles H. 1979. Christianity in Cultures: A study in Dynamic Biblical Theologizing in Cross–cultural Perspective. Maryknoll, NY: Orbis Books.

White, Ellen G. 1946. Evangelism.

Section III

Reflections from Former CEAR Directors

CHAPTER 15

CONTEXTUALIZATION IN PRACTICE: OPENING THE GLOBAL MISSION CENTER AND THE CHIANG MAI PAINTINGS

Clifton Maberly

INTRODUCTION

It was 1992. I was on study leave in Australia doing postgraduate research on the sociology of secularism when I was asked to set up a Buddhist study center for the Far Eastern Division[1]. I had already felt the need for such a center and promoted setting one up, but when I was actually asked to set it up my first thought was that we didn't know enough about Buddhism to begin authentically. Yes, we had Buddhists in Thailand who had become Adventists, even lower level Buddhist monks who were now pastors, but as far as I knew, no Adventist had built bridges between the two vastly different worlds. That was something I confirmed later in all Buddhist culture countries.

I had as much exposure to Buddhism as anyone with a non–Buddhist background. I had tried to understand Buddhism through its Western apologists at Andrews University; had haunted temples and temple services in my early years in Thailand, even going to layman's classes for Dhamma examinations under monks in a temple. However, as I was still struggling with the Thai language, I couldn't have passed. I had talked popular Buddhism with many ordinary Buddhists, and had even run public programs with Buddhist monk colleagues for

Thai society leaders—teachers and armed forces officers. But I really didn't know Buddhism as it was lived and taught by Buddhist monks and practiced by serious Buddhists– not enough to advise the church on Buddhist affairs. More importantly, I didn't have the connections that were needed to make an impact in the Buddhist world.

I could have just decided to do what was expected—prepare a doctrinal assault on Buddhism from an ivory tower, test various approaches in the field, then train others to use them in Buddhist evangelism. But I was sure none of us knew who we were speaking to, or that what we had to say was relevant. So I decided we'd better learn to live with Buddhist leaders first.

As soon as I was asked to set up the center I knew where I wanted to set it up; at the heart of Thai Buddhism in Thailand. Thailand is one of the 'most Buddhist' countries in the world—92% Buddhist at that time. It was also the country where the most 'Buddhists' had become Adventists, so why start elsewhere?

LOOKING TO SET UP

I chose to set up the center at the heart of mainstream Buddhism—beside the Mahachulalongkorn Rajavidyalaya University (MCU). MCU is the largest public Buddhist university in Thailand, and one of the largest in the world. For those who have been to Bangkok, it is near other centers of Thai culture—the Grand Palace, the Chapel of the Emerald Buddha, and Sanaam Luang, the Royal Park.

The university was "founded in 1887 by King Chulalongkorn with the purpose of establishing a major higher education institute for Buddhist monks, novices and laypeople with an emphasis on Buddhist studies as its main subjects." It has several undergraduate academic units: a faculty of Buddhist studies, a faculty of education, a faculty of humanities, a faculty of social sciences, and an international program. It also has a graduate school with master's programs in Buddhist studies and in philosophy. It also offers a PhD program in Buddhist studies. These days the Buddhism graduate and postgraduate programs are conducted in English as well as Thai.

The stated goal of the university is that it "aims to promote academic excellence in Buddhist Studies and other related subjects and to form a community of Buddhist scholars in Buddhism." Core Buddhist subjects are "incorporated in all majors." It is a real Buddhist center. It was also a university for Buddhist monks from all Theravada Buddhist countries. That is why it seemed to me to be a good place to locate our 'Buddhist center.'

In Thailand relationships always come before venues; neighbors come before neighborhoods. If I wanted to be neighbors with leading Buddhists I needed to acknowledge them first. I made an appointment to meet the highest–ranking member of the Sangha (the society of Buddhist monks) for the city of Bangkok, who also the abbot of Mahathat Temple at the heart of the university. He was a senior monk (82 years old) with dignity and learning. I explained that I had been asked to set up a study center to explore the similarities and differences between Adventism and Buddhism, and asked his blessing and suggestions. He was immediately supportive. He said that not enough was done to really know other religionists. He suggested I look for a place as near the university as possible—so there could be genuine interaction between us.

Maybe a note on the approachability of Buddhists is appropriate here. I knew that Buddhist leaders would be open to my approach. Buddhism is not a revealed religion, it does not have commandments or a revelation from a divine being, so each person is a seeker. There is seldom resistance to exploring new ideas, except in places where the aggressive confidence of those who 'have the truth' have affronted or pointedly ignored Buddhists. And in places where Buddhism is comfortably the majority religion, like Thailand, there is no defensiveness. Religions–of–the–book view other teachings with concern that we may be doing the 'wrong' thing' by opening ourselves up to other religions. Buddhists don't have that fear.

When I went for my appointment with the abbot out of respect I bowed to him. I had sorted out years before what to do in a case like this. When laymen go to ask advice or request help from a monk they always bow from a kneeling position, bowing three times with hands together, to the floor. Not feeling inclined to invent my own customs, I had decided I needed to follow suit. There were two issues in complete imitation of the gesture: 1) I had not taken my refuge in the triple jewels of the Buddha, the Dhamma (the teaching) and the Sangha (the practicing teachers), the notion behind the triple bow; and 2) I was not a layman in the presence of clergy.

In the absence of alternative forms of paying respect and as the Adventist Church had not addressed the issue, I decided to create my own alternative. I bowed in the traditional way, politely and respectfully, but merely once. I took as long as a regular believer would to bow three times. Over the years it had endeared me to many ranking Buddhists. Never once did they read it as insipient conversion, only as I intended it, as respect for their vocation, for their position vis–à–vis their followers, and genuine grate–fulness for their help. We should have no issue with 'who is the greatest'—since Jesus washed feet to overcome that fear.

I went from the abbot of Wat Mahathat to canvas the shops and buildings across from the university entrance for a place to lease, without success. Then I went into the lane I had asked others to explore for me. A man who was making images of a Buddhist saint suggested I ask a widow at the end of the lane. He said she had closed one of her shop houses since her husband died, refusing all offers to rent it. I went in and talked to her, told her about the conversation with the abbot, and she said she would be happy to let us have the premises for a nominal rent. She told me that her family had leased the property from the temple in perpetuity, so it was really Mahathat temple property and what better use for the property than for worthy religious purposes. So within hours we had a home—50 meters from the main entrance of one of most important Buddhist universities in the world, and on temple property.

The name "Buddhist Study Center" would not work well. We wanted to attract Buddhist scholars from the center of Buddhist studies nearby to our little center, so we called it a Center for the Study of Religion and Culture, "*Soon Suksa Sasana lae Wattanatham.*"

RELATIONSHIP WITH THE UNIVERSITY

When I went to open a bank account for the center, I struck the difficulty that our self–styled Center for the Study of Religion and Culture was not a registered entity. I asked the bank if there was any way around that, and they suggested that if I could get a guarantee from the chancellor of the Mahachulalongkorn University they would open the account. So I introduced myself to the chancellor, a very high ranking, and very astute Buddhist scholar, and he was happy to oblige. He wrote a letter recommending us to the bank and gave a standing guarantee for us. I was to meet with him many times over the next few years.

He later suggested that we would be a good resource for his graduate students. He encouraged the lecturers to assign their students to visit our center and consider doing comparative studies under our guidance. I asked him once how he would feel if monks converted to Christianity in the process. He said he trusted that we would never try to convert others when presenting our ideas and beliefs, and that if monks became convinced that Christianity was better, he hoped they would convert. It would be the only intellectually honest thing to do. And he concluded, that he hoped non–Buddhists who came to the center would be as open minded and honest.

So now we had a study center on temple property, a bank account per favor of a Buddhist university, and more support from the Sangha than we had from our own Mission.

A STUDY CENTER

I decided that to be true to the declared purpose of the center, it needed to be a genuine study center—with opportunities to study, debate and dialogue. First of all it needed a library. I had become familiar with all the English offerings of the university library, and they definitely leaned towards polemics against Christians. The writing of all the detractors of Christianity were there, but little from those who had seriously compared religions.

The library began with my own collection of cross–cultural and cross–religious studies. I threw in all my missiology, anthropology and sociology texts. I had the usual theology texts and commentaries, so quickly purchased the equivalent for Buddhism, Hindus and Islam—so each had its doctrinal studies for the believer section. I felt it needed to be filled out on the 'culture' side, and was fortunate to get access to academic texts distributed by Asia Books—a foundation that solicited academic texts from publishers and made academic books available to education institutions that could not afford them. I was able to get hundreds of books on various aspects of culture and science.

The library ended up having eclectic feel; appropriate for a center for the study of religion and culture.

Over the next few years, wherever I went I collected books relevant to the study of religion and culture. I even took a trip from Sri Lanka to Madras to purchase books from the great selection printed in India on the subject of the religions we would study.

It had also become apparent that the Buddhist university was under supplied in information technology as the scholars had little access to computers and electronic data. So we set about to have a computer lab for the study of religion and culture. I was able to get donated computers from shops in the computer markets—they liked our goals. We soon had about ten, all networked and with an impressive collection of religion and cultural data onboard or on CD's.

THE SHAPE OF THE CENTER ITSELF

The shop house was in disrepair. It had been a budget hair–dressing salon for decades, but was now stripped of its equipment. I decided to visit the offices of the university, and the residences of the monk scholars before making decisions about the redecorating.

It was immediately apparent that there was an attention to other–worldliness in all those venues. There was no difference in the feel of the space of the simplest or the highest ranking. The office of the university librarian was minimalist—nothing had been spent on interior decorating, even the walls were looking the worse for wear. The furniture was solid, but the chairs barely comfortable. Some rooms had bare incandescent bulbs.

My instinct was to strip the town house from top to bottom, give it a repaint or wallpaper it; upgrade the light fittings, set it up with modern office furnishings, but all that would have been counterproductive. Where did that urge come from anyway—from my mission or from some other ranking of values? It is what an Australian would do. It was imperative that I did not listen to my own values, but rather note and imitate theirs. I had found that the best décor is the décor that draws no attention to itself. So I collected used and abandoned furniture from the warehouses of our institutions, kept lighting simple, and made no attempt to match the furniture. And I very quickly reaped the benefits of those decisions.

As soon as the sign was hung out front, Center for the Study of Religion and Culture, I had curious visitors. Buddhist monks would come cautiously in the door, looking around at the developments. Soon they asked what religion I was, and whether I was Christian—it is assumed that westerners are most likely to be Christians. I said I was, but the center was for interactive exploration of religion with living practitioners, including them. They inevitably asked where the funding was coming from for the center. Some even asked if we being funded by the Vatican.

A leaked document had caused a scandal that still reverberated. A Catholic study document on how to win Buddhists had fallen into the hands of some conservative Buddhist monks. Ironically it was just the kind of document the church was hoping we would produce at this center—a summary of Buddhism, its common points with Catholicism, and strategies for winning Buddhists. It included some radical contextualization, exploring an apologetic that credited the Buddha with being a servant of God, God's reformer in his age. The Buddhists were furious. It even suggested that the goal of mission is to make Thailand into a Christian country—outrageous! The document was printed with an introduction by an outraged monk, and sent to every temple and to every significant government official in the land. I had come across it in even the most out of the way places, and it certainly influenced the thinking of most Buddhists to watch out for the scheming Catholics; they will do anything to convert you and subvert the culture of the Thai people. It even affected the monk scholars from MCU, who cautiously peered through the doors to see if this was one of the devious strategies of the Catholics.

It was good to be able to deny Vatican support, and to point out all of the things donated by a range of supporters—from used and second–hand books, used bookcases, old tables, chairs and dated computers, donated by schools, hospitals, foundations, computer vendors and individuals. The visitors were reassured. I am sure an up–to–date overfunded state–of–the–art center would have raised suspicions to an unworkable level. Reassured of our intent, the visitors would offer to find more things for the center. So more books and other resources were brought to the center by Buddhist monks!

Soon the center had a library and computer lab downstairs, a seminar room and interview carousels on the second floor; and guest rooms on the top floor—for volunteer staff and visiting scholars. And a series of contextualized temple–style Adventist end–of–time paintings featured on the walls. There was no doubt that this was a religious center.

These end–of–time paintings are the focus of this presentation, and serve to illustrate the challenges of contextualization.

THE PAINTINGS

There is a long story behind the end–of–time paintings.[2]

Art is central to religious experience in Buddhist cultures. One day I was invited to look at a temple ‘painting of the Great Life’ in a remote village in northeast Thailand. The abbot proudly rolled out the painting on the grass beside the preaching hall. It was nearly 50 meters long! Painted on 1.2 meter wide calico, it was a ‘cartoon’ of the events in the life of the Prince Vessantra life of the Buddha. It was used once a year for the Great Life Festival.

News of the off–season unrolling had gone through the village and dozens of children ran to the site. I was intrigued as they moved along the painting excitedly reminding each other of the stories. I was struck that for a once–a–year medium, it had been extraordinarily effective. I wondered how effective a "Great Christ Life" would be.

We located the artist of that scroll in his rice field, and he agreed to paint a 'great life' painting of Jesus for us. That was a brave challenge to take on. He had painted his "Great Life" scroll heavily indebted to other depictions he had seen. However he had never even heard the story of Jesus, let alone been exposed to illustrations of that story. I could have given him a set of our cradle roll picture rolls—I had used them to line church walls before. But I decided I wanted to see how a Thai villager would visualize the story for himself from the text. It took him five months to paint his 'Great Life of Jesus' scroll. Every week or so I sent a student to tell the next story. The result was a Thai village experience of the life and events of Jesus—partly 'borrowed' from the tradition of scroll paintings, partly original and distinctly like the life and environs of current village life. The effect on viewers was focused curiosity about what was happening—not on the images in the paintings. The 'western' picture rolls always distracted from the stories, and emphasized the foreignness of the religion—the same way Hindu images of their gods distract us from the essential teaching of Hinduism. But that's another issue, another story.

The scroll was completed in 1979, and was used for the next twenty years. It was used in villages and churches in three countries—Thailand, Cambodia and Laos. It has now been lost—its last known use in the Vientiane Church in Laos for Christmas around 1999.

The Thai church leaders at the time were not impressed with the scroll painting. The president of the Thailand Mission told me he was embarrassed by its crudity. He was a hobby western landscape artist himself.

It was in response to this criticism that the end–time paintings were attempted. I decided to commission a series of fine art paintings. And I decided the subject should be end of time expectations visually described in the Bible and in Ellen White's expanded commentaries.

I decided on the end–time story because the life of Jesus is well known and often illustrated—there are wonderful contextualized artwork on all aspects and events in the life of the historical Jesus. I would just be adding another version to many. However the Adventist understanding of how the world will end (and begin again) is a distinct contribution to the Christian revelation of the character of God—and nobody else was going to tell that story.

I also decided that visions of the future would be more appropriate subjects for an ancient art form. A revelation of the future could have been given in any era—and would certainly be envisioned by the 'seer' in the visual forms of his age—just as John the Revelator 'saw' his visions in Hebrew visual metaphors of his culture and time. So there was no reason we shouldn't 'imagine' the end–time predictions through a Thai medium.

The painting project took four years to complete with Thai artists 'translating' the visual biblical metaphors into the 'language' of a particular Thai school of painting. The process of developing these paintings is worth telling.

I looked for an artist who would be up to the challenge and was recommended to contact the head of the art department of the Chiangmai Teachers College. When I approached Achaan Suchaat Braappyri I could see he was not enthusiastic to take on such a daunting challenge. He knew what I didn't, that this was an extremely difficult task. We have just interviewed him, thirty years after he completed the series. We'll come back to his experience of creating the paintings later.

The completed paintings were masterpieces. One was exhibited in a national level exhibition of the works of the artists of north Thailand. They were seen and appreciated by a wide range of people, including hundreds of leading Buddhist scholars and monk students. The artwork always drew respect—well almost always, with the exception of some Adventist members and church leaders. And that is the other side of this story.

I had visualized displaying these paintings and the unique end–time expectations in Chiangmai church. I was the pastor there for five years. It was fortunate that the church needed expansion about the time the paintings were completed, and I designed a church to display the paintings—it had walls to hang the paintings. As long as I was there they graced the church, and we had a stream of people coming to the church "to see the paintings." Every week teachers brought classes of students, high school and university, on an outing to see the paintings. Buddhist monks came in groups and even as individuals to see the paintings they had heard about. I was their host, guide and art interpreter. I had the chance to talk them through this entirely new vision of how things were going to end. Entire classes of missionaries in training with other churches came to ponder the challenges of contextualization. Presenters in mission seminars brought their participants to see the paintings—including the missiologist Paul Heibert. Everyone was impressed with the art, and many intrigued by the teaching—well almost everyone.

I heard no reaction to the paintings from the church members while I was there—but in retrospect, no one volunteered to be their interpreter either. It turned out that some members were not happy with the paintings in their church from the beginning. Some time after I was transferred away from the church, to Thailand Mission as ministerial secretary, the paintings came down. A young teacher at our academy, a graduate from the Teachers College where Acaan Suchart was a teacher, called me to tell me the paintings were in danger of damage as the storeroom they had been kept in was being repainted, and they were not protecting the paintings from ceiling drips. I asked him to bring the paintings to Bangkok. That student is the pastor of Chiangmai church today— Suradej Tawinyangyuen. Some church leaders had not been comfortable with the Buddhist paintings in the church. The other contextual furnishings I introduced into the church have remained but the paintings didn't.

Something that saddened me years later was that I found out that the mission president whose criticism of the original contextualized 'Life of Jesus' scroll had disliked these paintings even more. He thought they were so syncretistic with Buddhist art that they lowered the uniqueness of Christianity. When I told him in his late retirement that his criticism of the crudeness of the scroll had led me to take on this fine art project, he said that was the worst thing he could wish to hear. I would not have told him of his part if I had anticipated the effect of the telling. However the reaction bears recording.

The other exceptions to universal acclaim were some concerned Buddhist laypeople. When the painting of the new earth was displayed at the exhibition of the works of Northern Thai artists, some attendees were not impressed. Some Buddhist were offended that Christians had 'stolen' Buddhist art, possibly were disrespecting the Buddha, and went and laid a formal complaint with the Buddhist authorities. I know how they felt. I had felt something similar when I walked past a Buddhist Sunday School in Sri Lanka and heard the children singing, "Buddha loves me this I know, for the Dhamma tells me so."

The ranking monk for northern Thailand called the painter and me for an interview, commissioned specialists to examine the paintings, and then called a meeting of both parties and gave his ruling—he said that the paintings were not Buddhist, had not used characters from any Buddhist narrative or stories, and made no disrespectful message about Buddha or Buddhism; that they were a different story, a different vision of what would happen at the end of time that had been painted in a particular Thai artistic medium. He told the Buddhist group that when Buddhism came to Thailand they used preexisting Thai art to tell their story. And although there was Thai art in every temple it did not mean Thai art was the intellectual property of Buddhism. In fact there were some unique adaptations of Thai art in this painting that should be appreciated. He ruled that Christians were as entitled to use Thai art as were Buddhists. The contending party accepted his ruling with apologies to us.

Some time later some local church leaders influenced the Chiangmai church to remove the shame of the 'Buddhist paintings.' And the divided reaction continues to this day. Perhaps we need the ruling of a patriarch.

After I had the paintings brought to Bangkok, I stored them at the mission office. I didn't know how to use them. I had commissioned them for hanging in a church.

After I went on study–leave to Australia, the mission got a new president, Steve Bassham. He and his educated Thai wife, Nancy, brought the paintings out of storage and displayed them around the mission office—with one dominating the president's office wall. Everyone was exposed to this positive 'ownership' of the medium and its message.

When I returned to Thailand, and after I had set up the Center for the Study of Religion on Culture I 'took back' the paintings and displayed them prominently above the computers on the first floor and featured the rest in the cross–religious meeting room on the second floor.[3]

Although this story began at an earlier time, the paintings were very much a part of the Center for the Study of Religion and Culture. They were the subject of much discussion with and by Buddhist scholars and leaders about the use of popular culture for the transmission of religious ideas; for heated discussions about contextualization and the ethics of borrowing art cross–culturally. More importantly the paintings were the vehicle for transmission of the Adventist view of the end of history and life after the end. Hundreds of significant Buddhist leaders came to see the paintings and listen to the alternative viewpoint of these visions of the end–of–time.

The place and role of the paintings in the 'Buddhist Center' is featured in the General Conference Global Mission documentary "Buddhist Neighbors" – a documentary that has been televised many times on Hope Channel and 3ABN. The paintings have been written about in Ministry and the Adventist Review magazines. They have been concrete illustrations of the challenges and dangers of contextualization for many courses in mission and contextualization.

These paintings have also been used in direct evangelism. A series of filmstrips and also slides were made and used in evangelistic campaigns in rural Thailand. A coffee table illustrated book and a message book were always envisioned, but were never undertaken. The paintings and their embedded message, their 'common ground,' their comparisons and contrasts with Buddhist expectations of the end–time are still there. Perhaps now maybe they can be shared in digital media.

PAINTING THE PAINTINGS – THE CHALLENGE OF ART

The first challenge in creating an artistic form to communicate ideas is to select the medium. I chose paintings because they are the most familiar medium for telling religious stories and for 'remembering' epics and their values. The net decision was to anchor the paintings to a particular tradition or style. I decided to use the same style as was used to tell the Buddhist story – Thai art.

I knew this would be a problem, but there weren't many options. If the style was too foreign the result would emphasize the foreign origins of the ideas depicted and would also convey the message that a person need move away from Thainess to accept the teaching. I decided to put the biblical view of the end of the world in an art style that was familiar to Thai people so they would focus on the truth portrayed in the paintings.

I then found that it wasn't sufficient to say that we would use Thai art because it is not monolithic. There are many different styles of Thai painting. It has many traditions, has been through many periods and has given rise to many schools of art.

We needed to anchor the story in one tradition. Suchaart took me aroung to various temples including Wat Pra Singh in Chiangmai which is famous for the two different schools of paintings used on its opposing walls. We needed to anchor the story in one tradition. Suchaart took me around various temples to discuss the different schools. He sent me to Naan Province to see his preferred style for our project—the Naan Lanna tradition. The art was beautiful—the most aesthetic I had ever seen. We agreed to work through that tradition.

All narrative art has its rules for depicting the time line of their stories. Thai art had no special flow for its stories. The story–line is read by the storyteller not the painting. All the elements of the event are there to be unpacked, but there are no clues to the order they should be unpacked, except that the story generally flows from right to left. But then there are events that are happening simultaneously shown in more than one place. The viewer who knows the story, or the storyteller if the viewer is unfamiliar with the story, brings each incident out in its turn. We decided to tell our story in a similar way.

As an authentic artist, not a copyist, Suchaat wanted to do something new with the Naan Lanna style—he asked if he could try adding perspective to the tradition. Thai art is traditionally two dimensional—the characters at the back of the storyline are located higher, but are the same size as the ones in the front. And there is no depth of field. These paintings would be a twist on that style.

Not being an artist, I had never faced the challenges of putting everything in images. Most of us are word–artists—we work hard to craft our talks and sermons to persuade our various listeners. But putting an idea onto a canvas is much more demanding. Every image, every color, every detail must be decided.

Suchaat started the project with an exploration of character types that had no Thai art countertypes, and which types may distort the story. I would bring all the texts that 'described' a particular player—like angels. We would read and discuss them. Deciding visual forms is different than describing functions. Suchaat was very familiar with western art—he taught the subject. He could paint in most of the styles of western art. But we had set our limits, and now we needed to explore the points of connection and disconnection between the characters who would inhabit our stories.

In the case of 'angels' our viewers would be familiar with Thai 'angels'—beings from the lower heavens, people who were living their reward for good karma after serving their sentences for bad karma in the hells. The roles of thewada in the lives of humans were understood. But biblical 'angels' were not those creatures. Theyare a unique creation; manifesting themselves in forms appropriate to their roles. Because the Hebrews were not encouraged to illustrate heaven in art, there are no clear traditions on what angels are really like. They appear as they are expected to appear. Our viewers would be Thais viewing a story that included creatures never conceived of, depicted in an art form already settled two hundred years before. How should we depict this kind of angel:

> *Angels of heaven are sent forth to minister to those who shall be heirs of salvation... angels of heaven are passing throughout the length and breadth of the earth, seeking to comfort the sorrowing, to protect the imperilled, to win the hearts of men to Christ. Not one is neglected or passed by. God is no respecter of persons, and He has an equal care for all the souls He has created (White 1898:639).*

Suchaat would explore with sketches, and we would meet again to discuss the appropriateness of the different alternatives—how do angels transport, what would be their demeanor, how should they be dressed, what are the signifiers and indicators of their type and role. We decided on wings—because it was the most consistent element of angel art metaphors in the Bible (but not usually apparent when they appeared to people) and to distinguish them from thewada. It was a link the western tradition of angel portrayal, but should not be out–of–place in the painting. Suchaat suggested transparent wings—not substantial wings. Heavenly beings transport by a power we have no access to. The wings would be signifiers not the mechanics of transportation.

Then we would explore demons, and so on.

We spent the most time exploring the depiction of post resurrection Jesus. Long ago depictions of Jesus had settled into a particular style—a style that would be discordant in a Thai Lanna painting. What would we do with this description:

> *I turned around to see the voice that was speaking to me. And when I turned I saw seven golden lampstands, and among the lampstands was someone like a son of man, dressed in a robe reaching down to his feet and with a golden sash around his chest. The hair on his head was white like wool, as white as snow, and his eyes were like blazing fire. His feet were like bronze glowing in a furnace, and his voice was like the sound of rushing waters. In his right hand he held seven stars, and coming out of his mouth was a sharp, double–edged sword. His face was like*

> *the sun shining in all its brilliance. When I saw him, I fell at his feet as though dead (Rev 1:12–17, NIV).*

Or this:

> *Then I saw a great white throne and him who was seated on it. The earth and the heavens fled from his presence, and there was no place for them (Rev 20:11 NIV).*

Once we had established some guides for illustrating the most unfamiliar and contrasting characters in the story, Suchaat said he was ready. He began to sketch in the first painting—a painting depicting the events occurring between the close of probation to the feast of the birds. How he did that I have no idea—the creativity of an artist is inaccessible to me.

I need to explain our complementary roles in the creation of these paintings: I was the caretaker of the story, and Suchaat was the artist. I never interfered with Suchaat's decision on how to put the story into its visual form. While we often talked through the elements and implications of the verbal metaphors of the visions, more and more I just supplied the text and Suchaat thought them through on his own. His contribution to the storytelling was massive—he tried to be faithful to the visions, and also to the aesthetics of narrative art. These are the works of an artist wrestling to bring together literary descriptions from a range of texts and expressing them in a detail demanding artistic form.

We tried to involve other artists—the second painting was done by Mr. X one of his former students, then art teacher on the college of art. While it faithfully depicted what I told him were the elements of the story, he did not immerse himself in the challenge of contextual art storytelling. We came to the conclusion that only Suchaat could complete the series. The last two paintings improved in aesthetics and in depth of meaning. The last painting—the new earth, is a masterpiece in both senses. It was the painting displayed in the exhibition for the works of Northern Thai artists that drew the protests by concerned Buddhists.

The description of the stories in the paintings has never been put to paper. There has always been an oral storytelling adapted to the understanding and interest of the viewer/listeners. I have told the story to a number of caretakers over the years, but much of the detail has been lost. I am working with Suchaat to write a joint report on what we tried to portray and say through these paintings, and tell about the obstacles faced and solutions attempted in telling this story to our primary intended viewer/listeners—Buddhist Thais.

THE END–TIME IN CHRISTIAN CONCEPTION AND ART

A biblical vision of the end–time period of human history has been recorded consistently over a long period—particularly in the writings of Hebrew prophets of the eighth to sixth centuries B.C.E. (the major and minor prophets) through to the writings of John the Revelator at the end of the first century C.E. The account has been commentated on through the Christian era, and illustrated often, usually as future real 'historical' events. This historicist approach reads visions of the future as presenting the course of future history from the time of the vision through to the end of the age. Often the end–of–the age was understood as referring to the age of the commentators.

Particular attention was given to the end–of–time by the Great Advent Movement of the Americas and Europe in the mid–19th century, although due to the pressure of what they believed was the imminent end of the world, there was no leisure in which to develop new illustrations during that period.

The inheritors of the end–time focus were Seventh–day Adventists. For some time they were the primary proponents of end–time specifics—and have illustrated it in many ways in their 'message' publications. Most of the illustrations remained clearly within the tradition of western religious illustration. Adventists believe that the world has entered into the end time period already, and the remaining events will take place in the near future. While 'knowledge' of the future storyline has no merit in itself, Adventists believe many of the revealed details have a bearing on our understanding of the character of God, can protect us from tempting wrong views, and encourage us to persevere in our religious life and survive the events.

For the most part, mainline Christianity steered clear of end–time particularities. For some it was because they read the texts with a preterist focus—that 'prophecies' of the 'end–time' referred to traumatic religious events in the immediate future (or recent past) of the time of their composing.

Many settled on idealist interpretations of 'end–time' visions:

> *While the Apocalypse thus embraces the whole period of the Christian dispensation, it sets before us within this period the action of great principles and not special incidents; we are not to look in the Apocalypse for special events, both for the exhibition of the principles which govern the history of both the world and the Church (Milligan 1889:153–4).*

Many mainline Christians avoided a focus on the end–of–time, because of their experience of or awareness of embarrassing failed end–time predictions by various Christian and partially Christian groups.

More recently with the explosion of futurist /premillenialist /dispensationalist interpretations of the texts on end–of–time events, particularly on the anticipated rapture, there has been an ever increasing range of depictions of end–time visions—in illustration and in film.

If we take our focus away from the differences between the various Christian views of the end–time, we can see what they hold in common. For the most part Christians believe in the resurrection from the dead; in a future judgment; in an eternal state in which believers will be with God, and unbelievers will not. Most agree on the importance of the study of prophecy and its edification for believer. All Christians wait for the return of our Lord and together would say, "Amen. Come, Lord Jesus!" (Rev 22:20, NIV 2011).

These four paintings come out of the expanded historicist interpretation of end–time prophecies held by the Seventh–day Adventist Church. They were created to share the benefits of this revealed prediction of the end of the world and the establishment of the new earth with Thai people unfamiliar with this viewpoint.

THE END–TIME IN THAI BUDDHIST CONCEPT AND ART

The view of eternity presented in these paintings is in conscious contrast to the expectations of Buddhist people. The Buddhist beliefs with regard to the post–death future of the individual were retained from the Hindu teaching. It includes kamma—the teaching that what we do now will inevitably impact our future; if we do good we will be rewarded with good; if we do evil we will be punished with something bad. This life is hard, usually unfair, and often tragic. The hope of all Thais is for a better time of it next time around—a better reincarnation. It is apparent that appropriate reward and punishment is not resolved in this life—so the unfinished business must be completed through a series of future existences.

The vision of future existences has been often illustrated in Thai Buddhist art. An important event in moving to future existences is the judgment scene of Yomprabaan. After death the 'soul' has to attend to a judgment reading, an explanation of the reasons for and conditions of the next life destiny from the guardian that stands between the world of earth and the hells. In Thai understanding punishment must be given before rewards can be awarded. The initial punishment phase can be punishment in one of the four forms of existence in this world—in a human life affected by past actions; as a sentient animal, as a hungry ghost, or as a restless ghost. More reprehensive living needs to be punished through periods in appropriate hells. After the account of bad and evil has been settled, the rewards for the good done can be given.

While ideally we can spend a period in one of the lower sentient heavens, most Thais are more focused on a better human existence—to be experienced after a limited 'punishment' on the four worlds, or after hell, or after a delay 'vacation' in a pleasurable heaven. And it is to that better rebirth they set their hopes. It is not necessary to depict a better life as a human—we have all tasted and observed what we would like next time around. Art is not needed for that vision.

But this is not the Buddhist ideal either.

The reforming teaching of the Siddhartha Gautama was to encourage all people with the possibility of achieving a perfect final ending this time around. He warned that rebirth would never lead to a final resolution of suffering or achievement of release. He said: "You cannot by going come to that place." He taught that if they applied their minds and lives to ideal living there would be no reincarnation. The Buddha said that Nibbana can be found – "in this six–foot body with its sense impressions and its thought and ideas." So what is the nature of this Nibbana, this final new beginning? How could it be depicted in art?

Nibbana cannot be depicted. I am not aware of any painting of that "new earth." It is so unlike present existence that it cannot be conceived. It can only be tasted through blissful imageless experiences of peaceful detachment.

The fourth painting on the Biblical teaching on the 'earth–made–new' is a radical contrast to the Nibbana vision. We were aware of how different that vision was. I have had educated Buddhist scholars immediately see the difference that was 'painted in' and have commented on how radical this vision is of 'eternal life.' It has given rise to discussions of what would have to be different in order to make such a solution possible. From the Buddhist perspective this present existence, this universe, is so flawed that nothing can be retained in a final solution. The Bible does address these issues, and can explain how radical redemption is possible. And the Biblical redeemed universe is easily depicted—it is this life with the flaws removed:

> *And I heard a loud voice from the throne saying, "Look! God's dwelling place is now among the people, and he will dwell with them. They will be his people, and God himself will be with them and be their God. 'He will wipe every tear from their eyes. There will be no more death' or mourning or crying or pain, for the old order of things has passed away" (Rev 21:3–4 NIV).*

That is the renewed earth depicted in the fourth painting. Before looking at that 'revelation' in detail, we need to look at another depictable almost–heaven illustrated in Thai art—the era of Maitreya Buddha.

In Buddhism the cosmos is envisioned as having its own cycle of birth and rebirth. During each cycle of existence everything is always degrading. When the universe enters a critical stage in this disorder a Buddha appears to give the universe a renewed start.

In this current 'existence of the universe, this kalpa, five Buddhas have been needed. Three had rescued the universe from premature dissolution before our Buddha, Siddhartha Gautama, was born, in the sixth century B.C.E.. However the effect of his rediscovery of truth and his ideal practice of it was expected to wear off over time. The periods between Buddhas gets shorter and shorter as we approach the end–time of the universe's cycle. Some have said this period would last 5000 years, but that there were factors that could considerably shorten the period of effectiveness. There is a text which records the Buddha saying that ordination of women would shorten the effectiveness of true teaching by half, to 2,500 years. If that is so, the era of the next Buddha is upon us.

The next and last Buddha will be Maitreya Buddha—in Thailand popularly called Pra Arya Maitreyo, or Pra Sean (called Miruk, Miruku, and Mile Fo in other traditions). Maitreya (Pali, Metteyya) bodhisattva, who is said to dwell in Tusita heaven, is known as the "future buddha" because he will appear in this world to reestablish Buddhism (the truth about the nature of the universe) after all vestiges of the current dispensation of Sakyamuni Buddha have vanished.

Many rural Buddhists, especially in the northeast, work to acquire special merit in order to be born here on earth in that distant era when Maitreya would at last attain Buddhahood. They see that time as a future Golden Age. They long to be born as human beings in that blessed age. The arrival of Maitreya is preceded by a vast cleansing that would see a cosmic battle between bodhisattvas and demons, a cleansing by fire, followed by the 'creation' of a pure and perfect world. An encounter with Maitreya in that world will bring instant and easy enlightenment.

It is interesting that the desire to be born into the age of Maitreya has been the main motivation for northeastern Buddhists listening to the story of the last great life of the Buddha, as depicted on the Last–Life scroll that was the stimulus for this project to illustrate Adventist beliefs through Thai art. Traditionally Isaan Thais have believed that the merit accrued by listening to that story applies directly to rebirth in the age of Maitreya.

The world of Maitreya is not heaven—it is this world renewed. Once reborn in this world cleansed by fire Maitreya will inhabit a royal city, Ketumati, that also shares some features of other pure lands. The features most well known in Thailand are its gold and silver trees, under which all wishes are met—alleviating the suffering caused through inaccessibility or rivalry. Historically, the worship of Maitreya has served as the seed both for general utopian longing and armed movements meant to usher in the millennium

In some ways the golden age of the Buddha–to–come bears some resemblance to the new earth predicted in the Bible. However this golden age is just a staging post. After the era of Maitreya the universe will collapse in on itself, and will emerge on the other side, with all those whose business was not finished in the previous kalpa. In the Biblical portrayal it is God who dwells with them, not a pious boddhisatva working short–term to assist the redemption of others like himself.

> *On each side of the river stood the tree of life, bearing twelve crops of fruit, yielding its fruit every month. And the leaves of the tree are for the healing of the nations. No longer will there be any curse. The throne of God and of the Lamb will be in the city... (Rev 22:2–3 NIV).*

The ideal future and final existence portrayed in the fourth painting is distinctly different from the expectations of Thai Buddhists portrayed in Thai visions of the end–of–time. It can give pause for reflection and discussion on the possibility of a radical redemption of the world and of us.

THE NARRATIVE OF THE SERIES OF PAINTINGS

There is no need for a detailed telling of the narrative of the paintings for Adventist viewers. They are a familiar story. To assist those who will explain the images below is a summary of the narrative:

The First Painting - After the Close of Probation

The first change from the world we know is the withdrawal of the reign of the Holy Spirit and the restraining protection of the angels 'of the four winds' subsequent to the conclusion of the redemption effort. The redeemed and unredeemable are sealed into their destinies.

The artist, Suchaat, chose to depict this as a period of darkness. The events take place inside the mouth of 'the dragon.' The world descends into chaos, accelerated by seven last plagues poured into the mixture by seven angels. Whatever the specifics of the plagues will be, the painting clearly depicts the reaction of the unrighteous to the plagues. Spurred on by the whispering of the false prophet demon, the unrighteous are depicted cursing God and heaven for their troubles. Soon they will divert their blame to the righteous.

Below a divider that indicates another series of events occurring at the same time, but separated from the accelerating chaos, is the situation of the righteous during this period is a depiction of the time of Jacob's trouble. The focus of the righteous is not on laying blame for the plagues, but on their own spiritual readiness for the anticipated second coming. The artist has portrayed the children of light protected from the chaos, and nurtured by angels. However their faces reflect their spiritual anxiety. The withdrawal of the Spirit has robbed them of affirmation of their acceptance by God. They experience the withdrawal of God as Christ did on the cross when he asked, "Why have you forsaken me?"

At the moment that the unrighteous decide to take out their frustration on the people of God, the heavens and a voice from heaven affirms that the righteous are still beloved and warns the unrighteous of the impending return of the savior. Angels that excel in strength defend the righteous.

On the far side of the painting a dark cloud 'the size of a man's hand' expands and the rescuing army of the rider on the white horse appears travelling to the earth. The painter told us recently that he intended it to be a 'tunnel' opening the world of light to the world descending into darkness. Light will snatch the children of light from the impending destruction of the world.

The rider on the white horse is depicted with all the signs John describes from his vision:

> *I saw heaven standing open and there before me was a white horse, whose rider is called Faithful and True. With justice he judges and wages war. His eyes are like blazing fire, and on his head are many crowns. He has a name written on him that no one knows but he himself. He is dressed in a robe dipped in blood, and his name is the Word of God. The armies of heaven were following him, riding on white horses and dressed in fine linen, white and clean. Coming out of his mouth is a sharp sword with which to strike down the nations. "He will rule them with an iron sceptre." He treads the winepress of the fury of the wrath of God Almighty. On his robe and on his thigh he has this name written: king of kings and lord of lords (Rev 19:11–16 NIV)*

Some of the heavenly army are angels who sweep down to assist the living and risen righteous join the rescuing host 'in the air.'

The unrighteous flee from the face of the descending avenger, and seek shelter in the shattering mountains. Birds of carrion circle, indicating the end of human life on the earth.

The Second Painting: From the Arrival in Heaven

This painting was created by a student of Achaan Suchaat. I was more involved in the putting together of this painting. Texts dealing with the 'millennium' between the second coming rescue and the final resolution are few. The images for this chapter are taken from a number of visions [Visions given to E.G. White and documented in the final chapters of The Great Controversy]. The painting takes up the story with the arrival in the 'temporary' abode of the righteous during the next phase of the end–of–the–world.

The 'redeemed' receive crowns, worship with music, bear flags of victory and take up their roles in the executing judgment. The center of the process is dominated by the two on the central throne— one unable to be described or depicted, and the other is the lamb (Jesus). In the foreground are the seven flames of the Spirit. The throne is surrounded by the 'representatives' of the other worlds—the lion, eagle, bovine and humanoid creatures, visibly impressed by the justice of the acts of God.' The redeemed affirm God's judgment which divides all the peoples of earth into two classes—the redeemed and the unredeemed. Angels are shown moving among the redeemed sharing the records they have made and inviting full scrutiny of the decisions made. The redeemed confirm every decision as just and true.

In the background is the final home of the redeemed, the New Jerusalem still under construction. The future tree of life is sprouting across the stream that will become the river of life. Somehow the redeemed are sustained in a 'heaven' that is not intended as their future home.

The scene in heaven is separated from the interim earth—not merely by a barrier but by a gate reinforced with chains. On earth the dragon from the bottomless pit, the 'unmaker' roams the devastated earth with his minions. As fallen beings their state and relations are not genial—without their pet projects to subvert humans they turn on each other.

THE THIRD PAINTING: FROM THE RESURRECTION OF THE UNREDEEMED

This painting, also by Achaan Suchaat, takes most of its imagery from the Great Controversy chapter: "The Controversy Ended."

> *The unrighteious dead are raised to life and are rallied by demons to join an attack to take the descending New Jerusalem. The army is composed of people from many ages.*

Satan, the mightiest of warriors, leads the van, and his angels unite their forces for this final struggle. Kings and warriors are in his train, and the multitudes follow in vast companies, each under its appointed leader. With military precision the serried ranks advance over the earth's broken and uneven surface to the City of God. (White 1911:664)

The notable elements of the painting are: 1) the contrast between the light of the righteous upper half of the painting contrasting with the darkness of the demonic sector below, 2) the completed city that settles down from heaven, international in character prepared as a bride for her wedding day, 3) on earth the cloak that hid the invisible world has lifted, so now men and demons are united together in their challenge, 4) Satan rides a battle elephant challenging all heaven (while his elephant bows in deference to the creator). The artist decided to include animals in the battle of Armageddon, as they are essential to the battle scenes in the art tradition we were using. He asked whether animals will survive the second coming devastation and felt uncomfortable with including animals in the punishment of humans. To emphasize the symbolic nature of the illustration, he included mythical beasts as well—with humans riding mythical beasts and demons riding natural beasts. Nothing is excluded from the conflict.

The narrative moves easily from the battle scenes to the great white throne poised in judgment on the sky, and the one who sits on the throne, his posture that of a righteous ruler.

The earth and the heavens fled from his presence, and there was no place for them (Rev 20:11 NIV).

The reading of the names from the book of life; the humble adoration of the saints; the panorama of the efforts of Christ to save them all; the bowing acknowledgement of all creatures; and the subsequent final crowning of Christ follow in succession. The punishing fire from heaven engulfs the unredeemable, and on the extreme left of the painting nothing remains but the cleansing fire.

And death and hell were cast into the lake of fire. This is the second death. And whosoever was not found written in the book of life was cast into the lake of fire (Rev 20:14–15, KJV).

The Fourth Painting: A Vision of the Earth Made New

And I saw a new heaven and a new earth: for the first heaven and the first earth were passed away; and there was no more sea... And I heard a great voice out of heaven saying, Behold, the tabernacle of God is with men, and he will dwell with them, and they shall be his people, and God himself shall be with them, and be their God. (Rev 21:1, 3, KJV)

The last painting, the third by Achaan Suchaat, takes its images from a range of end–time visions from the whole span of biblical prophecies—those that would have had their primary fulfilment in an ideal Israel, but always hinting at an ideal eternity. While the images were consistent with an ideal earth, we have no others to describe a real new earth. I think Ellen White would have approved our homely new earth:

A fear of making the future inheritance seem too material has led many to spiritualize away the very truths which lead us to look upon it as our home. Christ assured His disciples that He went to prepare mansions for them in the Father's house. Those who accept the teachings of God's word will not be wholly ignorant concerning the heavenly abode. (White 1911:674)

In the Bible the inheritance of the saved is called "a country." (Heb 11:14–16). There the heavenly Shepherd leads His flock to fountains of living waters. The tree of life yields its fruit every month, and the leaves of the tree are for the service of the nations. There are ever–flowing streams, clear as crystal, and beside them waving trees cast their shadows upon the paths prepared for the ransomed of the Lord. There the wide–spreading plains swell into hills of beauty, and the mountains of God rear their lofty summits. On those peaceful plains, beside those living streams, God's people, so long pilgrims and wanderers, shall find a home.

My people shall dwell in a peaceable habitation, and in sure dwellings, and in quiet resting places... Violence shall no more

> *be heard in thy land, wasting nor destruction within thy borders; but thou shalt call thy walls Salvation, and thy gates Praise... They shall build houses, and inhabit them; and they shall plant vineyards, and eat the fruit of them. They shall not build, and another inhabit; they shall not plant, and another eat... (Isa 32:18; 60:18; 65:21–22, KJV)*
>
> *Mine elect shall long enjoy the work of their hands. (White: 1911: 674, 675)*

Notable elements are the excluded sun; the included moon; the tree of life; the river of life; people involved in all the activities of a community within the conceptual time frame of the art tradition. Everywhere are small surprises—images of a community in harmony with each other and with the natural world. Angels can be seen busy with their supporting roles, but it is essentially a human world. It is a real earth redeemed.

Elements relating to the dwelling of God with man are the picture of God teaching some of the people—deliberately on their side (not authoritatively to all in the center); his 'home;' and his vacant throne. On stands bedside the throne are the masks God wore when relating to yet unredeemed people of earth—the mask of the lion and the mask of the lamb. No mask is needed any more as God lives with his people. The river of life has its source under the throne.

Central to Achaan Suchaat's ideal earth are two images, one of the nations bringing gifts of praise to the center of the city, and a beautiful sala[4] representing the unity of all flesh in their adoration:

> *People will come from the towns of Judah and the villages around Jerusalem, from the territory of Benjamin and the western foothills, from the hill country and the Negev, bringing burnt offerings and sacrifices, grain offerings and incense, and bringing thank offerings to the house of the Lord (Jer 17:26 NIV).*

The painter suggested that the central sala depicts the Sabbath—not the day but the function and meaning of the Sabbath—the rest from all care and grateful worship of God by the redeemed.

The fourth painting is bordered with a golden decorative border indicating it is a vision of the ideal—never before realized, but the hope of the nations. It is life as we would want to live if we could have all our wishes.

AFTER THE PAINTING

Presentations illustrated with details from the series have been used and shared with those who are evangelizing Buddhists in all the countries with similar art—Laos, Cambodia, Burma and Sri Lanka. We took as many as 50 close–ups from each of the four paintings. They have been used to stimulate thought on contextualization among people to whom the art is alien—in Australia, the US, Korea, Japan and in our seminaries. The explanation of the narrative of the end–of–time that should accompany this set of paintings has not yet been completed.

When the Center for the Study of Religion in Culture was closed, the Thailand Mission showed no interest in the paintings. They are cared for and on display in a private Adventist school in Bangkok—still informing inquirers about the Adventist vision of the end–of–the–world. However this kind of religious teaching art is only as good as its story tellers and without a contextualized telling, the paintings lose their ability to convict the people they were intended for—Buddhists in the Theravada tradition.

NOTES

1. *Editor's Note: The Far Eastern Division was an administrative division that has since been divided into the South–Asia Pacific Division and North–Asia Pacific Division.*

2. *Some of the following has been published in "Is Anthropology Practical," in A Man with a Vision, a Festschrift honoring Russell L. Staples, ed. Rudi Maier (Berrien Springs, Mich.: Department of World Mission, Andrews university, 2005*

3. *The mission president had changed in the meantime, and the*

new president was more than happy to see the paintings go—they represented the syncretism he was concerned about.

4. *A sala is a free–standing, open pavilion with stylized architecture where groups gather for listening to Monks teaching the Dhamma, village leaders call the townspeople to meetings, or simply a place to fellowship and relax.*

REFERENCES

Milligan, William. 1889. The Book of Revelation. London: Hodder and Stoughton.

White, Ellen G. 1898. The Desire of Ages.

White, Ellen G. 1911. The Great Controversy.

Chapter 16

Sharing Jesus with Buddhists

Scott Griswold

INTRODUCTION

I was startled the day my Cambodian friend told me, "Fleeing from the war into Vietnam, I stumbled into a Catholic church. There I saw for the first time the tortured figure of Jesus on the cross. I was shocked to learn that Christians worship this man. How could they even respect someone who obviously had such terrible karma?"

My friend looked at Jesus through Buddhist eyes, assuming His suffering must come from something bad He'd done in a previous life. This one man's confusion points us to the many other Buddhists who either don't know anything about Jesus or have major misunderstandings.

There are a lot of them. Tens of thousands of men have shaved their heads, donned orange robes, and devoted themselves as monks to the Buddhist path of good deeds and meditation. They hope to someday escape the cycle of suffering and rebirth. Millions more Buddhist lay–people depend on these monks for teaching, ceremonies, and blessings.

In fact their numbers are increasing in certain places. In many Asian countries Buddhism is reviving and growing. It is also significant to note that people in the West are turning to Buddhism in unprecedented numbers.

Seventh–day Adventists have typically found it difficult to reach Buddhists with the gospel. The Church has already been active in many Buddhist countries for over one hundred years without seeing many Buddhists become followers of Jesus. In such countries as Japan, Korea, Myanmar, Sri Lanka, Taiwan, and Thailand, there are few members who came from a Buddhist background. We have typically been more likely to bring into our fellowship other Christians, animists, and secular people.

We need to know what is making it difficult for Buddhists to come to Jesus and find better ways to share Him more effectively.

BARRIERS TO BUDDHISTS BELIEVING

One major barrier is the worldview or belief system of Buddhists. While Buddhism has many good moral teachings, at its core is the misguided belief that one can be saved by his or her works. The teaching of an eternal, supreme, personal, and loving God is left out. Concepts about life, death, and personhood such as karma, rebirth, and nirvana add to the confusion that makes it difficult to understand who Jesus is and what He can do to help.

Even the Buddhist view of their scriptures affects our use of the Bible to prove truth. They typically see their scriptures, not as an authority for belief and practice, but rather as encouragement towards finding one's own truth. In general, Buddhists think differently from those we have typically shared the gospel with such as other Christians, Jews, Muslims, and animists.

Another barrier is the reality that many Buddhists live in countries where all their family members and neighbors are Buddhists. Becoming a Christian often feels like a betrayal of family and country. In a few places there is serious persecution of Christians. The busyness and pressures of life along with an ever–growing barrage of fascinating entertainment add further barriers.

Often Buddhists are prejudiced against Christianity. They see it as a religion that is less moral and less spiritual than Buddhism. Sometimes this happens because of Christians nearby whose lives do not represent Jesus. Other times it's because Buddhists associate Christianity with the West, including its politics and materialism or even the immorality and violence of the movies produced there. These things from so–called Christian countries influence Buddhists to see Christianity as inferior to their religion.

Christian witnesses among Buddhists must often face the challenge of freezing, rugged mountains; congested cities; difficult languages; or repressive governments. Christians have not taken this mission field seriously enough and so the sin and laziness of God's people is another barrier to the gospel reaching Buddhists.

Beyond all of this, evil spirits are fighting against the knowledge of God and the natural human heart is simply not inclined towards Jesus. These are barriers with which we must contend.

In light of Buddhists' desperate need and Jesus' loving and passionate mandate for us to take the gospel to the entire world, we are called to ask, "How can we better present Jesus Christ to Buddhists?"

ONLY THROUGH THE POWER OF THE HOLY SPIRIT

Jesus clearly answers our question in His promise of the Holy Spirit as the means for taking the gospel to the ends of the earth (Acts 1:8). This is not a simplistic statement that ends in a quick prayer for the Holy Spirit and a return to searching elsewhere for some special method for reaching Buddhists. The Holy Spirit is the method, but He reveals Christ through various methods. This is His job. As Jesus said, "He will glorify me, for he will take what is mine and declare it to you" (John 16:14 ESV). We must search the Bible to know those ways and apply them to Buddhist people.

First, we can examine the gospels for how the Holy Spirit led Jesus to reveal His identity. Secondly, we can search the book of Acts and the epistles to see how the Holy Spirit worked through the disciples to reveal Jesus.

We will look at the following methods of the Holy Spirit which are effective for revealing Christ to Buddhists: 1) The power of prayer, 2) The Christ–like character of the messenger, 3) The loving unity of the church, 4) The leading through progressive truth, 5) The empowered proclamation of the Word, 6) The empowerment to heal and set free, 7) The conviction of sinners, 8) The ministry of the new covenant.

1 – THE POWER OF PRAYER

It requires a miracle of the Holy Spirit for any Buddhist (or anyone) to come to true conversion. Solid belief and trust in Jesus as the only eternal and divine Savior who has come in human flesh is a divine work of God in the human heart. Jesus clearly indicated that Peter knew Him as this, only by revelation from the Father (Mat 16:17). Paul declared that such spiritual things are only discerned because of God's Spirit showing them (1 Cor 12:3; 2:11–16).

If we truly believe that God alone can reveal Jesus to Buddhists, then prayer will be our greatest priority and method. It was by prayer and dependence on His Father that Jesus did His works of ministry. It was after the disciples prayed that the Holy Spirit came and thousands were led to Christ. The importance of prayer is repeated in Acts numerous times.

To be truly effective in presenting Christ to Buddhists we must pray for a miracle of revelation by the Holy Spirit in every attempt to witness. Prayers of dependence will permeate every other method that follows.

2 – THE CHRIST–LIKE CHARACTER OF THE MESSENGER

Jesus admirable character attracted many people. Kindness and generosity, justice and mercy, peacefulness and devotion were combined in a very attractive balance. When the Holy Spirit was poured out on the disciples they had "favor with all the people," "gladness and simplicity of heart," and "shared whatever they had with those in need". The fruit of the Spirit is "love, joy, peace" and many more attractive qualities (Gal 5:22–23). Through these examples we can see that the Holy Spirit leads people to belief in Jesus by revealing Christ's beautiful character (John 16:14). Buddhists will be drawn to Jesus as His character is seen both by the stories of Jesus we tell and the Christ–like lives that we live.

Jesus' character is naturally magnetic, but part of the attraction for Buddhists is that many of His qualities match the values their religion teaches. It's helpful to know what Buddhists value and then present Jesus emphasizing similar qualities. Below are a number of examples.

Compassion and moral purity are both significant aspects in the character of Buddha. The way Jesus treated the woman caught in adultery is an excellent example of how He masterfully combined the call to total moral purity with merciful compassion.

The sacrifice of position and power is a major part of Buddha's story and is repeated by monks who give up marriage, personal possessions, and entertainment to live a simple life seeking enlightenment. Jesus' life as a celibate teacher, traveling in simplicity with disciples who were dependent on people's hospitality, is similar to that with which Buddhists are familiar. Jesus' birth and death especially show this quality.

Millions of Buddha images portray Buddha in various positions of complete calm. In fact, serious Buddhists are attempting to put aside and not be controlled by any desire or situation. The stories of Jesus' calm under the religious leaders' verbal and physical attacks show His similar quality of peacefulness. His peace in the boat and the calming of the storm also demonstrates this.

In presenting the attractiveness of Jesus to Buddhists, our character will say more than any story we tell. If we want to be effective, we must let the Holy Spirit fill us with a Christ–like character.

This method has been effective in the conversion of many Buddhists at Seventh–day Adventist schools such as the Chiang Mai Adventist Academy in Thailand. Young people have reported that they came to believe in Jesus primarily through contact with various caring Christians, especially their teachers. Christ–like character was a significant reason for their attraction to Jesus.[1]

3 – THE LOVING UNITY OF THE CHURCH

Jesus said that unity among Christians would actually make it possible for the world to believe He is the one sent by God (John 17:21, 23). True love and cooperation is so rare in the world that when Buddhists see it they will be convinced it is supernatural and believe what these people preach about Christ.

Many modern Buddhists are against organized religion. They see it tied to money–making, power–grabbing and the extremism that leads to suicide bombings. They recall Christianity's horrific history of persecuting and murdering heretics for the sake of "truth." However, we can demonstrate in our church relationships a true love that reflects Jesus, which is what they need instead of religion.

Harmony and peace are important values of most Buddhists. Buddhists are often known as peaceable people. "Do not murder," is one of their five top precepts. Forgiving ones enemy and remaining unmoved by others praise or hatred is the standard. However, many Buddhists readily admit how difficult it is to do this. When they see us care for each other and forgive our enemies as Jesus so readily did, they will be drawn toward belief in Him.

Buddha rejected the caste system of India. He called people to live without prejudice. Jesus was kind towards the rich and the poor, the educated and the ignorant, as well as every ethnic group. His care for and inclusion of women will be appreciated by Buddhist women who sometimes feel undervalued because most Buddhist countries insist that only men can be ordained as monks and become enlightened. This inclusiveness can be shown in our churches as we consistently reject prejudice and welcome every type of person to our fellowship.

I remember the delight of one Buddhist lady who came to our

house church with her mentally handicapped son. She had been chased away from other gatherings because of his problems, but had heard from a new convert that this group of Christians didn't care whether people were rich or poor, educated or of low status. She deeply appreciated the kindness shown to her and her son. When he became unruly and damaged property, she was awed by the forgiveness extended. A church that loves each other and welcomes anyone is one of the Holy Spirit's methods for revealing Jesus to Buddhists.

4 – THE LEADING THROUGH PROGRESSIVE TRUTH IN PRESENTING JESUS

Because Buddha lived before Jesus was born on earth, there is nothing in the Buddhist scriptures concerning Him. Besides this, due to insufficient witnessing, the vast majority of Buddhists have little or no concept of who Jesus is. As witnesses for Jesus we have much to say. Jesus is teacher, healer, exorcist, compassionate friend, radical reformer, prophet, the Savior from sin, mediating priest, Creator, and the eternal God. We cannot demonstrate all this at once and so we must choose what to reveal and when. One of the Holy Spirit's methods is to present progressive truth, starting with what the audience can appreciate and moving towards that which is more difficult to understand or believe. Jesus stated it like this, "I still have many things to say to you, but you cannot bear them now. When the Spirit of truth comes, he will guide you into all the truth, for he will not speak on his own authority, but whatever he hears he will speak, and he will declare to you the things that are to come." (John 16:12–13 ESV).

The Gospel of Mark demonstrates this when it introduces Jesus, bit by bit, showing Him preaching, casting out evil spirits, and healing the sick (chapter 1). Jesus does not announce His identity as the Son of God and the Christ. In fact, when evil spirits say that He is the Son of God, He makes them be quiet (3:11–12). When the disciples declare that He is the Christ, He warns them not to tell anyone (8:29–30).

By the end of Mark, Jesus' identity as Son of God and Savior is clear. The Father Himself declares that Jesus is His beloved Son (9:7).

The centurion could see the same even when Jesus was on the cross (15:39). According to Mark's presentation, Jesus revealed His identity progressively.[2]

Luke's gospel also gives a similar gradual introduction of Jesus to the multitudes through His character, actions, and teachings. Both Mark and Luke were likely written for Gentile audiences.[3] Gentiles would find it hard to believe that a man could also be the supreme God. They must be drawn towards this belief through qualities of Jesus that were easier to appreciate. This would be true also of Buddhists.

Below is a progression I have found logical to some Buddhists I have worked with. It starts with His miracles, teachings, and admirable character and moves towards His divinity and role as Savior. One need not follow the progression rigidly, but simply be aware that the Holy Spirit often moves from the varied needs and interests of Buddhists, while progressively leading them on to know the whole truth about Him. We can cooperate with the Spirit by being aware of this and bringing it into our teaching.

7) Jesus as Savior

6) Jesus as Judge

5) Jesus as Creator

4) Jesus as Teacher Regarding the Living God

3) Jesus and His Admirable Character

2) Jesus as Teacher of Morality

1) Jesus as Miracle–Worker

As Buddhists come to appreciate Jesus' character and actions in ways that are familiar to them, it will be easier for them to believe the truths about His divinity such as His eternal nature, His omnipresence, omnipotence, and omniscience.

"Omniscience carries special relevance to a Buddhist,"[4] with many of them believing that after enlightenment, Buddha possessed all knowledge and wisdom. They need to move towards recognizing that Jesus truly possessed all these things before coming to earth and giving them up. It must become clear that Jesus was not another Buddha seeking enlightenment in His incarnation. This will happen as we share the fuller story and as we pray for the Holy Spirit to open minds and hearts to understanding and belief.

5 – THE LEADING THROUGH PROGRESSIVE TRUTH IN JESUS' TEACHINGS

Besides presenting Jesus progressively, we can also present His teachings progressively, moving from what is similar to what is unique. Both Buddha and Jesus taught openly in temples, towns, and in nature. Both of them frequently used stories and parables. There are also close similarities in some of their teachings.

Most of the themes in Jesus' Sermon on the Mount (Mat 5–7) have clear connections to Buddhist ways of thinking. Jesus called the people beyond rejecting murder and adultery to purity of thought without lust or hatred (5:21–30). Buddhism emphasizes such purity and right thinking. Jesus emphasized loving ones enemies, forgiving those who have caused hurt (5:43–48; 6:14–15). Buddhism teaches harmony and forgiveness. Jesus urged that charitable deeds, praying, and fasting be done in secret (6:1–18). Buddhism teaches the importance of correct motives and detachment from selfishness and pride. Jesus called people to stop seeking earthly treasures (6:19–24). Buddhism rejects materialism, frequently speaking of the transient nature of everything in the world.

Parables of Jesus that have some similar emphases to Buddhism are: the seed and the four soils, the wheat and the tares, hidden treasure, the pearl of great price (all in Matthew 13), the rich fool (Luke 12:13–21), and the parable of the sheep and the goats (Mat 25).

We can focus on the areas of similarities that Buddhists already value when we first share Jesus' teachings. This helps them develop a respect for Jesus as a great teacher. It helps them overcome any assumptions they may have that Christianity is less moral than Buddhism. Then they will be more ready to hear about His unique teachings.

However, we must not only talk about similarities, otherwise Buddhists are likely to assume they have no real need to study or follow Jesus since they already have Buddha and his teachings. They must soon hear that which is startlingly new and refreshing, the very things they need for salvation.

In the Sermon on the Mount there is a major emphasis that is entirely missing in Buddhism. It is the essential teaching about a trusting relationship with the living God. Jesus' moral teaching is not merely connected to purifying oneself or living in harmony with people. He relates basically everything to God the Father. Good works are done to glorify the Father (5:16). Loving ones enemies comes out of the truth that the Father gives rain and sunshine to the good and the bad (5:45). People are to do charitable deeds, pray, and fast to the Father (6:4, 6, 8, 9, 18). He is the one to be served instead of money (6:24). In fact Jesus says the final judgment will be decided by whether one has done "the will of My Father" (7:21).

Here we can see Jesus' style of progressive teaching. He taught people by moving them from their basic understanding of morality to a deeper morality that is in the context of a relationship with God. We can also help Buddhists know this essential truth of a relationship with the supreme God, by progressing from Jesus' moral teachings to His unique teachings about the Father.

This progressive truth approach can be used with Buddhists in conversations and sermons, and in the way we write pamphlets, Bible studies, and web sites. They will find it easier to believe in Jesus as God and Savior the more they see Him through the morality they already value.[5]

6 – THE EMPOWERED PROCLAMATION OF THE WORD

Despite our emphasis that many Buddhists have never heard about Jesus, there are a large number who have. Some have studied the Bible or have formed various opinions about Him in other ways. Some Buddhists simply view Jesus as a good human. Other Buddhists see Him as a Bodhisattva, who is an enlightened being who has power to help people. In general, Buddhists are likely to be very inclusive in their beliefs. They may be happy to put up a statue or picture of Him along with their Buddha image and the elephant god from India. They may even value Jesus as an enlightened Buddha. These same people are likely to be surprised or even offended to hear a Christian say that Jesus is the only way for salvation. This sounds arrogant and ignorant to them as they have a great value of other teachers and ways.

When we meet Buddhists who have an incorrect view of Jesus we must care enough to tell them the truth. We know that there is coming a time of final deception regarding Jesus. Satan himself will appear and deceive many. Therefore, there is a need for clarity in our presentations regarding Christ.

For this there is clear Biblical precedent. In the book of John we see a much more direct presentation of truth about Jesus' identity than in Mark and Luke.[6] The religious leaders were not being won by His miracles, teaching, or kindness, and Jesus determined to not leave them without a clear message. A study of the book of Acts reveals many sermons that directly spoke of Jesus as the Christ.

It is not easy to share with Buddhists the truths about Jesus as Creator, as the Resurrected one, alive from the dead, and as the high priest in heaven. We must try out best with good apologetics and explanations. However, these will not be sufficient to generate faith. For this God has promised the Holy Spirit to empower the proclamation of the word.

In all of these we see a solid dependence on the Holy Spirit to empower them for the proclaiming of the Word of God. Jesus was anointed by the Spirit for preaching (Luke 4:18). The direct result of Pentecost was mighty preaching through Peter in which thousands were converted (Acts 2). We can expect that Buddhists will come to believe in Jesus when the word of God is taught, not by human wisdom alone, but by the Holy Spirit's power.

Paul emphasized this in the context of presenting Jesus when He said, "And my speech and my preaching were not with persuasive words of human wisdom, but in demonstration of the Spirit and of power" (1 Cor 2:4). In all our answers to Buddhists, we must have a complete prayerful reliance on the Holy Spirit to lead them to understanding and belief. God has promised the Holy Spirit will help us know what to say (Mat 10:19–20).

This does not mean that there is no logic in our words as that would be senseless. Peter is very logical in His preaching of Jesus as the fulfillment of prophecy and as the Christ who the people crucified (Acts 2:14–39; 3:12–26; 4:8–12; 19–20; 5:29–32). Paul gives a vigorous defense of Jesus as the Christ among the Jews in various synagogues (Acts 9:20, 27; 13:16–41), and presents a carefully crafted talk to the philosophers at Athens (Acts 17:16–34). His statement in 1 Corinthians 2 simply shows us that our confidence must never be in our logic, but in what the Holy Spirit can do.

When the Holy Spirit empowers preaching, the words are spoken not only boldness, but with deep love.[7] Paul said, "Remember that for three years I did not cease to warn everyone night and day with tears" (Acts 20:31). Jesus spoke passionately as a mother hen who was earnestly seeking to protect her children from danger (Mat 23:37–39).

This means that in answering Buddhists' questions, we should be in earnest while determinedly avoiding a proud, combative spirit. Debate for the purpose of winning arguments is not effective in winning hearts. Most Buddhists are taught to have a calm, peaceful spirit and can easily be turned away by heated speeches. Whole dissertations have been written to show the value of approaching Buddhists with a meek spirit (Majudhon, Nantachai 1997; Majudhon, Ubolwan 1997). In every situation it is best to express compassion and true interest, relying on the Holy Spirit to change their hearts and help them understand. We should focus on the positive declarations of our points.[8]

Behind every question and objection is a Buddhist person. Therefore we should seek to answer that person's needs rather than just his or her intellectual wonderings. One of the ways to do this is through sharing our stories of what God has done for us. Many witnessing among Buddhists have found this to be more effective than purely logical explanations.[9]

7 – THE EMPOWERMENT TO HEAL AND SET FREE

Especially in Southeast Asia, Buddhism does not emphasize praying to gods. In fact the Buddha called people away from the gods, spirits, and magic in India to depend on themselves—their own good works and meditation. This creates a void for many Buddhists. In basically every Buddhist culture there are many Buddhists seeking for spiritual power. Shrines or idols for Hindu gods and local spirits are seen frequently, even inside Buddhist temples. Encounters with ghosts and spirits are commonly reported.

This creates an opening for a God who works miracles to help them now. We can be confident that God also desires to have us pray and see miracles that will lead Buddhists to Christ. This is the Holy Spirit's method of empowering to heal and set free.

One of the first ways Jesus revealed Himself was through miracles of healing or deliverance from evil spirits. A survey of the book of Acts also reveals that the gospel often went forward through such miracles. In our talking about Jesus with our Buddhist friends, one of the best places to start is with the stories of Jesus' miracles. To those Buddhists who believe in the supernatural already, these stories will ring true.

Beyond stories, we can pray for and expect miracles from God in order to reach Buddhists today. Christians in many places are seeing Buddhists converted as they pray for their problems and teach them to ask God for help. In fact, one study of 259 people, primarily from Buddhist backgrounds, it was found that "the majority, 48.4 percent, of Buddhists who have become Christians indicated that their personal experience with God was the main factor for their decision to accept Christ as their Savior" (Phetchareun 2005:96).

Seventh–day Adventists teaching includes the belief that the gifts of the Spirit continue to the end of time, which include healing and miracles (1 Cor 12:9).[10] Sometimes we avoid such things because we have a clear recognition that at the end of time Satan will work with lying wonders even through professed Christians. (2 Thes 2:9–10). This is a real concern and we must be extremely watchful for counterfeit movements. Nevertheless, God has a special end–time plan of healing ministry through which we can show Jesus to Buddhists as healer.11

In Cambodia, global pioneers have frequently seen God answer prayers for physical healing and for the casting out of evil spirits. Many Buddhists have become believers in Jesus, confident that He is alive, powerful, and personally interested in them. I can picture the peace and smile of one lady I personally saw find freedom after she tried to attack my wife with knives. There are many places, especially among tantric Buddhism (in places such as Tibet) where so–called Buddhist practitioners actually visualize demons and call for them to come. We can help them find true freedom in Jesus.

Miracles come in a wide variety of forms. Some come as answers to prayer such as receiving protection during an accident, finding a job to help with finances, or the resolution of family conflict.

Others experience visions or dreams where Jesus is seen or heard. A Thai Buddhist attending a health program at Mission Health Promotion Center had a vision of Jesus in his room urging him to read the book Ministry of Healing which lay beside his bed.

Buddhists are searching for power and we have the privilege of helping them see Jesus through stories and present–day experiences with His miracles, even while teaching them about truth so as to avoid counterfeit miracles.

8 – THE CONVICTION OF SINNERS

The Holy Spirit plays a crucial role in revealing Christ by convicting people of sin, righteousness, and judgment (John 16:8–11). He works directly on people's hearts and through His witnesses' words and actions. We can partner with the Holy Spirit to bring conviction to Buddhists. This is so important since they cannot truly see and know Jesus until they recognize their need.

The landlady of our house was surprised when I mentioned that we are all sinners needing a Savior. "I haven't sinned," she said. I was confused until she clarified that she had not broken the five precepts of Buddhism, neither killing, stealing, lying, committing adultery, nor drinking alcohol.

The Holy Spirit worked to convict this kind, noble lady as she saw a higher standard of unselfish service and devotion to God in my wife. The landlady finally recognized that she too was a sinner and sought forgiveness through Jesus.

Other Buddhists may be more aware of their failures, but don't think too seriously about it. One effective worker among Buddhists often asks people if they have kept the five precepts of Buddhism. They typically admit that they haven't. He reminds them of the potential consequences, including hell. God has used him to lead many Buddhists to their need for a Savior (Cioccolanti 2007:71,84).

Christians and Buddhists share some similar concepts of sin, righteousness, and judgment in Buddhism. Buddha clearly taught the law of karma. Many Buddhists understand this to mean that they will receive the consequences from their good or bad actions in this life, in heaven or hell, and in the next life. They also think that everything good they experience and everything bad they suffer comes from something they did in a previous life.

However, many are not very motivated by this threat of punishment. Life often seems very unfair and this can create doubt in the Buddhist's mind regarding the danger of sin and the value of doing good. In Southeast Asia there is a saying, "Do good and receive good; do bad and receive bad." But a well–known saying has been added: "We did good, but it flew away, and it's running after those who've done evil." This can lead to a careless attitude towards sin.

Most Buddhists don't have a sense that there is a supreme being who will make sure the judgment of sin and right–doing happens. As we present Jesus to Buddhists as the Judge who ensures justice, the Holy Spirit can use this to bring a greater sense of conviction. Paul suggested this method when he wrote, "For we must all appear before the judgment seat of Christ, that each one may receive the things done in the body, according to what he has done, whether good or bad. Knowing, therefore, the terror of the Lord, we persuade men" (2 Cor 5:10–11). Paul first presented Jesus to the men of Athens as judge (Acts 17:31). Peter did also when speaking to Cornelius' household who became some of the first Roman converts (Acts 10:42).

Buddhists already have an emphasis on judgment and justice. They can easily understand that in order to have true justice there must be a living, fair judge. As they learn that there is a holy, righteous and trustworthy judge, their conviction of sin will increase. They will be ready for the good news that this judge is Jesus, the compassionate one they've come to admire.

9 – THE MINISTRY OF THE NEW COVENANT

After all the work of the Holy Spirit to draw Buddhists to Christ, there is still the need for conversion. Jesus made it clear that no one can enter heaven without the new birth that the Holy Spirit provides (John 3:5–6). This is also connected to the New Covenant in which God forgives sins, brings people into a relationship with Him and writes the law upon their hearts (Hebb8:8–12; Eze 36:26). We must pray for this and share the truth of the cross with Buddhists.

The Biblical records shows that Jesus' death and resurrection was seen by the majority only after they knew Him as miraculous healer, teacher, and as a compassionate person. So also, it is easier to share Jesus as Savior with Buddhists once they've come to appreciate His teachings, power, and admirable character. As previously mentioned, the initial response of many Buddhists to Jesus on the cross is one of misunderstanding with questions that assume Jesus had bad karma. If we will share His life of perfection and communicate clearly who He was before His incarnation, it will be easier for them to understand that Jesus died for the sins of others, not His own.

However, the story of the cross itself truly does have a great drawing power for Buddhists (John 12:32). I was visiting a layman in a Buddhists temple. He was very humble and had committed himself totally to Buddhism. I wanted very much to share Jesus with him, but my Thai language was too limited. Imagine my surprise, when he, seeing my attempt, began to speak about Jesus on the cross. "Whenever I'm angry at someone," he said, "I think of Jesus on the cross. As I contemplate the way He did not get angry at the soldier, but instead forgave them, all my anger melts away."

We should tell the story of the cross to Buddhists by emphasizing Jesus' character, connecting it to characteristics they highly value. His compassion can be seen in how He treated the sorrowing women and the dying thief. His self control and patience can be seen in His silence and peacefulness under the verbal attacks of the religious leaders and the physical torture. His care for His mother while He was in pain will also be significant to those who highly value honoring their parents.

The depth of His sacrificial character will be seen the more clearly we can explain the depth of pain and suffering He chose in receiving our sins, and the separation that came between Him and His Father. We should show clearly that Jesus knew in advance that all this suffering was coming, and yet still chose it. Though He had the power and the perfect right to escape all earthly suffering, He embraced it in order to bring to an end the vicious cycle of sin. This will also help them understand that this suffering did not come upon Him because of His own bad actions.

As we share the beauty of Jesus' character on the cross, many Buddhists will be able to say with the centurion, "Certainly this was a righteous Man!" (Luke 23:47, NKJV).

Another significant aspect of the cross is described in Col 2:15 and Rev 12:11. Satan and the evil powers were at the cross to tempt Jesus and stop His work of salvation. Jesus won this battle and overcame them. People can find victory over evil spirits and all temptations through Jesus. For the many Buddhists who live in awareness and fear of spirits, this is a significant part of the story that we should share. In fact the whole story of Jesus can be effectively shared with such Buddhists in the context of the great controversy theme.

The idea that Jesus died as a substitute for our sins is a concept that initially seems to go against Buddhist teaching. Buddhism teaches that each person must pay for his or her own sins and no one else can do this. Some sects of Buddhism are very adamant about this. However, when we share this story of Jesus' death we can point Buddhists to examples in history and even recent news where an individual sacrificed his life to save someone. They can understand this concept. Especially as they come to appreciate Jesus' character and believe in His divinity it is easier for them to trust that Jesus' death provides a way to forgive their sins.

Grace for the repentant sinner is a major difference between the teaching of Buddha and Jesus that we can best share after they've heard the truth of what Jesus did for them. Jesus said, "'I desire mercy, and not sacrifice.' For I came not to call the righteous, but sinners" (Matt 9:13, KJV). Jesus told such parables as the prodigal son, the lost sheep, the lost coin (Luke 15), the great supper (Luke 14:16–24) and the generous vineyard owner (Mat 20:1–16).

This is the good news that is missing in Buddhism. On one weekend I met a Buddhist man who had come to church for the first time. He had experienced a stroke and was partly paralyzed. I watched the tears stream down his face as he heard about Jesus' death and how He could forgive any sin. This man had been involved in terrible crimes, in particular the trafficking of children into prostitution. He felt that his paralysis was because of his sins and eagerly grasped at the hope of forgiveness through Jesus' mercy. Like him, many other Buddhists have also found hope and eternal life through the presentation of Jesus as substitute.

One more important aspect of Jesus' death that is important to Buddhists is the truth that through the cross we can die to selfishness and live a new life of generous love. This truth, so clearly expressed in Rom 6, Gal 2:20, and 2 Cor 5:14–21, is significant because many Buddhists are working hard to detach themselves from their desires and be freed from the impurities of selfishness.

This answers the concerns of those Buddhists who express that Christianity's idea of the forgiveness of sins is too easy, even immoral. They see many Christians continuing on in a lifestyle of sin while claiming God's forgiveness. But the true gospel is one of repentance and faith. Baptism is a death of self and a rising to new life. So we can share these deeper truths of the cross and know that they will speak to Buddhists.

In general, the story of Jesus on the cross is an attractive story for Buddhists. We should tell it often, weaving the various parts of the story in ways that will speak to the interests and needs of the Buddhists to whom we are talking. We must invite them to ask God for forgiveness and a new life. Jesus can be known as Savior among them as we rely on the Holy Spirit and move forward to share the wonderful story.

SUMMARY

There is so much beauty in the person of Jesus that is extremely special and necessary for Buddhist people. There are many connections to Buddhist values that we can start from as we present Him. There is much that Buddhists are lacking that they can find in Jesus.

There is therefore no lack on the part of God or His people for the work among Buddhists. We can press forward, praying earnestly for a greater movement of the Spirit in all these areas. The methods of the Holy Spirit are today just as valuable and valid as in the days of the apostles. We must earnestly pray, seek to show His character in our lives and churches, and then boldly and lovingly tell the truth about our Teacher, Miracle–Worker, God, and Savior. The Holy Spirit will surely reveal Jesus as the Christ to Buddhists.

NOTES

1. *Two different dissertations have addressed this issue. Surachet Insom examined Chiang Mai Adventist Academy and wrote, "One of the factors which lead former Buddhists and animists to become Adventist is the teachers' dedication and love for the souls of the students" (Surachet Insom. November 2008. A Comparative Study between the Teaching and Compassion Model of Jesus with Buddhists in Thailand. Adventist International Institute of Advanced Studies Theological Seminary dissertation). Khamsay Phetchareun looked at Mission College and the Thai Ekamai church in Bangkok. He wrote, "In 2003 a study was conducted on 259 people, 155 Christians and 104 Buddhists....This study reveals that the majority of Buddhists (55 percent) learned to know about Christianity through Christian family members and friends. Since the study was conducted at church institutions, 36.8 percent indicated that they learned about Christianity from Christian institutions. It is important to understand that institutions cannot share the message, but rather it is the people in the institutions." (Khamsay Phetchareun. June 2005, Presenting the Gospel Message in Thailand, Andrews University dissertation).*

2. *"The Sun of Righteousness did not burst upon the world in splendor, to dazzle the senses with His glory. It is written of Christ, 'His going forth is prepared as the morning.' Hosea 6:3. Quietly and gently the daylight breaks upon the earth, dispelling the shadow of darkness, and waking the world to life. So did the Sun of Righteousness arise, 'with healing in His wings'. Malachi 4:2" (The Desire of Ages, 261).*

3. *"Much internal evidence supports the suggestion that the Gospel (Mark) was written for a non–Jewish audience" (Andrews Study Bible, 1293, see also 1326).*

4. *Wagner, Paul. Good News for Buddhists, privately published manuscript, p. 12.*

5. *In presenting Jesus as a great teacher we may encounter some Buddhists who think that Jesus' teaching and practice is shallow, lacking in the area of meditation and specific skills for purifying the mind. This is the opportunity to point them again to the special difference in His teachings. Jesus taught prayer and trust in a living God who has power to purify their hearts. Beyond this is the importance of the death and resurrection of Jesus, along with His ongoing intercession for inner transformation.*

6. *In quite serious contrast to the synoptic gospels, John boldly declares his purpose: "These are written that you may believe that Jesus is the Christ, the Son of God, and that believing you may have life in His name" (20:30). From the very beginning of the book, Jesus is described as Creator and eternal God (1:1–4). The disciple Nathaniel declares, "You are the Son of God!" (1:49). A searching Pharisee, Nicodemus, hears about the Son of God and salvation. One town of Samaritans are quite quick to recognize Jesus as "the Christ, the Savior of the world" (4:43). Even more, Jesus refers to Himself very boldly with the many "I AM" statements (6:35,43; 8:12; 10:7,9,11, 14; 11:25; 14:6; 15:1,5) to the point that He is nearly stoned for making Himself to be like Jehovah, the great I AM (8:58).*

This direct approach seen in John may also be related to the fact that John is writing years after the other gospels. More is now known about Jesus. Many are not sure if it is believable. Others are not clear enough on Jesus' identity. Therefore God makes it clearer through John.

7. *"The Savior knew that no argument, however logical, would melt hard hearts or break through the crust of worldliness and selfishness. He knew that His disciples must receive the heavenly endowment (the Holy Spirit); that the gospel would be effective only as it was proclaimed by hearts made warm and lips made eloquent by a living knowledge of Him who is the way, the truth, and the life" (Acts of the Apostles, 31).*

"After the descent of the Holy Spirit, the disciples were so filled with love for Him and for those for whom He died, that hearts were melted by the words they spoke and the prayers they offered. They spoke in the power of the Spirit; and under the influence of that power, thousands were converted" (Acts of the Apostles, 22).

8. *"Often, as you seek to present the truth, opposition will be aroused; but if you seek to meet the opposition with argument, you will only multiply it, and that you cannot afford to do. Hold to the affirmative. Angels of God are watching you, and they understand how to impress those whose opposition you refuse to meet with argument. Dwell not on the negative points of questions that arise, but gather to your minds affirmative truths, and fasten them there by much earnest prayer and heart–consecration" (Christian Service, 126).*

"So it should be now. The people of the world are worshiping false gods. They are to be turned from their false worship, not by hearing denunciation of their idols, but by beholding something better. God's goodness is to be made known. 'Ye are My witnesses, saith the Lord, that I am God.' Isa. 43:12" (Christ's Object Lessons, 299).

9. *"Our confession of His faithfulness is Heaven's chosen agency for revealing Christ to the world. We are to acknowledge His grace as made known through the holy men of old; but that which will be most effectual is the testimony of our own experience.... These precious acknowledgments to the praise of the glory of His grace, when supported by a Christ–like life, have an irresistible pow-*

er that works for the salvation of souls" (Desire of Ages 347).

10. *"Christ has empowered His church to do the same work that He did during His ministry. Today He is the same compassionate physician that He was while on this earth. We should let the afflicted understand that in Him there is healing balm for every disease, restoring power for every infirmity. His disciples in this time are to pray for the sick as verily as His disciples of old prayed. And recoveries will follow, for 'the prayer of faith shall save the sick.' James 5:15. We need the Holy Spirit's power, the calm assurance of faith that can claim God's promises" (Counsels on Health, 210).*

A further study and application of Ellen White's counsel regarding miraculous healing will be helpful to show how a combination of instruction in healthful living, care for the sick, leading them to repentance, and praying for miracles can best show Jesus' love.

REFERENCE LIST

Cioccolanti, Steve. 2007. Buddha to Jesus: An Insider's View of Buddhism & Christianity. See page 71 and 84.

Majudhon, Nantachai. 1997. Meekness: A New Approach to Christian Witness to the Thai People. D. Miss. Diss., Asbury Theological Seminary.

Mejudhon, Ubolwan. 1997. The Way of Meekness: Being Christian and Thai in the Thai Way. D. Miss. diss., Asbury Theological Seminary.

Phetchareun, Khamsay. June 2005. Presenting the Gospel Message in Thailand, Andrews University dissertation, page 96.

Appendix

Conference Recommendation:

Focusing on Excellent Grief Care and More Appropriate Bereavement Rituals

The following recommendations were voted by the delegates to the Mission Issues Leadership Conference on May 22, 2014 at Thailand Adventist Mission in Bangkok, Thailand. This conference was hosted by the Global Mission Center for East Asian Religions and the delegates were officers, departmental leaders, pastors, church members, and supporting missionaries in Cambodia, Laos, Malaysia, Myanmar, Philippines, Singapore, Sri Lanka, Taiwan, Thailand, the United States, and Vietnam.

Voted Recommendations

INASMUCH as we agree that the cultures of Eastern Asian religions focus particularly on death and afterlife, and inasmuch as these cultures deal with death through sensory rituals rather than through propositional doctrines more familiar to us:

WE RECOMMEND that each region should appoint a research team (including members with research, pastoral and administrative expertise) with a mandate to research, discuss, test and propose (within a specified time limit) the following:

1. Ways for the Adventist church to have a deeply meaningful care ministry to the grieving in their communities as a defining identity—and not just to the grieving in their own church

community.

2. Guidelines for an appropriate and appreciated participation of Adventists in the bereavement rituals of their non-Adventist family and neighbours—rituals associated with death, post-death and ancestors.

3. New Adventist rituals, procedures and facilities that are biblically appropriate and meaningful within the home cultures of Adventist communities: articulating grief, dealing with the dead and the remains, and honouring and remembering the deceased—remembering to make room for meaningful satisfying participation of non-believer mourners in our services.

Further

WE RECOMMEND that the administration of each region

1. Support the proposals of the research team by facilitating the acceptance and support of the whole church regionally;

2. In a systematic way, teach and train current churches to adopt the new initiatives; and

3. Incorporate the new initiatives into official church and ministerial manuals and into the curriculum of ministerial training.

Index

O

P

Q

R

S

T

V

W

Scripture Index

Note: page numbers appear in italic.

BOOKS IN THE GLOBAL MISSION SERIES:

Winning Hearts
Leading Buddhists to Faith in God
Edited by **Gregory** and **Amy Whitsett**

It's Time
Voices from the Front Lines of Urban Mission
Edited by
Bettina Krause

Ministering to Mourners
Funeral Rituals and Christian Witness in East Asian Contexts
Edited by **Gregory** and **Amy Whitsett**

Narrative, Meaning, and Truth
Fulfilling the Mission in Relativistic Contexts
Edited by
Bruce A. Bauer and **Kleber D. Gonçalves**

The Ephesus Model
A Biblical Framework for Urban Mission
Jeffrey McAuliffe and **Robert McAuliffe**

God's Mission to the Nations
An Old Testament Study Applied in the South Asian Context
Andrew Tompkins

Mission to the Cities
A Sourcebook for Adventist Urban Church Mission
Edited by
James H. Park

New York City, A Symbol
Foundational Principles for Adventist Urban Mission
Compiled by
John Luppens

www.globalmissioncenters.org

www.ingramcontent.com/pod-product-compliance
Lightning Source LLC
LaVergne TN
LVHW010053110826
845155LV00028B/320

* 9 7 8 1 9 4 3 5 0 7 4 6 7 *